Still More Wandering Back-Roads West Virginia

with Carl E. Feather

*Volume IV of the
Wandering Back-Roads West Virginia
with Carl E. Feather series*

Still More Wandering Back-Roads West Virginia
Volume 4 of the *Wandering Back-Roads West Virginia with Carl E. Feather* series
By Carl E. Feather
Author of *My Fathers' Land* and *Mountain People in a Flat Land*

Published by The Feather Cottage/Feather Cottage Media
6 Seaford Lane, Bruceton Mills WV 26525
Thefeathercottage.com / carl@thefeathercottage.com

Copyright 2025 Carl E. Feather / Feather Cottage Media

"Wandering Back-Roads West Virginia" is copyrighted by Carl E. Feather, TX9-390-448, May 15, 2024.

All rights reserved. No part of this book may be reproduced in any form or by any electronic or mechanical means, including information storage and retrieval systems and audio book, without permission in writing from the publisher, except by reviewers, who may quote brief passages in a review.

ISNB: 979-8-9907539-1-4 (paperback)
Library of Congress Control Number: 2025904181
Printed and bound in the USA
First Printing June 2025

AI was not used to create the text, images or design of this book.

Goldenseal magazine is a publication of the West Virginia Department of Arts, Culture, & History, The Cultural Center, 1900 Kanawha Blvd., E., Charleston, WV 25305-0300.

All photos in this book, unless otherwise noted, are by the author, Carl E. Feather, and copyrighted by the same.
Front cover image:
The Locust Heights and Western Railroad, Clarksburg, W.Va., 2008, by Carl E. Feather.

Other books by Carl E. Feather

Mountain People in a Flat Land:
Appalachian Migration to Northeast Ohio, 1940-1965
Ohio University Press

Covered Bridges of Ashtabula County, Ohio
Hidden History of Ashtabula County, Ohio
Arcadia

Ashtabula County: A Field Guide

Ashtabula Harbor, Ohio:
A History of the World's Greatest Iron Ore Receiving Port

Pleasure Grounds: 150 Years of Geneva-on-the-Lake,
Ohio's First Summer Resort

My Fathers' Land: Palatinate Immigration
to North-Central West Virginia

Wandering Back-Roads West Virginia (4 volumes)

Wandering Tucker County, West Virginia (2026)

Wandering Route 50, West Virginia (2027)

A Gathering of Feathers (Lenox Memorial Cemetery Feather burials)

Feather Cottage Media

Order Feather Cottage Media books online at
books.by/feather-cottage-media

Dedication

To my high-school assistant principal and fellow West Virginian,
Hiram "Bill" Lynch,
&
the foremost historian of Ashtabula County, Ohio,
Norma Waters,

*in appreciation of your decades of interest in my work
and support in many ways.
You have been an inspiration to me,
role models for hard work and dedication,
and, most importantly, cherished friends.*

Acknowledgments

Most of the chapters in this book originated as stories that were written for *GOLDENSEAL* magazine by the author. These stories have been updated to reflect the status of the places/owners as of the book's publication date of June 2025. Readers interested in visiting the places discussed are strongly encouraged to check with the online resources prior to setting out on their own wanderings.

A debt of gratitude goes to my wife, Ruth, whose day job helped make possible this book series. She heard most of these stories long before they were put to print, but still expressed a newfound interest upon reading them. Her patient understanding with my hearing disability has helped me navigate many a difficult situations at the venues where we peddle my stories and images. Most of all, I thank her for her love.

My son, Aaron E., and father, Carl J. Feather, continue to support my writing through their interest and encouragement.

The many people who were interviewed and photographed for this book are the true authors of the stories for which I am a scribe. Their lives and efforts created the places and traditions explored in this work. Thank you for patiently trusting me to enter your lives and report on my findings. May your works and stories live long after all of us are gone.

Contents

Introduction		11
1.	Last Train from Clarksburg	12
2.	Mountain State Castles	28
3.	Ghosts of Harpers Ferry	50
4.	Wandering Heirloom Orchards	62
5.	Arthurdale Memories	90
6.	'What Number, Please?'	110
7.	Wandering Centre Market	118
8.	Saturday Nights on Bunner Ridge	134
9.	Singing in the Hills	162
10.	The Buckwheat Stopped Here	174
11.	Organ Cave Speaks for Itself	188
12.	Last Ferry to Fly	198
13.	Virginia Furnace	212
14.	'Oh, Glorious Times!'	222
15.	New Directions for an Old Farm	238
16.	The Washingtons Slept Here	250
17.	Rosby, Roseby or Rosbby?	262
18.	A Sharp Landmark	272
19	The Pringles' Sycamore	286
19.	A Vision for Sweet Springs	292
20.	The Little House	308
21.	A Baby Boomer's Babies	318
Epilogue		335
Bibliography		337
Index		341
About the Author		361

Introduction

This is the fourth volume in the six-volume *Wandering Back-Roads West Virginia with Carl E. Feather* book series. The books are based upon the author's nearly 40 years of working as a freelance writer and photographer for *GOLDENSEAL* magazine, a publication of the West Virginia Department of Arts, Culture & History.

While the first three volumes focused mainly on people and their stories of growing up and living in The Mountain State, this volume's focus is on interesting places, traditions and landmarks in West Virginia. These places did not come about by divine creation or happenstance; accordingly, this book continues the series' focus on people, specifically the folks whose vision, hard work and passion created these gems off the beaten path.

This volume also introduces supplemental video content to enhance the reader's immersion in the places and people documented. Chapters that have associated documentary films are marked with a film reel symbol:

View these films online at the publisher's YouTube Channel: YouTube.com/@FeatherCottageMedia

The late Keith Mason sits in the cab of his beloved Locomotive No. 1 of the Locust Heights & Western Railroad. Keith and his friends built the locomotive and began running excursions on his backyard railroad in 1974. His family and friends continue to maintain and operate the railroad, referred to as "Clarksburg's Best Kept Secret." Photo from 2008.

Chapter 1

Last Train from Clarksburg

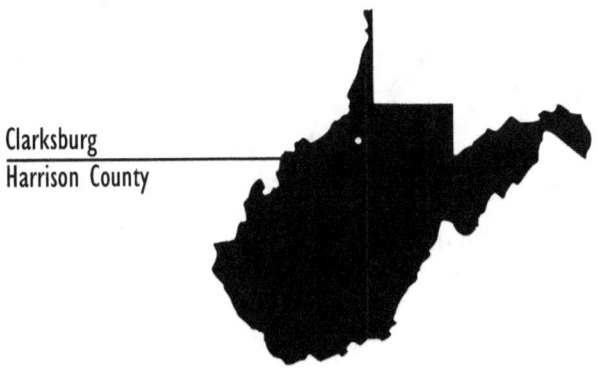

Clarksburg
Harrison County

Some men enjoy building barbecue pits, patios, garages and workshops in their backyards.

Keith Mason built a steam locomotive and the railroad on which to run it.

Keith died in 2016 after a long battle with Parkinson's Disease, but the little locomotive and railroad that he and his buddies built continue to operate under the ownership of his widow and the passion of his daughters, grandson and volunteers.

The scenery on this ¾-mile excursion is prosaic woodlands and fields, certainly not on the scale or grandeur of the Cass Scenic Railroad or Potomac Eagle. A ride on the LH&W is all about the train, its legacy and the crew of volunteers and family that keep it running.

Repeat riders account for many of the thousands of people who annually climb aboard the caboose and open-air passenger car each year, often with grandchildren in tow. In a reversal of the typical parent-introduces-offspring norm, my wife and I introduced the railroad to my 92-year-old father in 2024. It was my third visit and coincided with what was the railroad's

The excursion train consists of the locomotive, a lumber car converted to accommodate passengers, and the caboose. The railroad passes through a residential neighborhood, fields and forest. Rides depart on Wednesday evenings during the summer/early fall and take about 30 minutes for the round trip.

50th anniversary. I returned several times that summer and fall to film its operation and interview the principals: Jean Mason; Tammy Mason Molina and her husband, Duane; Tammy's son, Tre Roach, and his wife, Sarah Grace; and volunteers.

Devotees stay in touch with the railroad and its schedule through a Facebook page maintained by Tammy. Volunteers, Keith's loving family, and rider donations sustain this labor of love and legacy. In 2024, Jean Mason, in her mid-80s, was still mowing the 30 acres of fields and spraying the right-of-way for weeds, handling the riders' reception area and baking snacks for the volunteers.

"I keep busy, so I don't have time to think about (being tired)," she told me. As with the others who volunteer to keep the railroad going, Jean views her contributions as memorials to her late husband. Her grandson inherited that value from his mother and grandmother.

"I don't see how anybody could be born into this and not want to do it," Tre Roach said. "It's an opportunity that not many people get in this life."

The hobby railroad's name is a nod to the line's direction of travel and the subdivision of Locust Heights, where Jean and Keith Mason made their

The crew of the Locust Heights & Western Railroad in 2006 pose with Keith Mason (in cab) and the locomotive he built in 1974. From left are Bill Brady, Worthy Hall, Mark Ware, Tom Proud, Kevin Snyder, Tammy Mason Roach (Molina) and Tre Roach. Also assisting at that time were Gerald Corder and Dave Schwartz.

home. Tammy said her parents purchased the former strip mine parcel in 1958; it hosts the homes of several family members, including hers and Jean's. Keith and Jean had three daughters: Tammy, Michele D. and Kristi (Brady), who had friends living in the subdivision. To keep them occupied, their father built a playhouse for them in 1969.

Keith's father, Kenneth, was a machinist and in business with Keith, who apprenticed under him and studied mechanical engineering at West Virginia University. Mason Machine Shop, Inc., prospered as it provided services to regional industries. But Tammy said her father always found time for his passions of steam power, railroading and family. Jean is from Pendleton County, and the family enjoyed weekend visits back home in the mountains. But on weekday evenings, Keith hunkered down in the machine shop to tinker with his railroad and sawmill machinery.

"Any spare time he had was spent with the train," said Tammy, who grew up with the machine shop across the street from their residence. "He'd come home for dinner, and he went back over to the shop and worked until 11:30 at night doing all his hobbies. So, it was a passion. He was never far from home; we knew where to find him."

Jean Mason didn't even have to walk across the street to summon her husband for dinner or a family matter. Keith rigged up a train whistle that Jean could activate from the house and be heard across the property.

As his daughters outgrew the playhouse, Keith literally elevated it to a higher purpose by putting it on a pair of trucks (the wheel assemblies) from a narrow-gauge mining car. They constructed a short section of grade and track on which to display the caboose, but a companion steam locomotive and a longer line on which to run them were inevitable.

"We had an old (flat) car that had run on the railroad, and he fixed it up," Jean said. "(Keith) said, 'I got to build a steam engine, and I really like the Swamp Angel up in Cranesville Swamp, so, I think I will pattern it after that Class A Climax.'"

With photographs and drawings of the 1890s-era logging locomotive to guide them, Keith and friends built the engine that Tre would affectionately call "Big Black." Back in 2006, when I first visited the railroad, Keith told me that his 5.5-ton version was, at 20 feet long, slightly smaller than the original Climax locomotive. Keith's version had a chain-sprocket gear drive rather than the conventional gear drive, and while some Climax engines had U-shaped wheels that ran on "pole rails," he opted for the narrow-gauge set of wheels that came from lumber carts used at a sawmill near Franklin.

The original boiler came off a steam winch that Keith located near Roanoke, Va. It was replaced in 2001 at a cost of $10,000. About the time Keith passed away, the replacement boiler developed issues; the huge expense of repairing it threatened the railroad's existence. Donations and volunteers came through, and the Mason Climax is now on its third boiler.

The engine's original two upright cylinders, manufactured by J. F. Byers, came from a steam winch Keith located in Ohio. The link-and-pin couplers were salvaged from logging cars used by Ely Thomas Lumber Company in Jetsville (Nicholas County). The bell came from an antique store. Several whistles have been used on the locomotive, including one made by Mark Ware, a volunteer engineer on the railroad.

"Pretty much the only thing that he didn't build were the boiler and the

A swampy area had to be bridged before the railroad could be extended into the former strip mine area. Two trestles have been built over it in the railroad's history.

engines," said Tre Roach, recalling his conversations with his grandfather. "The engines were totally re-machined before they were installed on the locomotive. All the gear and drive line, frame, woodwork . . . everything was fabricated or created (in the Mason Machine Shop). It's had slight modifications over the years like everything else. There were things that (Keith) thought he could have been done better, and he improved upon them over the years. It has changed a little bit since its first design, but it still has its roots, and it is still a very reliable engine.

"My granddad was very keen on tight tolerances on everything and keeping everything in good condition, good lubrication," Tre added. "People see our engine and say, 'Boy, it's got a lot of oil and grease on it.' And I'm like, 'Yeah, but that oil and grease protect it from rust and everything.'"

During my visit in 2006, Keith recalled the months of construction and testing as the engine came together in his machine shop. "We ran (the engine) back and forth on the shop floor using compressed air and worked the bugs out of it that way," Keith recalled. The engine's maiden run went off without a hitch thanks to the testing that preceded its run on a short section of track between a log yard and sawmill near the machine shop.

The sawmill was another one of Keith's hobbies. Powered with vintage steam equipment, the mill cut the ties for the inevitable railroad that was built as far as a swamp by 1976. The 5-foot-long ties were cut from discarded utility-company logs. An elaborate system that conveyed the poles from a log rail car to the sawmill took advantage of the railroad's infrastructure. A boiler failure brought an end to the sawmill after 33 years, but it served the railroad well during its lifespan.

Keith and his buddies scoured the region for rails with which to extend the line toward a former strip mine. "A lot of the rails came from a sawmill in Franklin," Keith told me. But a swamp had to be bridged before the line could reach the farthest points of their property. The volunteer crew built a 40-foot-long trestle over this swamp in 1977. Nineteen years later, they replaced the original structure that made possible the line's extension up a 4 ¼-percent grade to a forest and field.

Completed in 2003, the extension was made possible by harvesting locust trees that grew in the area. The steam-powered mill was used to cut the logs into railroad ties.

All this activity attracted the Masons' neighbors, who were offered rides on the flat car and caboose pulled by Mason Climax No. 1.

"My first recollections of it are of coming out every Wednesday evening when his friends were here running the sawmill," said Tammy, who was born in 1969 and grew up with the railroad. "Every now and then, we'd be able to catch a train ride. And it was just really cool that my dad had a train. How many kids can say their dad has a train?"

Word of the railroad spread beyond the subdivision, and the Wednesday-night work sessions morphed into excursions. "(Initially) that was the night that all of his friends gave up with their families to come saw logs at the mill," Tammy said. "And so, when we started with the train (rides), Wednesday stuck. That's the night when everybody always knew where to find my dad, my family and most of his friends."

This cadre grew into a full-fledged railroad crew of firemen, brakemen, conductors and laborers. Brakeman Tom Proud joined the crew in 1985 and was still showing up for duty 40 years later.

"My employer did business with Keith Mason in the machine shop, and they sent me out here one day to pick up some material," Tom said. "And I saw the railroad and asked about it. At the time Keith Mason wasn't here, but he did show up while I was out here looking around and said, 'Yeah, come out of Wednesday nights. We operate.' So, I didn't know whether to

Tom Proud joined the group of railroad volunteers back in 1985. His jobs include brakeman and conductor. He said ensuring passenger safety is the most important assignment of each volunteer.

come out as a tourist or come out as a worker. So, I just wore something, and if it got dirty, it wasn't going to hurt me any."

Tom spent the evening shoveling sawdust out of the mill. "So that started it," Tom said while taking a break from his duties at the back of the caboose. "I kind of like being the brakeman, especially in the summer, because of the heat from the boiler. And I like being the conductor. A lot of people don't realize (the conductor) is in charge of the movement of the train. The engineer and fireman are responsible for moving the train, but the conductor is a position of responsibility."

Tom takes his role seriously and keeps a watchful eye out for any safety issues.

"We're all about safety," Tom said. "And thank goodness, we haven't had any major accidents or problems. People are people and kids like to climb on the tracks, so there will be instances when someone falls or gets stung by a bee or this or that. But when the train is moving, we want everybody seated, because if you happen to fall off or go between the cars or something, that's not good for anybody. I would say safety is our primary concern."

Unlike Keith Mason, who had no railroaders in his family, Tom Proud's

Riding the Locust Heights & Western Railroad excursion is made even more special when passengers can snag a sweet spot on the caboose platform. Keith Mason built the caboose as a playhouse for his daughters and later repurposed it for his railroad. Photo from 2024 season.

father worked for the Western Maryland Railroad at Thomas. "My dad started out on the section gang and worked his way up to fireman," Tom said. "He's one of the few (enlisted men) I know of who, during the Second

The Wednesday night crew gets together in the Mason Machine Shop building in the winter months to swap ideas, stories and family news. From left in the front row are Randy Harpold, John Gorby, Bill Kapphan, Tom Proud, Sarah Grace Roach holding Mason Kenneth Roach, Tre Roach; In the back row are Dave Scott, Jean Mason, Will Brady, Mark Ware, Kyla Brady, Kristi Mason Brady, Gerald Corder, and Tammy Mason Molina. The crew also includes Tammy's husband, Duane Molina and Austin Morrison. Photo from February 26, 2025 gathering.

World War, (worked) in a railway shop and did something in the military that he did as a civilian."

Tom worked for a utility company but "always liked trains."

"And I just fit in here. I like the people and the camaraderie," Tom said. Through sweat, regular attendance and the inspiration of Keith Mason, this fraternity has created bonds as strong as the rails on which their work runs.

"A lot of the guys who have been here for years, that I've grown to know them, are like family to me," Tre said. "I don't know what I'd do without them. It's hard to think about that sometimes."

Tom, who lives in Bridgeport, rarely misses a Wednesday or Saturday work session on the railroad, although he was 79 in 2024. "If the work is here, it's gotta be done. Somebody has to do it," Tom said. "I plan to do this until I fall over or I can't anymore . . . a lot of us are getting older and

Tre Roach grew up around his grandfather's railroad and trained under him to be engineer and caretaker. Photo from 2024.

slower, and we need to get some young blood involved in it in order to continue it."

Tre, born in 1998, said the "next closest guy (on the crew) to me is 65. I try to make it as easy for them as possible. I want them to be here. I don't care if they come here and don't do a thing, to just enjoy and hang out and have fun like they did with my granddad in past years. I just want them to have the best time they can possibly have and help however they want to."

Essential positions must be filled before the train runs an excursion. "It takes two for the engine, and we always have a brakeman. We usually have a couple of gentlemen on the caboose, just to keep an eye out on the flat car and caboose for safety," Tammy said. "And then, of course, we're back here doing tickets and making sure everybody's able enjoy themselves if they have to wait in line." Factoring in volunteers who direct traffic in the parking lot, Tammy said it takes a minimum of 14 for the Wednesday evening runs; more for holiday and Saturday events.

Only licensed individuals can operate the boiler. Tom, who also worked as a compensated employee on steam-powered excursion railroads, and Mark Ware handle the task. Mark has worked on the LH&W for more than 35 years and never drawn a paycheck.

Tre Roach, 8 years old at the time, smiles for the camera as he rides in the locomotive cab with Tom Proud. Photo from 2006.

"I enjoy it. I like trains, and I like to see the kids and the people come out," Mark said. "This is just like a family here. You get to doing it, you enjoy it, and you keep doing it."

What passengers do not see are the maintenance and preparation activities that occur long before the train leaves the station. The day before excursions, Tre cleans the locomotive, fills the water reserve, brushes out the flues and lubricates everything.

Two to three hours before the first run, which is usually 7 p.m., Tre starts the boiler's fire. After the excursions, he heeds his grandfather's advice and takes an hour or more to allow the boiler to cool, then fills it with fresh water, cleans out the ash and completes a proper shutdown.

"Then, the next day, I'll go through and get everything, all the major stuff cleaned out . . . just trying to preserve it. The boiler is going to wear out eventually, but the more we take care of it, the longer it's going to treat us better, the longer it's going to last."

The other aspect of railroading, maintaining the track and bed, is a

The Locust Heights & Western Railroad intersects an old service road to a gas well and abandoned strip mine, providing an excuse for blowing the whistle.

year-round task that often involves the physical labor of wrestling with ties and rails.

"First of all, you got to get the ties. We used to saw our own here," said Mark Ware. "And, of course, you have to go out on the track, find the bad ties, and jack up the track and pull them out, put in the new ones and spike them." Track work consumes many Saturdays in spring to ensure the line is ready for another season of excursions.

"This is hard work," Tre said. "You gotta wanna to do it."

When Tre speaks of the railroad, he speaks from the experience of having worked alongside its builder and engineer. "Tre never left my dad's side as a toddler," Tammy said. "As soon as he could toddle, he was here every Wednesday night."

"I was always shadowing him," Tre said. "I was always up there when he was up there. I remember he'd blow the whistle a lot, and then he'd let me come around and blow it every now and then. And we had a very unique whistle sound—a variation of two longs and a short, or a long in there—we'd just have a little fun with it."

With a departure time of 7 p.m., the Wednesday evening excursions leave in the dark as the season winds down. The Halloween excursion is particularly popular with families who come out for the festive, spooky atmosphere.

Tre still remembers the thrill of blowing that whistle when they rang in the new millennium.

"I remember my granddad holding me up to blow the whistle on that midnight," Tre said. "I guess my earliest memory is of being hot and complaining (about being) in the engine, and ringing the bell. I stayed there because I wanted to be around everybody."

By the time Tre was 6, Keith allowed him to run, under supervision, the gasoline-powered Vulcan engine that serves as a backup to the steam locomotive. "It was just me and him with the locomotive," Tre said. "We ran it out the track probably halfway."

Running the Mason Climax was another story, however.

"I never did fire for him much because I was a little young to do it. Just because you're the grandson, doesn't mean I got to skip any of the levels," he adds.

Tre and Mark Ware filled the engineer's role when Keith's illness prevented him from handling the task.

"Then granddad got to enjoy watching me learn to fire and run it a little bit, too," Tre said. "No one dared enough to run it as hard as he did.

He didn't cut it any slack. He run her hard. And that's how steam engines were meant to be run, to be run for all they got."

Tammy said her father was in constant pain from the Parkinson's but insisted upon being present for the summer excursions.

"I brought him over every week, and I mean every week, even when he was in a wheelchair," Jean said. The crew made sure that Keith remained in the engineer's seat for as long as it was physically possible for him.

"He was diagnosed when he was 57. The first years were not as hard for him … he was determined to still be able to get up in the engine and engineer. He continued to do that for 12 years after he was diagnosed, until he couldn't physically get on the train anymore," Tammy said. "But even then, he never missed a Wednesday. He would be in his wheelchair or power chair. And we still called him the boss. We still all looked up to him. He would sit here, and he loved listening to the whistle from afar. He missed being on the engine, but hearing it made him very, very happy."

Keith Mason made his final ride on the LH&W several months before he died on October 12, 2016—a Wednesday.

"When my dad passed, I worried. I was like, 'Are (the volunteers) still going to want to do this?' And Tre said, 'I'm not giving up. We're going to continue. We're going to do this.' And all those guys said, 'Absolutely!'" Tammy recalls. "They are dedicated. I cannot stress enough how important they are to us."

Tammy feels that her father would be proud of what the family and volunteers have done with the railroad since he vacated the engineer's seat.

"I think he'd be in shock at some of the things we've accomplished. The amount of people who have come and brought their families and their children, and then their grandchildren and now their great-grandchildren," she said. "I think he would be astounded at some of the crowds that we've had and some of the thing's we accomplished, like the Christmas runs."

Jean said the railroad and its inherent responsibilities will pass to Tre, who also will have to manage its financial challenges. Income comes from the $5-per-person donation requested from riders. Tammy said donations go toward the biggest expense, liability insurance, and whatever is left over goes for coal (the engine burns about 150 pounds per night), which is increasingly expensive and ironically difficult to source in a state known

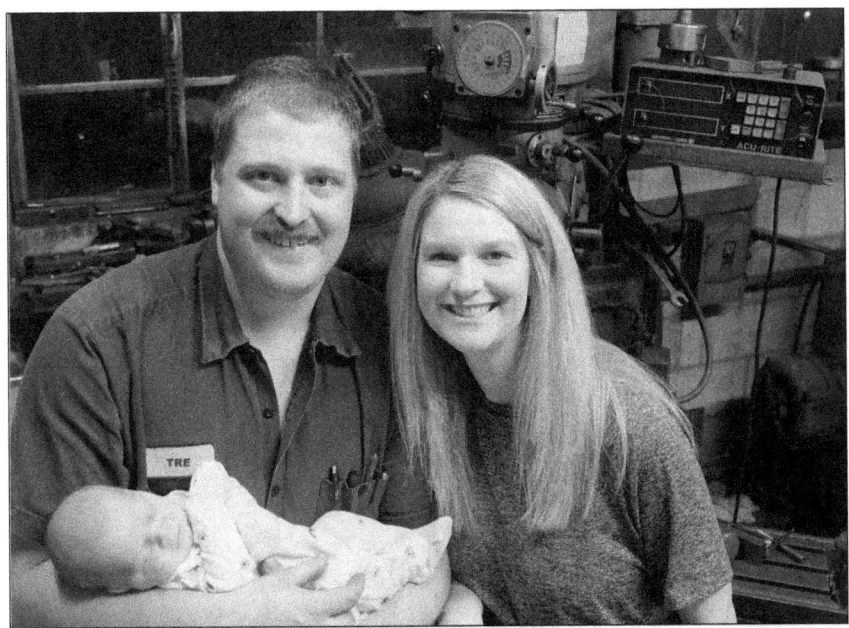

Tre Roach holds his son and the next generation of Mason-family engineers and machinists: Mason Kenneth Roach, 5 weeks old in this photograph from February 26, 2025, in the Mason Machine Shop, Clarksburg. Sarah Grace Roach, Mason's mother and Tre's wife smiles approvingly.

for coal mining. There are lubricants, parts, fuels and all the other non-personnel expenses involved in running a steam railroad, as well.

The most important asset, a desire to keep it operating, may have come into the railroad's lineage on January 22, 2025, when Tre and his wife, Sarah Grace, welcomed their son, Mason Kenneth, into the world. Destined to grow up as Tre did with the ringing of a train's bell in his ears and piercing odor of coal smoke in his nostrils, Mason was born—on a Wednesday—into one of West Virginia's best kept back-roads secrets.

"We love our state, and we're glad to be just a little part of it," Tammy said. Most of the people who live here call us the 'hidden secret of Clarksburg.'"

Follow the Locust Heights and Western Railroad on Facebook to receive updates on the operating schedule and special events.

The beautiful Berkeley Castle in Berkeley Springs overlooks the town that is known for history, art and quirky residents. Rosa Suit, for whom the castle was built, was right at home with this crowd.

Chapter 2

Mountain State Castles

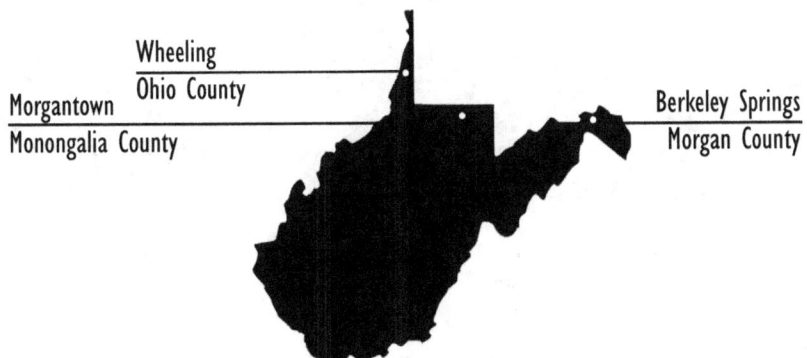

A ndrew Gosline had never been to Berkeley Springs nor heard of its castle until one day in early 2002, when he stumbled upon an intriguing announcement in *The Wall Street Journal*.

"I saw an ad for an auction in Berkeley Springs. I'd never heard of it," Andrew told me during a visit to his castle in 2008. A health care/data entrepreneur, Andrew was living in Jupiter Island, Fla., at the time. Intrigued by the property and the auction's attractive terms, Andrew registered for the May 4, 2002, sale. As the bidding began, Andrew and his two older sons, Andrew and Matthew, took their place by the massive stone fireplace in the front room. Roughly two dozen individuals with the potential to bid were present.

"I really didn't expect to buy it," Andrew said, standing by the same fireplace from which he did his bidding. "It's just one of those things you get caught up in."

After a few minutes of bidding, Andrew Gosline became the owner. "It was amazingly short," Andrew said. "My older son looked at me and said, 'Dad, I think you just bought a castle.' I fell in love with it."

Nearly a decade later, Andrew remained fascinated and captivated by

Andrew Gosline purchased the Berkeley Castle at an auction in 2002. He was photographed on the grand staircase in 2008.

both his purchase and the Morgan County town of Bath, more commonly known as Berkeley Springs. His castle, perched on a ridge overlooking the town's iconic springs and bathhouse, has stood here since the early 1890s. Built from native sandstone, it is the only Norman castle in the United States.

Andrew and his Doberman pinscher, Duke, were the 8,500-square-foot castle's only residents, except in the summer, when his youngest son, Mark, came to visit.

Although the castle was open to tourists from the 1950s to 2000, Andrew maintained it as a private residence, except for the annual Berkeley Springs Yule Tea, when a 14-foot-tall live Christmas tree was brought into the great room and decorated for the season. The castle also served as a backdrop for weddings during his ownership.

Tourists who had visited the castle decades earlier, when it was operated as a for-profit attraction, occasionally knocked on the castle door seeking a guided tour. Shortly after moving in, Andrew left the front door unlocked for a friend who planned to stop by, then headed upstairs to shower. Upon stepping out of the shower into his bedroom, he was startled to see a stranger

A portrait of Samuel Taylor Suit came with the Berkeley Castle purchase. Andrew Gosline stands in the castle's dining room, over which Suit kept watch.

standing there. On the main floor, the intruder's wife and children were poking around as they looked for a tour guide.

"I said 'This is my house.' And he said, 'Oh, I'm sorry!'" Andrew said recalling the experience that was embarrassing for both the visitor and owner.

"I find I have to keep the doors locked. The people try to come in and walk through," Andrew said.

Listed on the National Register of Historic Places, the castle enchants and entreats visitors with its history, architecture, romantic origins and legends. Samuel Taylor Suit was 55 when he began the project in 1885. Suit, a Republican, had lucrative careers in the stock market, distilling, railroads, dock management and politics. He served in the Maryland Senate from 1873 to 1877 and was ambassador to England under Ulysses S. Grant and Rutherford B. Hayes.

Following the Civil War, Suit purchased several hundred acres outside Washington, D.C. and established the Maryland town that bears his name.

Construction of the Berkeley Castle began in 1885. Each successive owner made additions/changes to fine tune the structure to their needs and times.

Suitland was home to his business, S.T. Suit, Fruit Grower and Distiller, which produced fruit brandies and a rye whiskey marketed in brown jugs.

He made his home in "Suit Land," a mansion modeled after an English manor house. On this estate, Suit raised a special breed of white ponies that he gave as gifts to the children of his friends. Often referred to as "Colonel," an honorary title from his Civil War days in Kentucky, Suit was a sentimental, loving person with a soft spot for young people, especially females.

His first wife died after giving birth to their son. His second, Aurelia, the daughter of a life insurance company's president, was 11 years his junior. Their 20-year marriage, while good for Suit's social standing, was contentious and ended in divorce in 1879.

Three years earlier, while Suit was away serving as a judge of agriculture at the Centennial Exposition in Philadelphia, his mansion burned to the ground. He went bankrupt and never rebuilt. However, Suit quickly regained his fortunes and eventually repurchased his Suit Land property.

In the late 1870s, while still married, Suit met and soon fell in love with Rosa Pelham, the debutante daughter of an Alabama congressman.

The castle overlooks the lovely town of Berkeley Springs, originally known as Bath. The warm springs attracted George Washington, whose stone tub can still be seen in the park.

Seventeen and beautiful, Rosa rejected his attempts at romance. Five years of pursuit followed, culminating with an 1883 meeting in Berkeley Springs.

Tradition holds that during this rendezvous, Rosa revealed that she always wanted to live in a castle. Suit promised to build one for her, a summer cottage on Warm Spring Ridge, overlooking the town, if she agreed to marry him.

They returned to Washington, D.C., and on September 4, 1883, married, just three days after the proposal. She was 22, he was 51. Three children were born to the couple.

Work began on the castle in 1885. The land was purchased from H. H. Boyd and had been part of the Fruit Hill Farm. A.D. Mullet, designer of the State, War and Navy Building (Eisenhower Executive Office Building) in Washington, D.C., performed the design work.

It was modeled, on half scale, after England's Berkeley Castle, where King Edward II was murdered in 1327. In the Berkeley Springs version, the great room measures 46-by-26 feet, has a 16-foot ceiling, hardwood floors and is flanked by stone fireplaces. A wide staircase, which becomes twisting halfway up the rise, leads to the second-floor bedrooms, library and solarium. The dining room and second-story library are paneled in carved Georgian pine. The turret rises three stories, providing reading nooks on the lower levels and a stunning overlook of the community from the top of the tower. Stone crosses are embedded in the turret's skin, and battlements trim the roof line. There is no moat; modern security systems fulfill that role much more efficiently.

In keeping with a summer-cottage concept, the kitchen, originally a pantry, was relatively small. A spacious dungeon—more likely a wine cellar—is carved into the limestone.

Built of native sandstone and lumber, the castle slowly took form as 100 German masons labored on the project. Each stone was hand cut and hauled to the site by horse and wagon. The Suits visited Berkeley Springs periodically to monitor the progress. Although the castle was still under construction, in the late summer of 1887 the Suit family spent a few days in the edifice. It was the only time Samuel Taylor Suit "resided" in his castle; he died September 1, 1888, in Washington, D.C.

Queen Rosa

Rosa and their three children, the youngest just 1 year old, inherited the unfinished work and most of its master's fortune. Rosa requested work resume on the castle, a condition for her inheritance of the property. In the interim, she divided her time between Berkeley Springs and Suit Land.

Rosa and her three children took up residency in the finished castle in May 1891. Total bill for the 13-room residence was around $100,000.

Blue-eyed, slender, 27 and wealthy, Rosa Suit had no problem attracting suitors to her castle door. She gave lavish parties and was known as "Queen Rosa" by both friends and those outside her circle.

"Mrs. Suit was elegantly attired in black crepe with an elegant train giving her a queenly air," wrote a reviewer in the *Morgan Mercury* newspaper of July 1891. "She was untiring in her efforts in order that her guests be well entertained, and made complete 'at home.' Not only the elite of our village were invited, but all of her friends received a cordial invitation to attend the festivities at her feudal home."

A caveat needs to be interjected at this point. Berkeley Springs was, in that era, a very rural community made up mostly of subsistence farmers.

Andrew Gosline looks at a portrait of Rosa Suit, the beautiful young woman who inspired construction of the castle. Queen Rosa lived the good life at Berkeley Castle, the site of parties and mysterious deaths.

It would not take a great deal of material wealth and flaunting of the same to create an air of royalty.

Although there were suitors, and scandalous stories of Rosa entertaining them, she never remarried. According to local gossip, one of her serious suitors was Malcolm Crichton, who owned Ravenswood, a large estate in the Eastern Panhandle.

One legend holds that one of Rosa's suitors fell or was pushed to his death from the castle roof; another suitor allegedly fell down the great staircase and was impaled on his umbrella. Some have claimed, perhaps to the enrichment of the castle's value, that the ghosts of unfortunate suitors haunt the place.

The castle was updated with electricity and running water in 1895. While modern conveniences made living in the castle more enjoyable, Rosa's extravagant spending, coupled with the Depression of 1893, brought tough times. The lawsuits and judgments overwhelmed Rosa's dwindling bank account. In 1902 she left the castle and moved into a small house she built

The third floor of the castle was very modern, with a large family room equipped with modern entertainment options and an outside entrance to the gardens.

along Sleepy Creek. That same year, she sold off her property holdings in Maryland to pay debts.

More financial problems followed when she invested in a bogus mining scheme centered on a thin seam of coal allegedly discovered near her home. With a ready market for it in nearby urban centers, the investment seemed like a sure bet. Rosa jumped in with borrowed money whose only returns were hardship and poverty. Dogged by creditors, her glory days behind her, Rosa rented the castle to raise cash. Neighbors along Sleepy Creek described her as poorly dressed and prone to act crazy.

The castle eventually went to auction to settle her debts. Her sons, Samuel Taylor Suit, Jr., and Pelham Suit, purchased it in 1909 for $4,265. In the interim, Rosa's father passed away, and she inherited his money. The funds allowed her to return to the castle and resume extravagant living for a few more years.

Poverty eventually caught up with Rosa. She was evicted from the citadel, and in 1916 the castle was sold to the Bank of Morgan County. Rosa moved into an old house and subsisted on gardening and raising chickens,

Andrew Gosline purchased Berkeley Castle in 2002. He was heavily invested in the Berkeley Springs community and committed to preserving its history and the iconic castle.

until her son, Pelham, took her to live with him in Idaho, where he was a park ranger. She died at the age of 90.

George Cunningham purchased the castle for $7,500 in 1923 and used it as a tearoom and for dances and social events. Taylor Voorhorst, a Washington writer, briefly attempted to make it into a writer's retreat in the late 1920s. Dr. Ward W. Keesecker of Berkeley County purchased it in 1936, opened it to tourists and made it the headquarters of Monte-Vita, a summer camp for boys.

It was during Keesecker's ownership that a row of bedrooms was added at the rear of the castle in the early 1950s. Standing on either side of the structure, the demarcation of old and new construction is evident by the difference in materials. The addition brought to 20 the number of rooms in the castle.

Water Bird and Henry Foil purchased it in 1954. Bird soon became the sole owner, and he and his family operated it as a tourist site until September 2000, when the castle and the contents went on the auction block.

It sold for $360,125 to Virginia Scientific Research, a paranormal group that evidently hoped to rent the building to ghost hunters. The plan failed. Locals say there are no ghosts in Berkeley Castle. The property sold again, to Associated Investors Group, LLC, which renovated it with new heating and cooling systems, an electrical upgrade, new roof and windows, and a commercial-grade kitchen.

Gosline years

Andrew Gosline said he paid about twice the price the castle brought at the 2000 auction. The only relics that came with it were two portraits of Rosa and one of Samuel Taylor Suit, which he displayed in the dining room and library, respectively.

He spent the first six months of ownership addressing structural issues, including failing mortar, which was allowing water to infiltrate the interior. Andrew said the biggest challenge was locating a reliable, knowledgeable stonemason qualified for the job. He found his answer in Dino Pretruci, who not only restored a century of haphazard patch jobs but also rebuilt walls and the gatehouse. When the castle was built, the road ran below the gatehouse; construction of the state highway in the 1930s went right through the castle property and isolated the entrance from the residence. Andrew said the structure was in bad condition, and the stonemason worked from vintage photographs to guide the restoration.

The roof also suffered years of neglect, and layers of tar paper had to be torn off to get to the beams, which had started to deteriorate from the standing water. When the rooms were added to the back of the castle, the addition created a barrier on the roof that interfered with proper drainage.

To preserve the exterior appearance of the castle, water flows from the roof through two copper downspouts that run along interior walls. Concealing modern infrastructure, such as electrical wires, outlets and plumbing lines, was a constant challenge

"Everything I have done to it has been to try to preserve it," Andrew told me. He reversed many of the "updates" the castle suffered at the hands of previous owners and was thankful not all their plans were enacted. At one point, a previous owner contemplated painting the dark paneling of the dining room to make it "more cheerful."

Andrew personalized the renovation by adding gargoyles to the

Andrew Gosline kept a telescope in his castle's turret, which provided a stunning view of the town below.

battlements because he enjoyed them and felt the castle needed that touch. He also had stone terraces and stairs built off the north and south sides of the second story.

By 2003, Andrew had adopted the castle as his home. His wife, however, did not share Andrew's passion for the citadel and disliked snow and the temperatures that accompanied it. They divorced, leaving just Andrew and his dog to roam the castle's 20 rooms and five-acres of grounds.

"There's plenty of room when it's only you and your dog," Andrew said.

It was an expensive home to operate with six air conditioning units to cool the massive rooms. Propane fueled the furnaces, which in the dead of winter burned through 2,000 gallons of fuel in 20 days. Andrew made a practice of idling the castle and going to Florida in the winter.

His favorite room was the second-floor solarium. "The best time of day here is in the early evening," Andrew said. "I enjoy sitting upstairs and reading. I enjoy the environment."

Much of his living space was on the third floor, where a modern, spacious family room was fully equipped with home-entertainment options.

Andrew described the castle's atmosphere as positive and imparting

Berkeley Castle owner Andrew Gosline with his son, Mark, outside the castle's upper level.

feelings of serenity, well-being and peace. It truly was a bulwark from the outside world. "You don't hear much in here," he said. The walls are close to two feet thick on the first level."

Although at least one former housekeeper would say otherwise, Andrew never sensed that his castle was haunted. Just to be sure, he agreed to allow a team of paranormal investigators access to the property. Their results were inconclusive. "One investigator supposedly saw traces of a ghost, or spirit," said Andrew, who personally did not believe in ghosts.

Likewise, he doubted the tunnel legends, especially one that linked the castle to the Potomac River. That would have been an incredible engineering feat as there are 6 miles of limestone between the castle and river. "It's not practical," Andrew said. Another legend claimed a tunnel ran between the castle and inn below it. "It's interesting because there are people who claim their grandfather or someone else they knew had seen it. I have not been able to locate anything like that," he said.

Andrew even had a well driller systematically drill down 6 feet along the front of the property in an effort to verify the legend. Most likely, the tunnel referred to a connecting passage that would have existed between the gatehouse and castle, before Route 9 cut through the property. The passageway reportedly collapsed during the highway construction.

In 2009 Andrew tackled another legend about his castle and traveled to the town of Bath, England, to tour the original Berkeley Castle. "The Berkeley Castle is a different design," he concluded. "It's more of a round castle. One side of the castle is close to this one, but it is a different type and much bigger."

The discovery in no way diminished his respect for what he owned. "I think it is an important part of the town and the history of Berkeley Springs," Andrew said of the castle. "You have to have a love of something like this to spend the money and time on it."

Unlike Rosa, however, Andrew understood that there was a limit to spending. "I don't want to end up raising chickens like she did," he said. "I'm much more cautious than that."

Andrew's favorite story about the castle and its original owners involved those dark times in Rosa's life when she was living in the poor part of town among the chickens. A group of citizens went to visit her, and as they sat and talked on the porch of her shack, one of them asked if she would have done anything differently or changed the way she lived if she were given a second chance.

"She said, 'No. She wouldn't have changed a thing; she had her memories,'" Andrew said.

Although he divided his time between Ormond Beach, Fla, and Berkeley

Springs, Andrew fully invested in his castle's home community. He also owned the Old Factory Antique Mall, Old Mill building and several other properties in Berkeley Springs. He clearly loved his castle and the town over which it kept watch.

Another chapter

Andrew died December 2, 2014, at the age of 74. True to its turbulent history, the castle entered yet another phase of controversy and intrigue.

The Berkeley Springs Castle Foundation purchased it in February 2020. Several online sources reported that the $1.4 million sale, without any bank financing, was to the white-nationalist, non-profit VDARE organization. At one point, the organization stated on a website that its purpose in owning the castle was as a "meeting place."

The purchase stirred the sentiments of some Berkeley Springs residents, who were interviewed for a March 19, 2020, story published by the Southern Poverty Law Center (SPLC). According to that article, VDARE was "founded by anti-immigration activist Peter Brimelow in 1999, the non-profit has grown in influence during the (first) Trump-era while simultaneously espousing more extreme, racist viewpoints." The author, Rachel Janik, suggested the Berkeley Springs location provided the group relatively close access to Washington, D.C., and its policymakers—it is about a two-hour drive to the district from Berkeley Springs. The group's purpose is to "defeat the post-1964 Immigration Act (Immigration and Nationality Act of 1965) disaster that has set America on a course of destruction."

In the winter of 2024, the castle's website, berkeleyspringscastle, stated only that it is owned by the Berkeley Springs Foundation and is available to rent for private events. The website's only mention of a tour opportunity was by volunteering for a spring community day, when participants could "contribute some elbow grease."

Lydia Brimelow, president of the foundation, wrote the website's posts. The SPLC identifies her as "the 38-year-old wife of VDARE founder Peter Brimelow, 75." In January 2025, there was on the VDARE.com website both text and video messages from Peter Brimelow announcing suspension of VDARE after 25 years.

In his lengthy post, Peter Brimelow stated: "One bright spot: The

Thoney Pietro, an Italian immigrant, built a castle for his family near Morgantown. The castle is now home to the Calvary Chapel Morgantown congregation.

Berkeley Springs Castle, which is where we're filming this, is owned by a separate foundation that is based in West Virginia. It will continue to host Dissident conferences as well as normie events like weddings and so on... —if any of you want to get married and battle the Great Replacement. "

A castle and a Bible walk

On the outskirts of Morgantown stands another castle built by a man who dearly loved his family and wanted to treat them like royalty.

Thoney Pietro, an Italian immigrant, began work on the structure in 1928 and completed it five years later. Pietro was a bricklayer who chose Morgantown as his home because it reminded him of Italy. He built brick streets, homes and halls throughout the town, but his most amazing work was his castle home on Tyronne Road.

The 23-room structure cost $200,000; Pietro taught unemployed men how to cut stone and hired them at $2.40 a day to labor on the fortress.

In 2006, Father June Mili welcomed me to the Good Counsel Friary that hosted a Bible walk on its Morgantown property. Afflicted with Parkinson's Disease, Father Mili was unable to maintain the Bible walk and sought a group to take over its restoration and maintenance. Although he lived on the castle campus, he'd never spent a night in the building.

In 1949, he donated his castle and about half of his estate to the Roman Catholic Church, which used it as a place to train missionaries. In 1955, a chapel was built, and in 1968, the Franciscans completed a separate building to house the priest, a library, conference rooms and offices. Collectively, it was known as the Good Counsel Friary.

I visited the property in 2006, when Father Jude Mili was resident priest and property guardian. Father Mili told me he never spent a night in the castle, and the vacant building was slowly succumbing to time. No problem. It was not the castle that I came to see; reports of a bizarre, dilapidated Bible walk in the forest behind the friary provided an excuse for this back-roads journey.

Father Mili apologized for the Bible walk's condition—weather and a lack of maintenance had led to several decapitations and dismemberments among the inhabitants.

Among the high-profile victims was Adam, that old progenitor himself, whose right hand was missing two fingers and head was attached with duct tape. The right hand of Ham, of Noah's Ark fame, was gone. Abraham had no fingers but fared better than the female figure next to him. She was prostrate with broken hands, puddles of water standing in her tunic's folds.

The situation in the New Testament section was equally distressing.

The Bible walk in the forest behind the friary was stocked with New York fashion mannequins resurrected as Bible characters. The figures were not weatherproofed and suffered from exposure to the elements. The walk no longer exists.

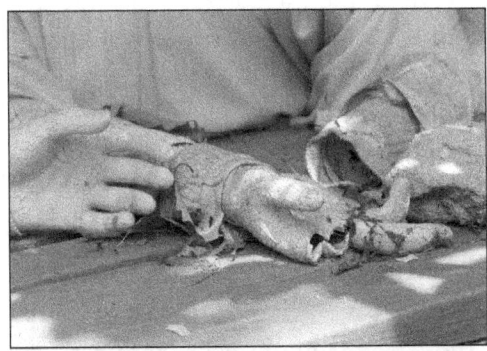

The Twelve Disciples' missing fingers and hands gave a new meaning to the words "Last Supper."

These religious figures started their lives as clothing store mannequins in the New York Bronx, and as the Bible predicts of all mortal creatures, they were returning to dust.

"We had two very bad winters, and they did a lot of damage (to the walk's figures)," Father Mili told me. "People still come to see it, but they are very disappointed and discouraged to see what has happened to it."

The friary was constructed as a house of study shortly after he arrived in 1968. A New England native, he came to Morgantown to head up the Franciscan ministry formed to provide newly ordained priests with a sanctuary where they could prepare for parish service. The timing was not divinely appointed, however. New priests were few and far between, and the house of preparation was soon converted to a retreat. By 2006, it was facing bankruptcy.

The Bible walk attraction came to these grounds in the early 1980s through a contact with Bill Warren, a Pittsburgh-area businessman who had built a Bible-themed walk around his home in Collier Township, near Bridgeville, Pa. Warren felt God had called him and his wife Gail to construct 30 biblical scenes that traced the story of redemption as presented in the Old and New Testaments.

Warren's project cost $200,000. He purchased from Bronx fashion companies dozens of mannequins predestined for biblical roles. Father Mili said Warren told him that his vehicle looked like the morgue with all those mannequins stacked inside it. Gail Warren researched the clothing that the historical figures would have worn and designed and sewed their coverings using sturdy materials like burlap and awning fabric. A scripture reference painted on a sheet of plywood was posted at each scene.

The couple's neighbors objected to the thousands of visitors going through the walk and took the Warrens to court. The judge determined the attraction violated zoning ordinances, and the Warrens went searching for a new host.

Through a series of events, Bill Warren and Father Mili became acquainted, and Warren offered the walk to the friary. Father Mili said they really didn't want it, but they agreed to pray about the request. "Each time we prayed for the Bible walk, it seemed like we'd get another letter from Bill Warren or someone would write to us about it," he said.

Warren and his family hauled most of the Bible walk mannequins to the friary and re-established it in the forest; 22 other figures went to Diamond Hill Cathedral in Mansfield, Ohio, where they became the cornerstone of the Living Bible Museum (biblewalk.us).

Father Mili melded the Warrens' donation with 14 marble Stations of the Cross formerly displayed in St. Peter's Shrine in Pittsburgh. "When it first came here, many people would come here to be healed," Father Mili said. "They came out of curiosity, and the Lord gave them the grace to be converted."

In 2006, the Bible walk needed some conversion of its own. Afflicted with Parkinson's Disease, Father Mili could no longer wander through the attraction, let alone maintain it. The mannequins needed repaired/replaced, their garments restored, their shelters rebuilt. The dozens of plywood signs that displayed Bible verses and annotations were peeling and crumbling. But Father Mili remained optimistic about the walk's future.

"I feel we are on holy ground on this place," he told me as we wrapped up the interview. "We've seen many, many miracles happen."

He died the following year.

In 2012, Calvary Chapel Morgantown purchased the 34-acre property. Vacant for nearly 15 years, the building suffered from water damage, as well as plumbing and electrical issues. Renovations began in 2014 and required nine months to complete.

"The castle is a great illustration of how we ourselves have been changed internally through a relationship with Jesus Christ," notes the church's website.

The heavily vandalized Bible walk, beyond salvation, was removed by the property's new owners.

Wheeling's castle

No discussion of West Virginia castles would be complete without mentioning the state's most abused castle, which stands in Wheeling's North Park (Mount Wood Overlook).

Built of concrete, the structure shared a common thread with the other

The concrete turret of Wheeling castle at Mount Wood provides a sweeping view of the Ohio River and the graffiti artists' mindsets

West Virginia castles in that a man's love for a woman inspired the work. This man, Dr. Andrew Jackson Harness, chose the perfect location overlooking the city and Ohio River. Unfortunately, in the other direction was Mount Wood Cemetery. The castle was to have a turret-like feature with windows that opened to a stunning view of the valley.

Dr. Harness established a sterling reputation for his doctoring abilities while practicing in Kentucky in the early 20th century. By 1916, he had relocated his practice and family to Fairmont. His medical talents were pressed into service in both the French and U.S. armies during World War I. His wife, Mable, and daughters Myrtle and Mary Louis, relocated to Wheeling during his absence.

A successful physician who never turned a patient away for lack of money to pay him, Dr. Harness planned to build at Mount Wood a home that would both celebrate his success and most likely provide a clinic. Construction got under way in the mid-1920s but was halted when Dr. Harness landed in some serious trouble: He unwittingly sold regulated narcotics to two undercover federal agents who posed as needy patients. The crux

Construction of the Wheeling castle was halted by the builder's prison term. It has provided a canvas for area graffiti artists and inspired many online legends about its builder and purpose.

of his crime was that he sold the drugs without collecting the proper tax. He was sentenced to 18 months in the federal penitentiary in Atlanta, Ga.

Given early release for good behavior, the doctor returned to West Virginia, where the family had relocated to Cabin Creek. Tragedy struck the Harness family in 1927 when Myrtle succumbed to heart disease. Mabel Louise married a Charleston man who went on to college in Florida, and the doctor and his family followed them to Miami.

Wherever he practiced, Dr. Harness was one to show compassion to all and continue his training and education. By the time he died January 30, 1946, the couple had begun to sell off their significant land holdings around Mount Wood. Evidently, the castle portion ended up being city owned.

There are many other versions of the Mount Wood Castle story floating around on the Internet, and they frequently paint Dr. Harness as a much more sinister individual. But this account, researched by Miranda Heitz for Archiving Wheeling, is by far the most thoroughly documented.

The uncompleted, concrete structure has been the target of graffiti artists for decades. A Guerrilla Gardening project sponsored by the Wheeling Arts Commission attempted to reclaim the castle for nature by growing moss in artistic patterns over the layers of spray paint.

The Wheeling Castle is at 53 Mount Wood Road, Wheeling. For more information on its neighbor, Mount Wood Cemetery, see Chapter 12, "Mount Wood Dentist," Wandering Back-Roads West Virginia, Volume 2.

The Thoney Pietro castle/church is at 493 Tyronne Road, Morgantown. The church's website includes a history of the building: ccmorgantown.com.

The O' Be JoyFull ghost tour departs from St. Peter's Roman Catholic Church at Harpers Ferry on a June Evening. Amelia Garland leads the tour that was started by Shirley Dougherty more than 50 years earlier.

Chapter 3

Ghosts of Harpers Ferry

Harpers Ferry
Jefferson County

A crepuscular shade crept across Maryland Heights' craggy face as Amelia Garland took her seat in front of St. Peter's Roman Catholic Church, Harpers Ferry. Carrying a black kerosene lantern with a sooty shade and wearing a long dress of similar tone, Amelia announced she was ready to accept payment for the O' Be JoyFull ghost tour, owned and operated by Amelia and her husband, Rick. The couple promote the tour as the oldest of its kind in the nation, 55 years in 2025.

This evening in early June, I was taking the tour with my wife, Ruth. It was my third tour, but the first for Ruth. My first and second tours were with their founder, the late Shirley Dougherty, who entered the afterlife on December 20, 2011, at the age of 83. She started the ghost tour in 1970 as a one-time, light-hearted event hosted by Neal Randell, a National Park Service interpreter who knew of Shirley's interest in the town's spooky heritage. That limited-edition walk turned into a two-year run of tours that Shirley hosted as a volunteer. After the park service shelved the attraction, Shirley revamped it as a commercial venture; her advertising was a small sign in front of Hot Dog Haven and word-of-mouth. She charged $2 a head.

The beautiful, historic town of Harpers Ferry at the confluence of the Shenandoah and Potomac rivers has a history boiled in bloodshed and violence, the perfect setting for ghost stories. Photo from 1984.

The ghost walk became a Harpers Ferry tradition. Shirley knew how to deliver a good story with the gravelly voice of a middle-aged woman who had smoked three packs a day since adolescence. Clothed in a long cotton dress with a dainty print, her gray hair piled atop her head in a bun and wire-rimmed glasses resting on her nose, Shirley led the adoring crowds with a kerosene lantern. The proximity of flame next to the abundant cotton pleats raised alarm among the participants once they heard Shirley's rendition of the Jenny ghost story, a staple of the walk Shirley related while pausing at the Iron House Inn on Potomac Street.

A resident of Loudon Heights at the time, Shirley leased the inn and operated a restaurant there with help from her son and daughter-in-law, Pat and Linda, who lived on the inn's second floor. Her story of Jenny had nothing to do with the inn, however. Jenny's story was staged on the railroad tracks that parallel Potomac Street until they cross the river and disappear in the 1921 Harpers Ferry railroad tunnel.

Shirley Dougherty knew how to hold a crowd spellbound during her ghost tour of Harpers Ferry. Photo from 2000.

The CSX line was the Baltimore and Ohio Railroad in Jenny's era and a key player in the Ferry's story as a town of strategic importance for Confederate and Union soldiers alike. Provisions, soldiers and materiel moved on these rails. The army that controlled the B&O and Harpers Ferry armory held strategic advantages across its namesake points—Baltimore and the Ohio River.

The Civil War is not at the core of Jenny's story, however. The tale was born one cold, obscure night in the mid-19th century. Jenny's abode was a storage shed near the Federal Armory. Poverty-cursed residents like Jenny made do with whatever shelter they could find in which to escape the dank, cold of winters of Harpers Ferry. Jenny, like Shirley, wore long, cotton dresses, except they were as ragged and scruffy as their wretched occupants.

That fateful night, Jenny drew too close to the fire in her shack as she attempted to drive the chill from her bones. An ember ignited the skirt of her dress; the flames crawled up her petticoat like a snake after prey and quickly engulfed Jenny, who grabbed her lantern and ran down the railroad tracks screaming. A locomotive coming from the opposite direction

The late Shirley Dougherty found her place in this life as an author and ghost-tour guide.

violently ended her suffering, but not her aura. For decades to come, engineers reported seeing a flaming, screaming ball of flesh and spirit heading toward the locomotive, followed by collision and a jolt of energy surging through the train. Upon stopping, no physical evidence of the encounter was found. It was said that engineers who previously encountered Jenny always approached Harpers Ferry with a profusion of caution and whistles.

"Watch the trains pass this point in the old Armory yard," Shirley

Amelia Garland pauses in front of the inn Shirley Dougherty once operated on Potomac Street, Harpers Ferry. As a historian, Amelia's versions of the stories that Shirley told are often at odds with Shirley's in the details.

wrote in her book, A *Ghostly Tour of Harpers Ferry*. "You will be able to tell which engineers have met screaming Jenny by the slack speed at which they guide their trains over this section of track."

Although embedded in Harpers Ferry lore like John Brown and floods, this fascinating tale is usually omitted during O' Be JoyFull's ghost tour. This evening, however, Amelia makes an exception, not so much to scare folks but to set the record straight in a town known for legends as steep as the peaks that surround it.

In the case of Jenny's story, which Amelia and Rick Garland extensively researched, the facts unravel the yarn from which Shirley knitted her living. "This is the most popular ghost story in Harpers Ferry. If you pick up a book on ghosts of Virginia or West Virginia or Harpers Ferry, 99 times out of 100, you will find this tale within its pages," Amelia said.

As to the reasons this story holds water like a presidential candidate's speech, the reader must take the walk. Sufficient to say, the Garlands' research revealed that Jenny, if that was indeed her name, never lived in Harpers Ferry but belongs to another Jefferson County railroad town.

"I am a historian at heart. I try to be as historically accurate as possible... I cannot in good conscience continue with Shirley's favorite story without throwing in that very important footnote at the end," Amelia said, exposing the errors in Shirley's version of the story. "But I do find it fascinating the power us ghost tour guides have and how we can alter the myths and legends of a town merely on a whim."

Shirley, who once said, "We've had some mighty strange people live in town; in fact, we still do," explored the human, gray areas of Harpers Ferry lore. The Garlands, who also operate a daytime historical tour, refer to Shirley's *Ghostly History of Harpers Ferry,* but detour when they reach the intersection of lore and history.

They came into the ghost-tour business on a whim. During the 1990s, Shirley mentored her granddaughter, Ann, to take over the walk. "But Ann was not as passionate about the whole ghost tour thing like Shirley was," Amelia said. "And Ann did the tour for about six or seven years or so. And then she walked into the Harpers Ferry Merchants Association meeting one evening and explained she was going to retire. And everybody in town objected, and they said, 'Ann, you cannot give this up. This is a tradition in Harpers Ferry that goes back over 40 years.' But Ann insisted she was going to retire, and she turned to me and my husband, and said, 'I want you to take it over.' So, my husband and I do our very best to keep Shirley's tradition alive."

A visitor may still find a copy of Shirley's classic 40-page booklet in one of the town's bookstores. In that work, Shirley shared her "favorite theory" for ghost sightings, which she linked to the energy force, or aura, that theoretically surrounds our bodies.

"This energy force turns inward when we are hurt or ill and helps to heal," Shirley wrote in the introduction. If one becomes terminally ill, the aura diminishes in step with the physical body's decline. But what happens to this energy field if death comes suddenly, violently, as often occurred in Harpers Ferry? Could what we describe as a "ghost" be that wandering life force still searching for its container that departed our realm centuries ago?

Interestingly, in all the years that Amelia and Rick have conducted both ghost and historical tours of Harpers Ferry, they've not encountered Shirley's ghost, although one might expect her to haunt them for having the chutzpah to challenge her work.

Amelia Garland's background in theater is evident as she leads her ghost walk.

"Shirley does not haunt her own ghost tour, but there are some people who would disagree with me in that regard," Amelia said. Later in the tour, Amelia remarked that among the many photos taken at the allegedly haunted spots and posted on the tour's Facebook page, there was one that jumped off the screen for those who knew Shirley Dougherty. In the comments section, they wrote "You know what? That looks like Grandma Shirley!"

Shirley was born in nearby Cumberland, Md., but formed a bond with Harpers Ferry at a young age. "The place has always fascinated me, even as a small child," she told me back in 1990. "As I grew older and started dating, I always wanted to go to Harpers Ferry on my dates."

Amelia grew up in a small town near Gettysburg, Pa., another Civil War town steeped in violence and sudden death. She said that growing up in that region and living in a 200-year-old house provided experiences that prepared her for leading ghost tours. Her background in musical theater equipped her to do something that Shirley thankfully did not attempt; Amelia sings the familiar "Battle Hymn of the Republic" as its original composition, "John Brown's Body."

Rick is a historian, licensed tour guide, musicologist, vocalist, pianist

Amelia Garland shares a ghost story from the steps of St. Peter's Roman Catholic Church in Harpers Ferry, June 2024.

and historical storyteller also rooted in Gettysburg, where he developed historical sing-a-long musical programs about American cultural history, the Civil War and Battle of Gettysburg. The Garlands' artistic talents intersect with their knowledge of paranormal activity in Harpers Ferry.

"Basically, in the ghost-hunting world, there are two kinds of hauntings," Amelia told our tour group. "The first kind of haunting we see all the time is known as residual-energy haunting. This could be something like footsteps walking up and down the staircase, or up and down the hallway. It's like a movie loop replaying itself over and over again."

Amelia said these kinds of hauntings might reflect an ordinary occurrence in the human's life or re-enact a traumatic event. The tour's launching point provides at least two examples: Father Costello and a mortally wounded Irish Catholic soldier.

The iconic stone church was used as a hospital during the battles for Harpers Ferry. During Stonewall Jackson's big campaign in 1862, a soldier with Irish heritage was brought to the piazza of St. Peter's for surgical intervention. There were soldiers with more extensive injuries ahead of him, but the suffering private took comfort in knowing his care would be administered within the walls of a Catholic church. He waited patiently for both treatment and last rites from Father Costello. As hospital aides carried him past the threshold of the church and into surgery, he whispered, "Thank you, God. I am saved."

Except he wasn't. The soldier died moments after crossing the threshold, and the incident became a convenient explanation for a common sighting on the church grounds.

"There have been many accounts of people claiming that they've seen what they've described as a golden ball of light, almost what looks like a really big orb emanating from the threshold of the church," Amelia said. "And those who are brave enough to come forward and investigate claim they hear somebody whispering with a thick Irish rouge repeating over and over again, saying, 'Thank you, God, I am saved' until it fades away."

Another frequent sighting on the St. Peter's property is that of Father Costello descending the path from the rectory to the church. The event occurs around 6 p.m., when priests offer the vespers, or evening prayers.

"They describe him as being dressed in all black, wearing a big black friar's cap and carrying a big heavy book," Amelia said. Some witnesses have spoken to the priest, but he aloofly walks right past them and disappears into the stone wall.

"And many people believe that apparition to be Father Michael Costello, who is still keeping an eye on his beloved St. Peter's Church," Amelia said.

She uses the story as a launch pad for more history about the church, Father Costello, John Brown and Luke Quinn, whose name is seldom heard in the same breath with "Harpers Ferry." While the death of John Brown's son, Oliver, and the freed slave, Dangerfield Newby, are common fare in narratives about Brown's raid, any casualties suffered by the Virginia militia under Col. Robert E. Lee are not. That person is Luke Quinn, the only Marine killed while quelling the raiders. Amelia said a flag flies over his grave in St. Peter's Cemetery, where Father Costello and Shirley Dougherty also rest.

As for Dangerfield Newby's remains, they were buried in the bowels of the wild hogs that frequented "Hog Alley" between Potomac and High streets. The alley was essentially a dump, where everything from the contents of chamber pots to food scraps were deposited. Dangerfield's lifeless, mutilated body was tossed in this alley, as well.

Hog Alley has a violent, macabre story tied to the John Brown Raid.

One of five Blacks in Brown's raiding party, Dangerfield incited the hatred of the townspeople after he killed George Turner, a friend of Lewis Washington and frequent visitor to the town, on October 17, 1859. One of the many ironies of this place was that weapons were plentiful but ammunition was scarce. Residents improvised with what they had, which in Dangerfield's case was a 6-inch-long spike propelled from a musket, delivering a very painful, fatal wound. Another irony—Dangerfield Newby was a former slave and freeman, but he was married to a slave whom he hoped to free through Brown's aggression.

The townspeople tossed Dangerfield's corpse in the alley, where it was dismembered, stabbed and abused. The appendages thus removed became dinner for the hogs that frequented the alley.

Amelia shared this story as we sat on a stone wall along Hog Alley. The lantern, previously a mood-setting accoutrement, by this point was a matter of safety for Amelia, who cited as her source of this ghastly tale the work of witness/author, Joseph Berry (1828-1905).

"The writer saw all this with his own eyes, as the saying is, and, at the risk of further criticism, he will remark that none of the good people of Harpers Ferry appeared to be at all squeamish about the quality or flavor of their pork that winter," Berry wrote in *The Strange Story of Harpers Ferry*. "Nobody thought on the subject or, if anybody did recall the episode, it was, no doubt, to give credit to the hogs for their rough treatment of the invaders." (Newby's remains were tossed into a packing crate along with the remains from several others killed in the raid and unceremoniously buried. They were exhumed in 1899 and reburied on the former John Brown Farm in New York.)

In a more recent story connected to the incident, Amelia shared an experience that her husband had while leading the tour.

"He had a woman stand up proudly, put her hands on her hips and declare that, 'Well, you know that human flesh tastes just like pork!' He stayed away from her the rest of the evening," Amelia told us.

Although nothing showed up in the images that I took of Amelia standing in Hog Alley that evening, other ghost-hunting tourists have captured some convincing proof that the place is haunted, perhaps by an intact Dangerfield Newby.

"In the 16 years I've been doing this, I've seen lots of interesting pictures," said Amelia. "Most of my favorites have been captured right here in Hog Alley. About 12 years ago, a gentleman was taking pictures of me, and in this picture, he caught the image of what appears to be a man dressed in black, wearing a hat, moving toward me. It was the first time a full-bodied apparition had ever been caught on my tour. I do genuinely believe that to be an image of Dangerfield Newby."

As previously mentioned, Amelia believes such apparitions result from residual-energy haunting. But the "holy grail of ghost hunting" is intellectual haunting, "where the ghost, or the spirit, or the entity, or the poltergeist—whatever you want to call it—maybe knows it is dead, maybe it doesn't, or maybe it is confused and wants to try to reach out to you to figure some things out. Or maybe it just wants to have a fun afterlife and just scare everybody it sees."

That's the afterlife Amelia wants.

"I have my whole afterlife planned out. I'm going to haunt my own ghost tour, and it's going to be awesome," she said.

For more information on the Harpers Ferry Ghost Tours, visit the website at harpersferryghost.20m.com and their Facebook (Meta) page, where tour participants post their haunting photos.

A Yellow Transparent apple tree, believed to be a century or more older, keeps watch over fledgling trees at the Paul and Karen Teets heirloom orchard in Preston County. The old tree is among those on the former dairy farm that donated scion wood for grafting on to rootstock, thus perpetuating the variety.

Chapter 4

Wandering Heirloom Orchards

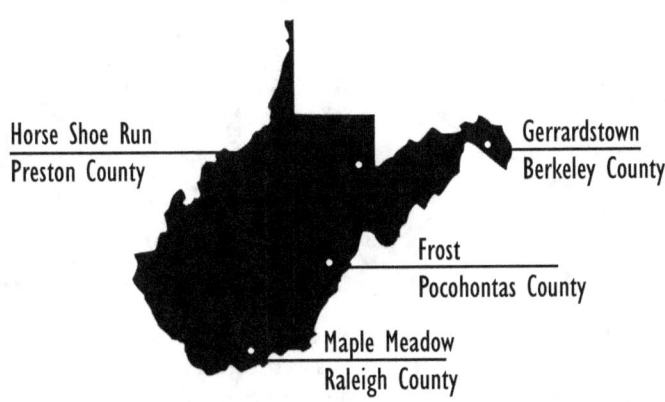

A ttribute it to a series of coincidences or my memories of eating fresh apple slices served from my maternal grandmother's paring knife, but my back-roads West Virginia wanderings have led me to many apple orchards.

I interviewed a descendant of apple royalty in Berkeley County and enjoyed the October fruit from a lone Grimes golden tree growing at the Brooke County location where its ancestor was discovered in 1802. Each fall I return to an old tree in Canaan Valley to get my fill of its blemished fruit and travel Route 50 to purchase new varieties from Romney orchards. We plan our trip to include a stop at the festival in Burlington, where the region's apples are laboriously cooked and stirred in copper kettles to produce apple butter for a good cause. As winter approaches, we once again travel Route 50 to Cool Springs Park, where we stuff a bushel bag full of apples hand picked from wood bins parked in front of the store.

In the front and side yard of our Bruceton Mills home, several heirloom varieties grow from scions donated by trees that once grew on my grandparents' turf. These varieties are referred to as "Carl Feather's Tree" and "Sissaboo Red"; they are heirlooms and their imperfect fruits will never

In this photograph from 1999, Carlos Manning checks the crop in his orchard, where many heirloom apple varieties were preserved. Known as the "Apple Savior," Carlos has inspired other landowners to rescue and raise heirloom varieties..

attain market quality. With the blessing of earth and sky, they someday will reward Thanksgiving guests with thick, aromatic slices of apple pie.

Although frequently blemished and misshapen, heirloom or antique varieties have the subtle flavors, scents and textures that many of the commercial varieties jettisoned on their way to the supermarket aisles. Consumers are conditioned to believe that the apple kingdom begins with Gala and Honeycrisp and ends with Red Delicious and Granny Smith. Hundreds of varieties that our grandparents knew will never tease our taste buds unless we still have access to those trees or know someone like Carlos Manning of Maple Meadow, near Bluefield.

In the modern history of West Virginia, no couple have done more to preserve the heritage of old apple varieties than Carlos and his wife, Mavis. National news outlets like NPR accurately have called Carlos the "Apple Savior" and "Modern Johnny Appleseed." The couple grew up on farms that included an apple orchard stocked with "antique" varieties like Wolf River, Black Ben Davis, Western Beauty, Winesap, Red Winter Pearmain, Rome Beauty, Old Mule and Rainbow.

The orchards met the homesteader's need for fresh and dried fruit, sauces, cider and vinegar. Each variety served a different purpose and provided a broad range of harvests from July's Yellow Transparent to August's Summer Rambo and October's Romes and Pearmains.

"That is how they survived; that was their food source," Carlos told me during my visit to his orchard in 1999.

A heavy equipment operator by day, Carlos desired to pay homage to the apples that grew on the Maple Meadow farm on which Mavis grew up. A perusal of nursery catalogs revealed that the varieties Mavis recalled from her childhood were unavailable from commercial nurseries. A classified advertisement in *The Old Farmer's Almanac* led them to Virginia orchard specialist Thomas Burford, who was propagating heirloom trees.

Carlos visited Burford in 1992 to learn about his work and acquire grafting skills. Simply planting seeds from an apple does not ensure the resulting tree will be true to its parent. However, by grafting onto to rootstock a piece of a donor tree's scion wood, the original variety can be replicated. Grafting is usually done when the donor tree and rootstock are dormant—late winter to early spring. Two types of grafts are commonly used:

❖ Tongue-and-whip involves trimming back the top of the rootstock and cutting a notch into the wood. The scion is likewise trimmed and the wood brought to a point— the "tongue" received by the split in the rootstock's wood.

❖ The cleft graft, which is faster to perform, works particularly well for smaller pieces of scion. The rootstock and scion are trimmed at 45-degree angles and their exposed surfaces matched.

Tongue-and-whip graft.

In both cases, the key to success is aligning the green cambium layers between the bark and wood. Because the cambium is the tree's "circulatory system," nourishment from the rootstock can flow across the graft to the scion, from which the new tree will eventually put forth limbs. Wax or a special tape is used to seal the graft, and the new tree goes into a potting

Heirloom apples may not be the prettiest fruits in the basket, but their external imperfections are forgotten as soon as their flavors register with the tongue. Carlos Manning holds three York Imperials.

media to grow for several months or longer before moving to a permanent home in an orchard.

Back in West Virginia, Carlos applied his new skills to scion collected from heritage farms.

"We started checking old farms and wherever I could remember old trees growing," Carlos said. "We located everything that we recalled having grown in that old orchard. Once we got started with it, it snowballed."

By the turn of the century, the Manning orchard and nursery had at least 350 varieties growing, the majority of them sourced from trees growing in West Virginia and Virginia. His father, Crockett Manning, assisted him in the search.

"Dad knew where a lot of them were at," Carlos said. "I was working in the mines a lot back then, and he helped me plant them and label them. Some of those trees (in the orchard) were planted at night by the headlights from my truck."

Leads were often short on details as folks recalled only an apple's name or characteristics, not the location of the tree that bore it. One of the legendary apples that he tracked down was Rainbow, a medium-sized, striped apple with exceptional flavor. The backstory of the apple was that

Carlos Manning examines one of the hundreds of heirloom apple varieties growing in his Maple Meadow orchard.

freed slaves from Southern plantations brought the variety north with them after the Civil War.

Jason Bailey, Carlos's nephew, remembered that an elderly gentleman used to stop him on his way home from school and offer a Rainbow apple from his tree. Jason showed Carlos where the man lived, and an old tree was located on the residential lot.

Today, the donor tree's heritage lives on in many heirloom orchards throughout Appalachia. "Once I get a tree started, there's no end to it," Carlos said. "You can keep taking cuttings off it and starting new trees."

Carlos funded his preservation work by selling hundreds of the heirloom trees. He kept a record of who purchased each tree in the event he needed to go back to a buyer for a donation of scion to propagate another mother tree.

While deer, insects and fungal diseases threaten all apple trees, the single biggest danger is the loss of farmland to residential and commercial development. Progress is a cancer that feeds upon our agricultural heritage.

"That's what this apple thing is all about, preserving our heritage," Carlos said.

His efforts received a boost from national media attention—Associated Press in 1999 and National Public Radio in 1998. Boxes of apples started arriving at his farm from readers and listeners who had a tree on their property and wanted Carlos to identify the fruit.

From dairy farm to orchard

One of those parcels came from Paul and Karen Teets of Preston County, who had June/July Sweet and Fall Rambo trees growing on their former dairy farm at Horse Shoe Run. The dairy farm was owned by Paul's late father, David. Paul and Karen took over the dairy aspect of the farm in 1979 and ran it with a herd that seldom exceeded three dozen—too small for profitability. Paul supplemented the farm income as a log truck and school bus driver, did carpentry work and whatever other odd jobs he could to maintain the wellbeing of the farm and their three children, Kevin, Aaron and Amanda. Karen worked off the farm at many different jobs, including the oil and gas industry.

The dairy operation reached a tipping point in 1986. "You either had to get bigger and put a lot of money into it or get out," Paul said.

They sold out. The farm was re-purposed for beef cattle and, after a few years of that business, the couple turned to wintering cattle for other producers. "Then we got out of cattle altogether," Paul said.

Concurrent with these ventures, Paul's father began planting fruit trees and berry vines in what had been the cow pasture. Enriched by the byproducts of that former use, the soil was kind and nurturing to whatever Dave entrusted to it.

"He just liked growing things," Paul said. "Dad bought several different kinds of pear trees and peach trees; blueberries and English walnuts."

The late Dave and Wilma Mae Henline Teets on their Horse Shoe Run dairy farm. It has been revived by their son and daughter-in-law, Paul and Karen Teets, as an heirloom apple orchard.

And apples. Lots of apples, including Fallawater, Fall Rambo, Grimes Goldens and black Ben Davis, whose flavors don't "zing" until February.

Dave recognized these trees as a legacy from the Blamble, Watring and Henline ancestors who'd owned and worked these farms since 1828, when pioneer Abraham Watring (Wudring) purchased the entire tract. In 1869 Abraham sold the eastern section of the farm to his son Benjamin; Don Blamble purchased it in 1892.

Paul and Karen Teets have transformed their former dairy farm at Horse Shoe Run, Preston County, into an heirloom fruit orchard. The hundreds of white buckets are receiving the root stock onto which scion was grafted several weeks earlier.

The west farm passed to Watring heirs and was sold to John Henline in 1896. John's granddaughter, Wilma Mae Henline, married David Teets in 1948, and in 1953, David and Wilma Mae purchased the eastern farm from Dan Blamble's heirs, thus becoming neighbors to her parents.

Following Lawrence Henline's death, David and Wilma Mae purchased the western farm, thus reuniting the two parcels under a common owner. In 2001, Paul's parents deeded the tracts to him and Karen.

All that is background to the second orchard that once grew on the hill above the Teets' farm on former Watring/Blamble land. Paul said his father told him the story of how Dan Blamble became mentally unstable toward the end of his life and dramatically dealt a death blow to the hilltop orchard in a tragic act of madness.

"He came in one day and said, 'I took care of them!'" Paul said. "He had taken an ax up there and girdled (the apple trees), but he didn't girdle the Fall Rambo. He killed all the trees except the Fall Rambo."

Fortunately, trees on the Henline farm, including the venerated Fallawater, were spared from Don Blamble's melee. Concerned about the loss of heirloom apple trees throughout the farming community, Dave took an interest in preserving those that remained in his domain. He worked with several contacts experienced with grafting, but none of those efforts produced viable trees.

That led him to Carlos, whose story was published in the Fall 2001 *Goldenseal* magazine. David envisioned an heirloom apple orchard where the cows once grazed, but he felt Paul ought to be the one to learn the grafting skills.

"Dad told me, 'Why don't you try grafting? You ought to be able to do that,'" Paul recalled.

Working with Carlos, Paul and David established a new generation of all but two of the heirloom varieties that grew on the farm, including the Fall Rambo on the hill.

"One of the apples (they didn't save) was one that mom made apple salad from," Paul said. "The apple would not turn brown in the salad. The other one was one that grew next to the chicken house and kept blowing over."

Tree by tree, an orchard spread across the former cow pasture.

"Dad kept saying, 'I'll never get (to eat) any of the apples from these trees, but you kids will have them.' But Dad ate a lot of the apples off the ones that he said he would not eat from because he lived to be 92. He just loved to grow them," Paul said.

Largely through happenstance, Paul and Karen took David Teets' passion to the next level. As neighbors learned of their ability to save

Paul Teets and son Kevin graft scion from the orchard on to rootstock in February; Karen Teets works in the background. Orders for the grafted trees are taken in October and delivered the following fall.

heirloom varieties and provide a variety of apples, they hired the couple to perpetuate trees from their family farms. This also allowed the couple to add more varieties to their own orchard.

While Paul and Karen try to match a "new" variety to a documented heirloom, the trees are often unique volunteers that came up from a seed rather than grafting and have unique, often intriguing characteristics. When no match can be determined, Paul assigns a moniker based upon the donor's name, location of the tree or other unique identifier. Thus, there are Kelly Farm, Eglon Post Office, Jobe Road, Scott Stemple, Jim 4 and Jim 5, Dr. Kines, Sissaboo Big Red and Pride of Preston varieties growing in the orchard. There's even a Carl Feather, taken from an apple tree that my paternal grandparents planted in their front yard in the 1930s.

Pride of Preston came from the Aurora Pike property of the late Clifford Stemple, whose grandfather once owned the land. Paul grafted scion wood from that tree, whose fruit is fine enough to earn it the "pride" honor for an entire county.

Sissaboo Big Red was brought to Paul's attention by a neighbor who hunts in that hollow along Route 219 north of Thomas in Tucker County. More recently, a second red apple from that area came to Paul's attention, and he offers it as "Railroad Red" because it was discovered along the abandoned railroad bed at William.

These old apples and the places where they are found intersect with Paul's childhood, when he and his father delivered eggs from their farm to Thomas, a bustling town back in the 1950s and 1960s. "We'd pass through William, Pierce, and as we went through there, we'd stop and sell eggs," Paul said. "We did that every Saturday night."

Dave Teets knew all the families who lived along this route, my maternal grandparents included, and could tell Paul where the husband worked, what kind of car they owned and their children's names. He had a story for just about each homestead between Horse Shoe Run and Thomas. Paul regrets he did not pay more attention or write them down as his father shared them years ago.

The trees thus honor the families whose stories, although lost, survive as misshapen fruit with russet, smooth, scabby or striped skin; some tart, some sweet; some juicy, some mealy; some who winter well and others who spoil quickly; some who excel as cider, some who shine in baked goods, and some best enjoyed right out of hand. Perhaps we love them because, in their personalities, quirks and qualities, they assume human characteristics. Or, more pragmatically, they simply taste better than the supermarket varieties shipped hundreds of miles and engineered to appeal to the eye rather than the palate.

Word of Paul's effort spread among neighbors who had a tree or two left in their old orchards and wanted to "save" it for the next generation. Several newspapers in the region picked up on his orchard story and gave the effort broader exposure. Paul said that before word of their effort was disseminated beyond Eglon and Aurora, they annually grafted 100 to 200 trees in late winter. In winter 2025, they grafted 500 apple and 50 pear trees.

Carlos Manning provides their rootstock and new varieties that have come into his inventory. Likewise, they share scions with Carlos and other growers.

Paul and Karen count close to 200 varieties growing in their orchard. Orders are placed in the fall and grafted in February. The freshly grafted rootstock is kept in a cool area until the end of March, when each fledgling tree is transplanted into a 5-gallon bucket filled with dirt from the barnyard.

Karen said accumulating the buckets needed for this operation is a huge task. Drywall contractors save their empty goop buckets for them, and Karen brakes for cat litter buckets and other usable containers discarded in roadside ditches and residential trash-collection piles.

"We scavenge buckets to plant in from every source we can find," she said. "It is handy for customers to take the trees in when they pick them up, then hold them until it is convenient to plant them. Sometimes we get our buckets back, sometimes not. Some customers start container gardens in them. That is O.K. We are often amused at people who preach about saving the planet but who live such wasteful lives. Around here, we salvage everything that still has any good in it. We repurpose everything we can."

By June, Paul can tell which grafts have failed; typically 20 percent or so don't take. The trees are ready for distribution and planting in November. Paul said planting a dormant tree gives it a better start than if it were planted in the spring, a timetable used by most mail-order sellers and garden centers.

Nearly a thousand five-gallon buckets have a huge footprint, but the former dairy farm's infrastructure can handle it. Paul stores the freshly grafted trees in the former cooler room. His cider press is in the former milk house, and the old milking parlor is used for grafting and storing cider and apples. A barn is a barn, essential for storing tractors and supplies, and its commodious bay accommodates large groups that attend educational events at the farm.

Paul's parents thus left future generations a practical, adaptable infrastructure in addition to the orchard. Likewise, Paul and Karen are working with their three children and eight grandchildren to create a sustainable succession plan for the 245-acre farm.

"That was Dad's dream, to have it for the future generations," Paul said.

Their daughter, Amanda, lives in a house on the former Henline portion of the farm. She operates a daycare there. Son Aaron lives down the road and is a civil engineer. Kevin lives in Cleveland, Ohio, and has three daughters. He and his wife, Elissa, plan to eventually move to the family farm, build a house and look for more ways to incorporate the orchard and farm's natural resources into a livelihood. The ideas range from agritourism centered on the orchard to selling scions for grafting and apple wood for smokers. Their goal is to make the move circa 2030.

Meanwhile, Paul and Karen tweak their operation and test the waters

Karen Teets sprinkles fertilizer on the freshly planted rootstock with the new scion grafted onto them. The couple recycles whenever possible, such as using discarded 5-gallon pails rather than buying standard nursery containers.

for value-added ventures. Karen cooks and cans about 250 pints of apple butter annually (in 2024 she sold it at the orchard for $5 a pint). Paul made 800 gallons of cider in 2024, a significant increase in production thanks to the purchase of a modern press. By selling their pastured horses, they freed up room for even more trees—Paul added a small planting of peach trees on the farm, too.

As with their mentor, Paul and Karen went from having a hobby to running a business rather quickly. Karen points out that there are large cash outlays for rootstock, grafting tape, fertilizer and other supplies that are recouped by selling trees. By recycling and repurposing, they have kept operating costs and prices at a minimum. It's more than a courtesy to their customers, it's a way of life.

"We could buy shiny new everything and look very professional," Karen said. "We could also raise our prices to pay for those things. That is not why we are doing this. We re-purpose everything we can because that is our philosophy and because it keeps our costs, and therefore our prices, down."

Paul said the orchard has reached the point that Carlos Manning warned him about years ago—he will have to decide if he's going to sell apples or trees. A small farm can't do both.

Regardless of which direction the orchard takes, Paul said he'd rather "wear out than rust out," and if his father's longevity is any predictor of his own mortality, Paul will be around for several more decades to keep memories, legacies and good eating alive on Preston County's rolling farmland.

"I have realized that apples mean more to people than just food," Karen said. "There is often a nostalgia to it. Many people still prefer what they ate as a child. I often hear stories that begin: 'My grandmother...'

"(A customer) searched for 30 years for a sweet July apple and came from New Hampshire to get July Sweet trees," Karen said. "We shipped her a box of apples that year, so she wouldn't have to wait any longer."

But her favorite lost-apple-found story involves a woman who unsuccessfully searched for a Sheep's Nose apple that she recalled from her childhood. After she died, the family discovered the variety among those in the Teets orchard.

"Her family got (some trees) from us and put (a Sheep's Nose apple) on her grave," Karen said.

Frost apples

Carlos's influence reaches all the way to Frost (Pocahontas County), where Charles "William" Young grows heirloom apples in one of the worst possible horticultural environments in the state.

"Frost. What does that tell you?" he asked me during a visit in 2021. "We get (frosts) earlier and later than most other places. If I was to have an orchard, I would not pick Frost, West Virginia, for it."

The location works because Bill is in the business of propagating and selling heirloom apple trees, not fruit. He's lived on this 30-acre mountainside tract since 1972, when he and his late wife Carole built their home there. Bill was just a few years into his three-decade-long career as principal of Green Bank Elementary-Middle School, a job he retired from in 2000.

The job was a seed that grew into an orchard. "It was one of those things that I did at school," he said. "I collected apples and made cider for the students."

The image of a school administrator pressing apples and serving the

Retired school principal Charles "William" Young is saving heirloom apples in Pocahontas County. He and his wife, Christina, operate Allendale Nurseries.

fresh cider to students probably runs counter to most readers' memories of their principals. But Bill had a philosophy that "there is a time to learn and a time to have fun," and he figured out that Halloween could be both. Unfortunately, the macabre element destroyed the potential for learning.

"We celebrated Halloween," he said. "But we were literally scaring the kids. I liked the idea of dressing up, but I didn't like scaring kids."

His staff came up with the concept of a heritage day that would retain Halloween's autumnal elements. They called it "Harvest Day." Held on the last Friday of October, the day introduced students to their Appalachian heritage through displays, demonstrations, presentations and activities. Bill chose cider-making for his contribution. "I knew some farmers that still had these old orchards, I mean we're talking really old apple varieties that I was using in my cider," he said. "And every year that I went back, there were fewer trees from which to get apples."

Disturbed by the loss of these old varieties, Bill took a course in grafting from Carlos, who conducted a workshop near Sugar Grove in Pendleton County in the 1990s.

Bill Young checks the health of trees in his Frost nursery. Carlos Manning taught Bill how to graft and a distant cousin in Virginia assisted him in identifying the varieties he perpetuated from Pocahontas County farms.

"I came away from that with a product. I had tried to learn how to graft by reading, but I needed the hands-on experience," he said.

Once he learned the grafting techniques, Bill went back to his Heritage Day apple sources for leads and scions.

"I went to the old orchard of (the late) Albert Wilfong, who owned a farm at Stony Bottom," Bill said. "I took cuttings from 24 varieties of apples." He also collected scions from several other orchards from which he had sourced cider apples for the school project. In most cases, he did two grafts from each tree so he'd have a backup in case disease or deer claimed one of them. As the number of trees in his orchard grew, the effort transitioned from a pastime to a retirement business of selling what he rescued.

"I wanted to keep these trees going," Bill said. "My intention was not to go into it as a business . . . but, once I started doing this, I realized this was something others would be interested in buying."

More than two decades after the scion was procured from Wilfong's orchard, the old varieties are growing in home orchards throughout the region. Several of the trees from that original collection retain the original nomenclature, such as "Albert No. 18," that Bill assigned when he collected the wood. For many others, he has found a close enough match that he's confident to formally recognize its heritage: Ben Davis, Baldwin, Golden Delicious, Roxberry Russet—nearly 250 in all, and still collecting. Bill makes a call on the variety's name after it bears fruit that can be compared to published sources. His bible for this work is *Apples: A Catalog of International Varieties*, by Bill's distant cousin, the aforementioned Thomas Burford of Monroe, Va., who mentored Carlos Manning. Tom took boxes of apples from his trees to Bill, and they worked through the book and Tom's experience to determine the formally recognized fruit. But the "volunteer" trees, which came up from seed rather than grafting, often defy classification. Unlike grafted trees, which assume the donor's characteristics, volunteers have a mixed lineage that all depends on the source of the pollen that contributed genetic material.

"It will be related to (the tree from which the apple came) but may not be true to it," Bill said.

He keeps meticulous records of each tree's lineage and could direct you to the orchard or farm where he collected the grandparent of the tree he's selling you. "I map every tree from which I take a cutting," Bill said. The mapping places both the original tree and the offspring in their respective locations.

He uses a cold-hardy rootstock of Russian origin. Most of the trees he grows for propagating scion wood and producing apples for his own use are on standard rootstock, which at maturity will require a ladder to reach the fruit. He uses semi-dwarf and standard for those he sells to the public and encourages standard unless space is an issue. "People around here don't want a small tree," he said.

His orchards are on the steep hills in front of and to the south of his Frost Road house; the nursery is along routes 92/84 at the bottom of the hill. Trees are planted in rows and in triangular patterns so at least 25 feet separate them.

Visitors will notice a wide path through the middle of his orchard below the house.

"When our kids were growing up, that was the sledding hill," he said. "We had a four-wheel-drive truck, and I'd pull them up the driveway. By the time I got down the hill in the truck, they'd be down on their sleds. Do you know how long kids will sled ride if they don't have to walk up

Bill Young and his wife, Christina, walk among the trees that donate scion wood for the Allendale Nursery trees. The hill doubles as a sledding path!

the hill? I still keep the sled-riding hill, and I (sled on) it occasionally. It's still a place to ride a sled."

Aside from providing the occasional frosty thrill ride, the property is home to Allendale Nurseries, named after a farm that his late wife's family owned in eastern Maryland. His business came into being around 2005 and has grown to offer more than 100 named varieties and thousands of grafted trees growing in the nursery. Like Paul and Karen Teets, Bill also grafts from trees with familial or sentimental histories. Two of his most popular trees are the Yellow Transparent and the Transparent Yellow. Both varieties come on early in the season and are favored for making applesauce.

Bill's Romanian wife, Cristina, assists Bill in this work (his first wife, Carole, died in 2011). Twice a year, they travel back to her native country, giving him a break from the work of growing the tastes and textures of Pocahontas County's apple heritage.

While retirement took the former principal and teacher out of the school, it has not taken the educator out of him. He patiently explores each potential buyer's expectations for the apples they want to grow. Lacking a "tasting room" where all the varieties could be sampled, Bill said this interview process is important. Does the buyer want an apple for fresh eating or baking? How important is disease resistance? Will the fruit be used immediately or expected to store well? What are the growing conditions and season length? Is a firm or soft flesh desired? Tart or sweet? Will the apple be used for fresh cider or hard?

If the apples are for making hard cider, their sugar content plays an important role in selection, which brought Bill to what he considers one of the most historically important apples in his collection: Roxberry Russet. As its name suggests, the small apple has a very textured skin, like that of an Asian pear. What it lacks in appearance and size it makes up for in acid and sugar content, attributes valued by the hard-cider maker. It also has a great heritage, dating back nearly 500 years in the colonies.

"It was the first named variety in the United States, and it's believed to have originally been planted in Roxberry, Massachusetts," he said. "It has stood the test of time."

The varieties he grows have expanded as he's listened to customer requests, although he won't grow those under patent.

"I started primarily with the heritage, heirloom apples, then I started adding newer varieties, such as Jonagold. Then I started to have clients who wanted certain varieties for hard cider," he said.

Thus, his work came back to where it started, his 40-year-old cider press, where many of the apples from the Allendale trees end up—he typically blends 20 varieties when making the beverage.

"A cider apple is, to me, any apple," he said. "My cider is made as a present that I give away because people enjoy drinking it." That includes the youngsters at the Green Bank school where he still volunteers for the Harvest Day he helped start.

Bill said his goal is to have each tree producing apples when visitors come to the orchard so they can walk the rows and sample fruit before placing an order for their trees. One thing they would have to recognize, however, is that the apples that grow on these trees are not like the ones in the supermarket, that come from trees bombarded by chemical sprays that enhance size and appearance. Like anything with a heritage, there are always a few well-earned blemishes and misshapen characters in the lot, but their stories and flavor more than make up for these "defects."

And the best apple is . . .

Raised on heirlooms and possessing access to hundreds of antique varieties, neither Paul nor Karen Teets can single out one favorite variety from this deep barrel. Paul said it is like when a person unfamiliar with the options tells him to "pick out a good apple for me."

"I have no idea what a good apple is," Paul said. "What I think is a good apple might not be so for another person. And every time you think you have a favorite, you get another."

It's a personal thing. "I like the Fall Rambo really well," Paul said. "I don't have any bottom teeth, and I don't like the hard, crispy apple, so I like softer apples like the Rambo."

If Karen were starting an orchard from scratch, she'd have five sections: antique, seedling, Limbertwig (varieties with limber, weeping branches and sweet, yet acidic-tasting fruit), cider and West Virginia apples.

"We feel obliged to keep West Virginia apples," Karen said.

Intended purpose has much to do with selecting the best trees for one's yard or farm. Karen, who handles the "research and development" side of the business, uses her kitchen as a laboratory for this research. Her favorites are:

- Gravenstein for apple pies;
- Baldwin for apple sauce;
- Cox's Orange Pippin for drying;
- Ashmead's Kernel for out-of-hand eating;
- Fall Rambo for all-around uses;
- Cortland for apple salad;
- June Sweet for canning/apple crisp;
- Fried Apple for, you guessed it, frying;
- Ben Davis for apple butter, but only after it has aged for several months;
- Fallawater, a large, green apple with great keeping characteristics. Properly stored, the Fallawater will keep throughout the winter. Our grandparents stored the apples in their grain bins, taking care to keep the fruits from touching each other for long-term storage.

The late Madge Miller married John Miller II, son of the Eastern panhandle's Apple King. Their home was in Gerrardstown, Berkeley County, where she was photographed in 2000.

Apple royalty

Apple lovers who want to stick with commercial varieties or not grow their own fruit find many options in the Eastern Panhandle. The Romney area is especially "fruitful" along Route 50, and this growing region extends to Winchester, Va. and the Shenandoah Valley.

One cannot study this region without sensing that Providence customized this soil, topography and climate to the apple's preferences, then brought the industry to fruition with the perfect combination of talent, markets and timing. The counties of Berkeley, Hampshire, Jefferson and Morgan produce most of the commercially grown apples in West Virginia (about 95 percent in 2000).

Limestone soil overlaid with a clay base that retains moisture is at the root of this suitability. An extended growing season and plenty of sunshine ensure that the fruit will grow to perfection. And the gentle, rolling landscape makes for relatively easy cultivation of the orchards and harvests.

Perceptive readers with some knowledge of oenology will note that these conditions also favor grape vines. And this region could have very well become a Napa Valley of West Virginia had it not been for Providence once again stepping in—this time in the form of a religious Presbyterian woman.

The potential winemaker was William Smith "W. S." "Peach" Miller; the righteous woman was his wife, Isabella Wilson McKown Miller.

The Millers were farmers with a large family that eventually included eight sons and three daughters. In the early 1850s, the couple lived on a 200-acre farm, "Prairie Dingle," two miles north of Gerrardstown in southern Berkeley County. The land provided W. S. and his family with plenty of food, but he desired a cash return, as well. He tinkered with a small orchard and vineyard planted in grapes, plums and peaches.

Early results were encouraging, but the grapes seemed most promising. Both vintners and saloon owners hailed the wine he produced, claiming it was as fine as anything from the Rhineland.

Neighbors enjoyed his output as well. While coming home from church on Sunday afternoon, Isabella spotted one of the neighbor's boys along the road and intoxicated with the fermented fruit of their land. Back home, Isabella challenged her husband's role in the lad's slide toward hell. She said, in so many words, "William, we cannot be responsible for making drunkards of our neighbors. You can either get rid of the wine press, or I go."

The following spring, the vines were removed and peach trees planted.

Madge Sherrard Miller (1914-2004) shared that story with me when I visited her at her home in Gerrardstown. The widow of W. S. Miller's grandson, John Miller II, Madge had spent most of her life immersed in the industry of growing and selling apples, as well as documenting its history in Berkeley County.

W. S. Miller was the father of the commercial apple industry in West Virginia. His son, John McKown Miller, was the "Apple King."

Over the generations, the Miller family slowly released its grip on the industry. When I met Madge in 2000, her son, John M. Miller III, was operating a 260-acre orchard near her home. It encompassed some of W. S. Miller's original holdings. A cousin, John Douglas Miller, was overseeing 270 acres of non-productive orchard land in the region. He lived in the original McKown house, "Marshy Dell."

These orchards were on the northern edge of a land feature known as Apple Pie Ridge, a 22-mile-long rise extending from Martinsburg south to

Apple harvest time in the Miller Orchards, 1902. John M. Miller is the man with his arms folded, center of photo. *From the collection of the late Madge Miller.*

Winchester. Scottish immigrant David Miller made his original purchase of land on Apple Pie Ridge in 1756. He eventually owned 1,370 acres in Berkeley County.

W. S. Miller, born in 1819, was his great-grandson. Once W. S. found his footing as a fruit grower rather than a vintner, he pursued the craft with gusto. By the close of the Civil War, he had 4,000 peach, apple, pear and plum trees. Apples soon overtook the other fruits, and when W.S. died in 1901, the Miller family was firmly enthroned as the Eastern Panhandle's apple royalty.

John M. owned several orchards in Berkeley County. In surrounding counties, other sons of W. S. made their mark, as well: Harry and Porter in Morgan County, Gilbert in Hampshire, Mineral, Hardy and Grant counties; and Gold in Berkeley County. Harry's land holdings ran into thousands of acres in both West Virginia and Maryland.

The men worked hard for their land, fame and profits. John Miller III told me that his grandfather, John M., broke and worked all the land with a team of horses. Even after tractors became available, John M. insisted upon working with his horses.

"He never did learn to drive anything," he told me. "He was just too old to learn how to use that stuff when it came along. He tried to drive (an automobile) several times, and instead of putting the brake on, he'd yell, 'Whoa!' He was strictly a horse man."

John Miller III said that his grandfather would wear down two horses during a workday. If he had to ride his horse to an orchard on the opposite side of the mountain, he'd release the horse once they got there and let the animal walk back by itself—he did not want to burden it with the owner's weight. John walked home.

His industriousness was legendary. Madge said U.S. Senator Harry F. Byrd of Virginia visited the orchard while John was at work in it. A fruit grower, the senator wanted to learn more about growing apples. John told Byrd he would share his knowledge but could not afford to stop plowing. The senator walked alongside John as he worked, but after several hours of trying to keep up with Miller, Byrd admitted defeat.

"Bryd said, 'I have a lot more questions, but Mr. Miller, you've gotten the best of me. I'll have to come back another time,'" Madge said. "(The senator) told that story several times. He used to say, 'I never met a man who outwork or out walk John M. Miller.'"

John M. Miller simply found joy and purpose in watching apple trees produce and finding ways to coax greater production from their branches. One cannot imagine a more fulfilling way to labor and live. "He enjoyed raising apples. That's why he was responsible for such a big growth in the apple business around here," Madge said.

By 1915, John M. Miller was the largest producer of apples in the Eastern fruit belt. He bought and sold several orchards and never tired of planting new ones. At the age of 68, he planted 250 acres. When he was in his early 80s, he owned 600 acres of orchards.

The threadbare clothing that he and his family wore obscured his true material wealth. "They said the best dressed he ever got was when he got married," Madge said. John M. purchased army surplus clothing for his workers and was known to wear the duds himself. He wore them when he went to a Martinsburg bank one day, which drew the attention of some women who were appalled at his shabby garb.

"Look at that man! Someone ought to buy him some clothing!" said one of the women. A man standing nearby overheard them and remarked,

John M. Miller III with one of the hundreds of trees in his commercial apple orchard in 2000. Those beautiful apples are the Rome variety.

"That's John McKown Miller. I don't believe he needs it. He owns nearly half of that bank!"

Unfortunately, John Miller invested heavily in the stock market and lost $250,000 overnight when it crashed in 1929.

"After the crash, he told (Fannie), 'We're a little short of money,'" John Miller told me. Fannie had set aside cash from the money he gave to

W.S. Miller was active in promoting fruit production on a state level. These badges are in the collection of his grandson, John Miller III.

purchase food for their camp kitchen. She walked around the house and gathered the precious currency from various stashes, including the hollow bedpost of the brass bed where they slept.

"She got it all out, and the money covered the whole dining room table," John Miller III said. The total was $60,000, which "saved the day."

Although John Miller was known to be frugal when it came to his own needs, he generously supported his local church and foreign missions. He refused to work on Sunday and would not allow his employees to violate the day's sacredness, as well.

The size of his harvest workforce was substantial, drawing laborers from as far away as Elkton, Va. From 1910 to World War I, he operated a labor camp at the Gerrardstown orchard that fed the harvesters three meals a day. Those who didn't have a home to return to at night were housed in shanties that John M. built in the orchard.

He paid his workers in cash from a small window in an office at the rear of his home. Madge told me that her father, a young schoolteacher living on a nearby farm, was John's paymaster. Wages were based upon the quantity of apples picked by each worker.

Madge married into this dynasty in 1939. John Miller II was the youngest son of the Apple King. His brother Frank took over the family's orchard after the father's death in 1937. Madge, a schoolteacher, had little time for the apple business between teaching and raising their children, Sarah and John M. III.

Family discord after John M.'s death led to a decline in the orchards and infrastructure, much of which was eventually sold off. John M. II and Frank ended up with the original Miller orchard in Gerrardstown. Madge said Golden Delicious was her husband's specialty, but in 1969, he set a record for the orchard when its York Imperial trees produced from 65 to 70 bushels each.

John Miller II died in 1973 at the age of 62 years. John III, who began working in the orchard at the age of 12, eventually took over the orchard.

The region's apple industry has suffered from D.C. urban sprawl, making the orchards more valuable as subdivisions than farmland. Competition from imported fruit, droughts and a shortage of seasonal labor have also challenged the industry. As the trees age beyond their productive lifespans, many orchard owners remove them and sell the land for housing and commercial development. Given the work and risks involved in the orchard business, one cannot blame them.

As Madge Miller told me decades ago, "I don't believe there are any John M. Millers left in this world anymore."

Back in the hills and hollers, in residential yards and orchards of micro-breweries, the state's apple story continues to come full circle. Thanks to the work of people like Carlos and Mavis Manning, Paul and Karen Teets, and William and Christina Young, consumers can recreate a portion of the table that refreshed our ancestors more than a century ago.

Carlos Manning may be reached by phone, 304-934-6558, or mail: Carlos Manning, 681 Maplewood Road, Lester WV 25865

Allendale Nursery has a website where heirloom trees can be ordered. Some "whips" can be mailed, but larger trees must be picked up in Frost. https:// allendalenursery.com or email them at charles.william.young@gmail.com.

Paul and Karen Teets typically hold an apple sampling and tree ordering day in October. Contact them at Teets Orchard and Nursery, 723 Hog Back Road, Eglon WV 26716. Email is kbteets@yahoo.com; phone is 304-698-6712. They offer apples, cider and trees grafted to order.

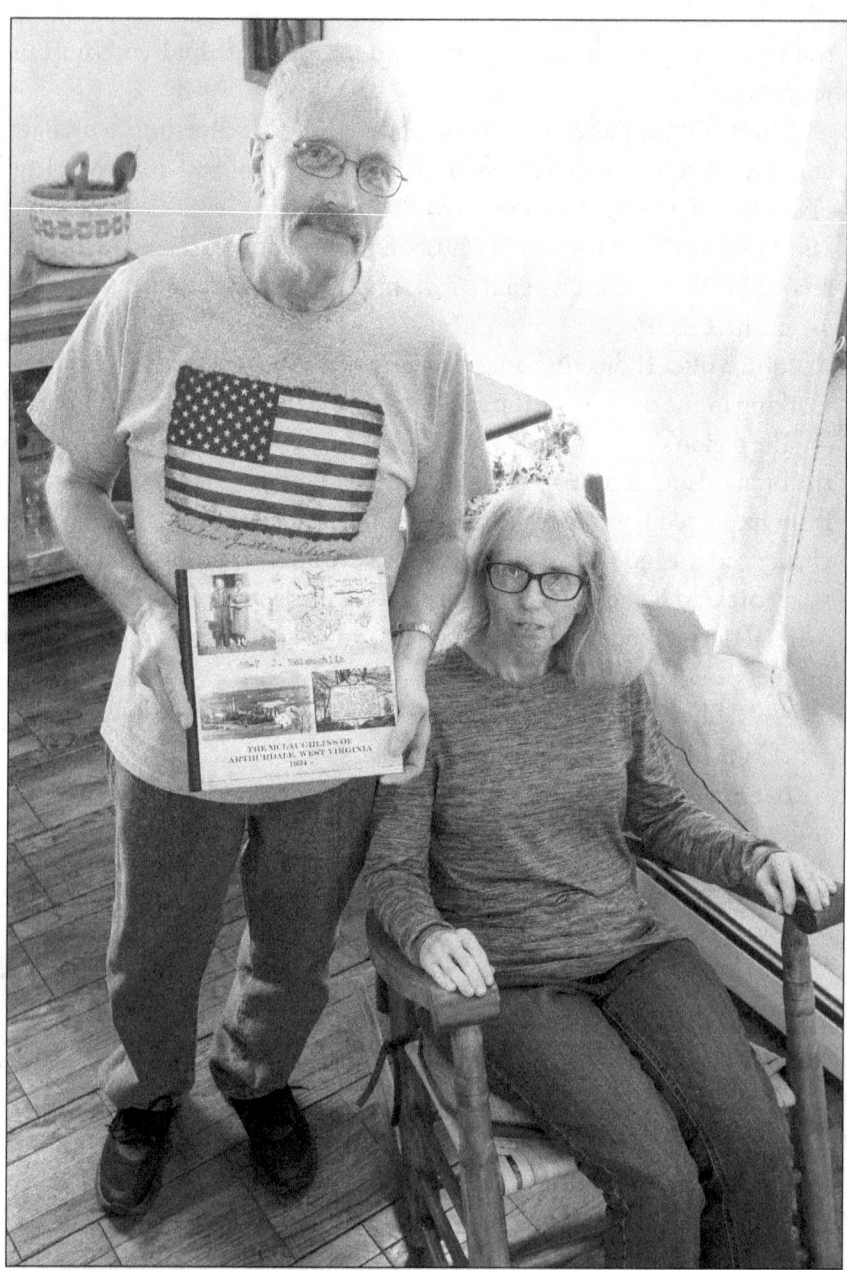

Robert and Wendy (Feather) McLaughlin have lived in Arthurdale since 1976, when Bob purchased the home of his paternal grandparents, Joseph Harvey and Nellie Jane (Hall) McLaughlin, who were Arthurdale homesteaders. Wendy is sitting in a rocking chair that came from Eleanor Roosevelt's guest room at Arthurdale. The New Deal community gave out-of-work coalminers a hand up and opportunity to own a home in a progressive community.

Chapter 5

Arthurdale Memories

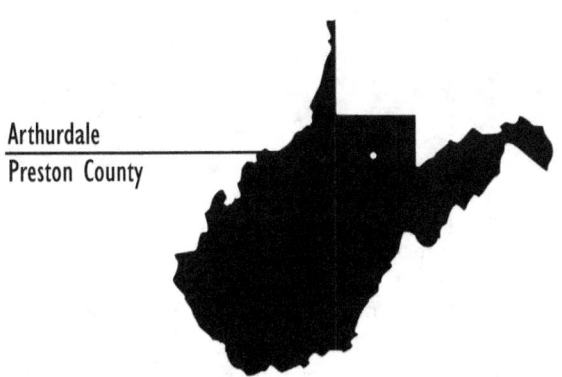

Of all the places Eleanor Roosevelt could have square danced with a commoner, she chose Preston County.

Arthurdale, to be specific. Located on Route 92, south of Reedsville and Morgantown, Arthurdale is simultaneously a residential community, federal experiment in top-down social engineering and National Register of Historic Places site.

Known as "Eleanor's Little Village," Arthurdale was the first lady's pet project of resettling poverty-afflicted, out-of-work coal miners in a self-supporting community built and administered as a New Deal project. Due to her personal stake in the project, the first lady made nearly three dozen visits to the community. During one such visit in May 1938, a photograph was captured as Mrs. Roosevelt danced with an Arthurdale resident in the Community Center.

You can walk through this center as part of the guided tour offered during Arthurdale Heritage's regular business hours (see the website for days, times and cost). During Arthurdale Heritage Day in July, the center hosts exhibits, authors and artisans (admission charged). If you are but a

A Hodgson house is owned by Arthurdale Heritage and has been restored to its original appearance. The prefabricated homes were built as summer cottages and were a poor choice for north-central West Virginia winters. Nevertheless, they were much better than most of the miners' housing at Scotts Run.

window-peeking, mildly curious tourist, just pull into the parking lot off Route 92, wander about the grounds and read the interpretive signage. The cluster of structures in this commons area includes a gasoline station, blacksmith shop, museum, gift shop and administrative offices.

Stretching across the landscape in all directions from this center are homes that were built in the mid-1930s for the resettled miners. Of the 165 homes built, 160 are on the National Register of Historic Places, along with the supporting structures in the community commons area.

The houses came in three styles:

Hodgson. Essentially prefabricated summer vacation cottages that were chosen for their immediate availability, the Hodgson houses began arriving in the late fall of 1933. Plagued by blunders such as building foundations that were too large for the houses, the Hodgsons also were mismatched for West Virginia winters. The one-story structures had pine frames clad with Oregon cedar, four to six rooms, electricity, indoor plumbing and a furnace. Despite being essentially summer cottages, Hodgsons were still a significant upgrade to the housing the homesteaders had prior to Arthurdale. Each house cost taxpayers $2,000 to $2,500. The houses came furnished right down to the towels and curtains. The five-acre lots

Arthurdale's community center faces Route 92 in Preston County. It and several other original buildings are on the National Register of Historic Places. It was in the community center hall that Eleanor Roosevelt square danced with homesteaders.

provided space for a cow shed/poultry house, pasture, garden and orchard to facilitate self-sufficiency.

Wagner. Named for their architect, Steward Wagner, these 75 houses ranged from one-and-half to two stories in height and were on cinder block foundations. The first story exterior was block, the second wood. They had the same lot improvements and amenities as the Hodgson houses in keeping with the concept of subsistence living.

Stone: Using stone quarried nearby, 40 houses were built as one-and-a-half story bungalows, two-story Tudor Revival and two-story Colonial Revival houses. They had five to seven rooms and featured a stone fireplace. There was no basement, but a root cellar was near the house. The last of these were built in 1937 and marked the end of Arthurdale's residential development under the New Deal.

All but two of the New Deal homes are privately held—a Hodgson house to the west of the center is owned by Arthurdale Heritage and has been restored to its original appearance. South of the center is a Wagner house originally owned by the Heinz family. It was acquired by Arthurdale Heritage in 1999. Otherwise, most of the houses in this development of narrow streets identified by letters of the alphabet have been drastically

Bob and Wendy McLaughlin stand outside their Wagner home in Arthurdale. His grandparents were original homesteaders. The couple have many improvements and several additions to the house during their decades of ownership.

modified and modernized from their original appearances. Without the signage and stunning portico of the Community Center, one could zip past the place without hardly noticing anything special about it.

An Arthurdale family

Only a handful of Arthurdale's current property owners can claim ancestors who were original homesteaders. Robert and Wendy McLaughlin are unique among them for both their connection and dedication to the Arthurdale saga. Bob's paternal grandparents, Joseph Harvey and Nellie Jane (Hall) McLaughlin, moved into their Wagner house, designated SR-7, in 1935. Bob's grandmother lived there until her failing health and mobility precluded independent living, at which point Bob and Wendy purchased the house in 1977.

"I've actually lived in this house longer than what my grandfather and grandmother did," Bob said during my visit there in 2025.

Bob's father, Robert Francis Sr., like many young men of Appalachia after World War II, migrated from West Virginia to Ohio for jobs. Bob grew up in Ohio, but after a stint in the Navy longed to return to the slower

Joseph Harvey and Nellie Jane (Hall) McLaughlin were living near Morgantown when they heard about the New Deal project south of Reedsville. Scraping by on whatever work they could find during The Depression, the couple qualified for a home in the community and moved into it in 1935 with their seven children. Their grandson, Bob, and his wife, Wendy, bought the house from Nellie Jane after Joseph died.

Photo courtesy of Bob McLaughlin and McLaughlin family ancestry researchers.

pace of life and mountain landscape of his grandparents. Their home held many special memories for Bob, who visited there as a child.

"That's where my grandfather used to sit, right over there," Bob said, motioning to a corner of the former living room, now the family's dining room. "A lot of times in the morning, I'll get up, sit in that spot and drink my coffee."

Memories of his childhood visits to Arthurdale and his grandparents' house remain vivid after 60 years.

"We'd jump out of the car, and the first thing my sister and I and my brother would do is run up that hill across the road, because in Ohio where we lived it was flat. We'd go up to the top of that hill and run down it as fast as we could," he recalled.

Memories were made indoors, as well.

"When I go upstairs (to the bedrooms), sometimes I'll think, 'This is the room where my dad slept, and this is the room where my aunt slept, and my grandmother and grandfather slept in this room.' The one bedroom upstairs is where my great-grandfather (Robert E. Lee Hall) died. He was born during the Civil War, and he died in that bedroom upstairs," Bob said. "So, there are a lot of memories with the house, and I would have hated to see it sold to anybody else."

Bob hands me a small, framed photo of an old log cabin in which his grandfather grew up. It stood at Harmony Grove, south of Morgantown, the area in which Bob's grandparents were living when the Arthurdale opportunity presented itself.

"They were so poor, that when The Depression came along, they didn't even know it. They just kept on living like they had been," Bob said.

His grandfather heard about the project being built south of Morgantown and applied for the program. Then he went back to his hardscrabble existence—working the family farm and picking up random laborer's jobs while his wife cared for the family and worked a few hours as a school janitor.

"They never heard anything back, and one day she told him maybe he should go down and check on it," Bob said. "So, he went somewhere in Morgantown and checked on it and found out they were approved and going to move to Arthurdale. They probably moved here in 1934, but not directly into the house. They lived in Bretz for a while; it was like a holding place there, while the house was being built. In 1935, they actually moved into the house. My dad was probably nine years old at the time."

His grandfather spent the intervening months working in Reedsville, where lumber for the stick-built Arthurdale homes was cut. A woodworker, he also built furniture for the project. When the McLaughlin family of nine moved into their house, it was fully furnished with furniture, towels, washing machine, curtains, stove and refrigerator.

"For my father, when they moved to Arthurdale, it was like moving into heaven," Bob recalls. "Everything was so much different from where they grew up in Harmony Grove. He loved Harmony Grove, and he had a lot of good thoughts about growing up there. But Arthurdale was just different. It was an opportunity that most people during The Depression never got. They had good schools, good friends, everything. It was just different."

A hand up

The FDR Administration launched this ambitious experiment of resettlement and progressive education on what had been the 1,018-acre farm of Richard Arthur. Purchased by the government for $48,500, the hilly parcel was joined by additional purchases that brought the community's total land mass to 1,200 acres. The purchase included Arthur's mansion, which spoke of the seller's once prosperous times as a Pittsburgh hotelier

The settlement was the first of roughly 100 such subsistence homesteading projects under the New Deal. For residents of Scotts Run near Morgantown, the help was perfect timing. Scotts Run, like many other coal camp communities, declined rapidly after the mid-1920's coal boom went bust due to increased efficiency in coal-burning locomotives, a shift to highway transportation and mechanization of the coal mines. The unemployed miners and families of Scotts Run were plunged into an "abyss of misery," wrote C.J. Maloney in *Back to the Land*. Many of the coal miners and their families were evicted from the coal company-owned housing that came with employment. Families were forced to survive in shanties without the most basic necessities. One journalist, after touring Scotts Run, described the community as "the damnedest cesspool of human misery I have ever seen."

First Lady Eleanor Roosevelt visited Scotts Run in August 1933 upon the urging of her friend, Lorena Hickok. Just two weeks later, FDR's administration was at work on a solution—Arthurdale, formally known as "The Reedsville Project." But the architects of this New Deal project wanted nothing to do with the existing town immediately to the north. Rather than build mutually beneficial water and sewage treatment facilities and schools, New Deal officials did it their way, resulting in each home having its own well on land known to have a poor water supply. And having schools dedicated to Arthurdale students provided a taxpayer-funded laboratory for testing progressive-education theories.

The concept of a communally organized, back-to-the-land settlement had been promoted by the first lady's husband two decades earlier, when he was a New York state senator. FDR introduced legislation to move New York poor onto rural farms. Responding to his wife's impressions of misery at Scotts Run, FDR updated the concept and wove it into his New Deal. Mrs. Roosevelt became the "Angel of Arthurdale," and $25 million of taxpayer funds were allocated to establishing the communities, of which Arthurdale was the poster child.

Soon after ground-breaking in the winter of 1933, 50 Hodgson houses were raised on the former farmland, followed by 75 Wagner homes and 40 stone houses. Government housing construction ended in 1937.

"People who moved here from abject poverty moved into a house with running water and electricity, a refrigerator and central heating, said

Each Arthurdale home came with modern appliances, like a stove and refrigerator, plus central hot water and heat. These were luxuries previously unknown to many of the homeowners who came from the "cesspool" of Scotts Run.

Elizabeth Satterfield, curator and director of education for Arthurdale Heritage. "Their children had excellent educations and had opportunities they never would have had elsewhere."

"It was to give people a hand up, to develop them as human beings, said Darlene Bolyard, whose parents came to Arthurdale as a young married couple in the late 1940s. Darlene grew up in Arthurdale, came home to it after a career in international business and lives in a Wagner house. She served as executive director of Arthurdale Heritage for a decade.

Arthurdale's housing, acreage for gardens and cows, and all the basic, modern amenities were perfectly timed for those afflicted with The Great Depression's misery. However, the concepts of subsistence, back-to-the-land living and an economy based upon communal farming, cottage industries and local markets were out of touch with the cultural and economic shifts that occurred between The Depression and close of World War II. The entire concept, hatched in the halls of academia rather than cornfields and general stores, was a mixed bag of poorly researched ideas, impractical implementations, and denials of agricultural, transportation and economic realities.

Visitors to Arthurdale can tour this Wagner home owned and restored by Athurdale Heritage. The interior (photo at left) has been restored and furnished with the items homesteaders received as part of the package.

The Scotts Run miners were not farmers; at best, the land produced vegetables for the homesteaders, but efforts to sell any excess, which was essentially government property, ran into issues. Bob's grandparents, although possessing subsistence-farming skills gained during their years of hardscrabble living, could not make a go of it on the five acres that came with their Wagner home.

Bob said the soil in this low, southern section of Arthurdale is clay. "It was not good for planting," he said. "In the summertime, when it dried up, it was hard as concrete."

A planting of buckwheat was made on the land with assistance from another farmer. "And they would harvest the buckwheat and in turn give (his family) all the buckwheat flour we wanted," Bob said. "This flour was stored in a small closet in one of the bedrooms."

Bob's grandparents had 10 children, born between 1921 and 1941. Several were born at Arthurdale, including the community's first set of twins, Linda and Glenda.

"Eleanor Roosevelt gave my grandmother a set of blankets as a gift

Bob and Wendy McLaughlin have tried to keep their Arthurdale home close to original. This little closet in a bedroom was where buckwheat flour was stored.

having the first set of twins born in Arthurdale," Bob said. The blankets are in the museum at the Arthurdale Heritage complex.

Bob's grandfather, unable to sustain a family of 12 on the five acres of poor soil, found employment as a woodworker. During World War II, he worked in the shipyards at Norfolk, Va. After the war, he worked for Southside Lumber in Morgantown until his retirement in 1951.

By then, it was evident that the vision of Arthurdale being a self-supporting community of sustainable agriculture and industry was out of sync with the post-war economy and laws of economics and manufacturing. Arthurdale factories turned out furniture, vacuum cleaners and radios for which there was no distribution network. The tractors built at Arthurdale were not designed for West Virginia's terrain. And there was no railroad connection at Arthurdale on which to move them to a suitable market. Even clothing produced at Arthurdale had few buyers in West Virginia.

"The manufacturers that ended up coming here ... the products they made weren't maybe accessible to the general American public and certainly people in West Virginia," Elizabeth Satterfield said, explaining the reasons for Arthurdale's economic struggles. "And Arthurdale at that time was

Arthurdale's blacksmith shop was one of the buildings that were saved and restored by Arthurdale Heritage. The shop is a stop on the public tours of the complex.

very isolated, it was not on a main rail line. There's not a major waterway here. Further, (back then), they were still in the middle of the Depression. People do not have the purchasing power that they do after a war. So, there were a lot of elements that contributed to the difficult economic times.

"During (World War II), manufacturing did pretty well here, but that's how it was across the country," she added. "Manufacturing struggled everywhere until World War II, which fully lifted us out of the Depression."

The Arthurdale schools had an even shorter life under federal jurisdiction. From 1934 to 1936, the schools were under the direction of Elsie Ripley Clapp, a student of John Dewey and proponent of progressive education. During Clapp's brief administration, the experiment emphasized experiential learning, individualism and using schools to build community. Bob said his father learned how to type, do home canning and cook while the schools were still under the New Deal's control. Although the Arthurdale schools were turned over to the Preston County Board of Education in 1936, Eleanor Roosevelt returned to the community annually to hand out diplomas—Bob still has his father's bearing her signature. In May 1938, FDR gave a commencement speech to Arthurdale High graduates.

As early as 1942, the program in charge of the settlements, the National Housing Agency/Federal Public Housing Authority, began withdrawing federal support and oversight. Homesteaders never owned their Arthurdale homes; they had paid a small monthly rent that included utilities. Bob said his grandparents' rent was $13.20. In 1947, the government offered homesteaders the opportunity to purchase their property. Many of the residents accepted the deal and eventually updated their abodes to late-20th century housing standards.

Robert McLaughlin said his grandparents paid $4,689 for their home and five acres. They eventually sold off all but .6 acres of the original plot. As the lots were subdivided, mobile homes and modern single-family structures were built alongside the classic stone, Wagner and Hodgson homes, which often underwent expansion and extensive remodeling to the point of being unrecognizable today. Arthurdale, aside from its historic significance and central-community infrastructure, transitioned into being one more post-World War II subdivision.

Wendy's story

Bob's wife, Wendy Feather McLaughlin, moved into this community with her parents from Lenox, also in Preston County, about the time she was entering elementary school.

"My dad worked at Sterling Faucet, which is in Reedsville," she said. "It was either 1959 or 1960 when we moved here to be closer to Dad's work. We lived on O Road, which is what we called 'up the hill.' That's where I grew up. We were not original homesteaders, but we lived in an original (Hodgson) Arthurdale home."

Wendy said Arthurdale's schools provided an education on par with that of other Preston County schools of the time. She graduated and earned a teaching degree from West Virginia University. Hired by the Preston County Board of Education, Wendy taught in the same buildings in which she had been educated as an elementary student.

"I taught mostly first grade, but also fourth, sixth, and, for one year, second," she said. "When I started, I taught first in the new building, then as time went on, I taught in the farthest building. It was the one I went to elementary school in."

The Arthurdale School buildings have survived and await restoration in 2025. The wooden buildings were designed to accommodate progressive educational theories that were at odds with the community's agrarian nature.

The original frame buildings still stand behind the new school, which is on Route 92 below the Presbyterian Church. The long row of buildings served only Arthurdale youngsters and were instrumental in coalescing a tight-knit community, even as the original homesteader families died off and their bond of gratitude faded.

Bob McLaughlin feels that, in his grandparents' time, Preston County residents outside Arthurdale viewed the homesteaders as "privileged."

"But I think those feelings went away over time, when the kids started growing up and dating some of the other kids from the communities around them," Bob said. "And then they combined the schools."

Although Wendy's family moved into Arthurdale at the tail end of the first-generation of homesteader ownership, the community was still tight-knit in the 1960s.

"We knew almost everybody else who lived in Arthurdale," she said. "We knew who lived in this house and that house because it was mostly still the original homes."

"There was a closeness and uniqueness to Arthurdale as far as the community goes. I never saw anything like it in Ohio," Bob added. "Everybody knew everybody else, and everybody seemed to know everything about each other. It was just a closeness and uniqueness, maybe because of Eleanor Roosevelt."

"It was a great place to grow up," Darlene Bolyard said. "Everybody embraced you. And everybody corrected you and minded after you. So, if you got in trouble, your parents would know about it even before you got home. And that was good . . . and we all, generally, went to church together. Our moms were homeroom mothers and did stuff together."

Investing the sweat

Jeff Zinn's grandparents, the late Cameron and Opal Radabaugh, and Luther and Marie Zinn, were original homesteaders. Jeff's parents also owned a home in Arthurdale, and Jeff's house and business are on land adjoining the original 1,200 acres. Born in 1961, he's been "back to the land" throughout his life. Although he graduated from Masontown's high school, Jeff progressed through the lower grades in Arthurdale's orignal school buildings.

While these structures continued to serve the Arthurdale children decades after federal support ended, the public buildings around which the community's social life and industry were built fell into disrepair in the hands of private owners.

"We all saw the center hall go from a fairly decent place until (when) private owners bought it, then it all went downhill," Jeff said. "All the buildings were dilapidated and falling. One of them had a little pizza shop and an apartment in it, and it caught on fire. So, everything was looking pretty bad by the time I was out of school (late 1970s)."

Jeff's father built and remodeled homes in the Arthurdale area. Jeff worked with him in the business and learned just about every construction trade, except masonry. Unknown to him, Jeff was being trained to help save one of the New Deal's most important historic sites, his hometown.

The turning point came in 1984, at a 50th-anniversary ice-cream social that brought many of Arthurdale's homesteading families back to their roots.

"So, everybody comes home to Arthurdale, and they come back to buildings that are completely falling apart and the roofs are caving in. And that's when Arthurdale Heritage really started. We were formally

Jeff Zinn's grandparents on both sides of his family were Arthurdale homesteaders. He gives back by managing and working on the myriad restoration projects Arthurdale Heritage has tackled for more than 40 years. He stands outside one of the Arthurdale Schools buildings.

incorporated (as a nonprofit) in 1985. But it started with that reunion," Darlene Bolyard said.

The fledgling organization had no money except the loose change contributed by homecoming guests. "There really wasn't seed funding," Darlene said. "It was volunteers who cared about the community that did almost all the labor, did the roofs, did the lists of things that needed done. The community and their children and their grandchildren all came together to restore the buildings."

Acquiring the buildings was the first order of business—the administration building and forge were purchased from the Brown family in 1986. A year later, a capital campaign raised $30,000 for the project and, in 1987, the mortgage on the structures was burned and a new roof put on the administration building. The Arthurdale Historic District was placed on the National Register of Historic Places in 1989.

Building by building, the heart of the community was acquired and restored to exacting historical standards. Grants were sparse in the early

Demonstrators help visitors connect with the lost skills of the 1930s during the Arthurdale Heritage Day in July. Fiber arts are among the skills demonstrated and perpetuated on the campus.

days; donations from the homesteaders' children and extended families funded the efforts.

"If you didn't volunteer to do something, you didn't get anything done," Darlene said. "If they bought lumber, they bought it out of their own pockets. And the women—they had fundraisers and encouraged their husbands and family to come and work."

More than a dozen Arthurdale buildings are owned by the heritage group. Jeff Zinn was involved in their restorations and many of the other projects, often serving as contractor, volunteer and donor. He contributed out of respect for his parents, the late Gerald and Maxine Zinn, who had five children.

Jeff said the combination of depending upon volunteer labor, keeping things historically accurate and the years of neglect made for some very time-consuming, nasty projects. He dug up and replaced old sewer lines, cleared an acre of old-growth pine trees and excavated neglected land from the former factory complex that stood behind the center hall. That project had to be done in a matter of a few weeks to ready it for a heritage festival and meet its funding source's terms. The project came along in early summer, when contractors were busy with other jobs, forcing Jeff to

The Arthurdale Museum (above) presents the settlement's story through displays of products manufactured in the community's government-sponsored factories. The output included target kites (right) that were used to train military warship crews and anti-aircraft gunners. Arthurdale's factory produced 75,000 of the kites with enemy-aircraft images printed on their surfaces.

work nights and weekends to meet the deadline. As if that pressure were not enough, some of his workers contracted COVID-19, and Jeff ended up working alone during a hot spell.

"It was all just rubble, grass and weeds," Jeff said. "It was awful. It all had to be dug out and then a base put in. Then we had to find stone masons that were qualified to restore some of the stonework. That's not easy ... I worked by myself. Never took a day off ... it was a nasty job, one of the most demanding because it had to be done (by the deadline)."

Elder "peer pressure" drew Jeff into this work. It was not just physical labor and contracting that he contributed. Jeff served as a board member and, in 1990, was elected president. It was about that time the board faced a huge decision. Valley Junior High, the former Arthurdale High School and last of the school buildings still being used by the Preston County Board of Education, was closing (the high school had been consolidated with Masontown in the late 1950s). And the board of education wanted Arthurdale Heritage to take on responsibility and ownership of the historic structures.

There were reservations and opposing opinions on the board as to the merits and dangers of assuming responsibility for more historic buildings. The Arthurdale Heritage Board wanted to accept the offer and move forward with restoration, but money and overextension of resources were grave concerns. "But yet, we didn't want them to be bulldozed," Darlene said. "They would have gone to private owners, and they would have been bulldozed and all the history would have been lost."

The board accepted the buildings but proceeded cautiously. Stabilization was prioritized over immediate restoration as the group studied repurposing options that would be consistent with their historical and educational heritage.

Carrying on the heritage

Bob and Wendy McLaughlin's home is steeped in family and Arthurdale heritage. Although they have added a living room to the back of the house and modernized the kitchen, their renovations and upgrades were made with a tolerance for the home's quirky construction methods and reverence for its heritage. Thus, the parquet floor in the dining room still heaves up in the summer because the joints are too tight, and the huge, porcelain bathtub in the upstairs bathroom was retained during a remodel. The plaster, more than an inch thick in places and over metal lathe, has survived electrical, heating and plumbing upgrades. Look closely and you can see the scars from water damage resulting from a poorly implemented chimney design that was common to the Wagner homes. And the tiny closet in which the family's buckwheat flour allocation was stored has been retained in one of the bedrooms. Where possible, the original copper wall plates still cover the switches and outlets.

Bob displays his grandparents' wind-up alarm clock next to the bed in the room in which they slept for decades. Several of the furniture pieces in their home were produced just up the road in the Arthurdale factory; it is likely his grandfather helped build them. A rocking chair in their dining room is said to have come from the guest room in which Eleanor Roosevelt stayed when she visited her beloved community. Several sections of the solid-maple countertop that Bob and Wendy upgraded to modern materials were made into cutting boards and given to family.

In July, when hundreds of history and festival hounds descend upon the community to celebrate Arthurdale Heritage Day, Wendy and Bob hold a familial celebration at SR-7. Bob cooks and serves crispy buckwheat cakes paired with sausage for nearly three dozen guests as the couple celebrate their Arthurdale heritage. His surviving twin aunts, who live out of state, make the pilgrimage to Arthurdale as infirmities permit. Their stories remind him just how "privileged" his Arthurdale ancestors were to be chosen for a project that has been both praised and criticized by historians and taxpayers.

For Bob and Wendy, who are among the community's longest-tenured residents, Arthurdale is more than fading petals of a New Deal bouquet arranged by a First Lady. It is perennial garden of hope nourished by memories, heritage and commitment.

"I'm not moving," Bob reiterated. "They will have to carry me out feet first."

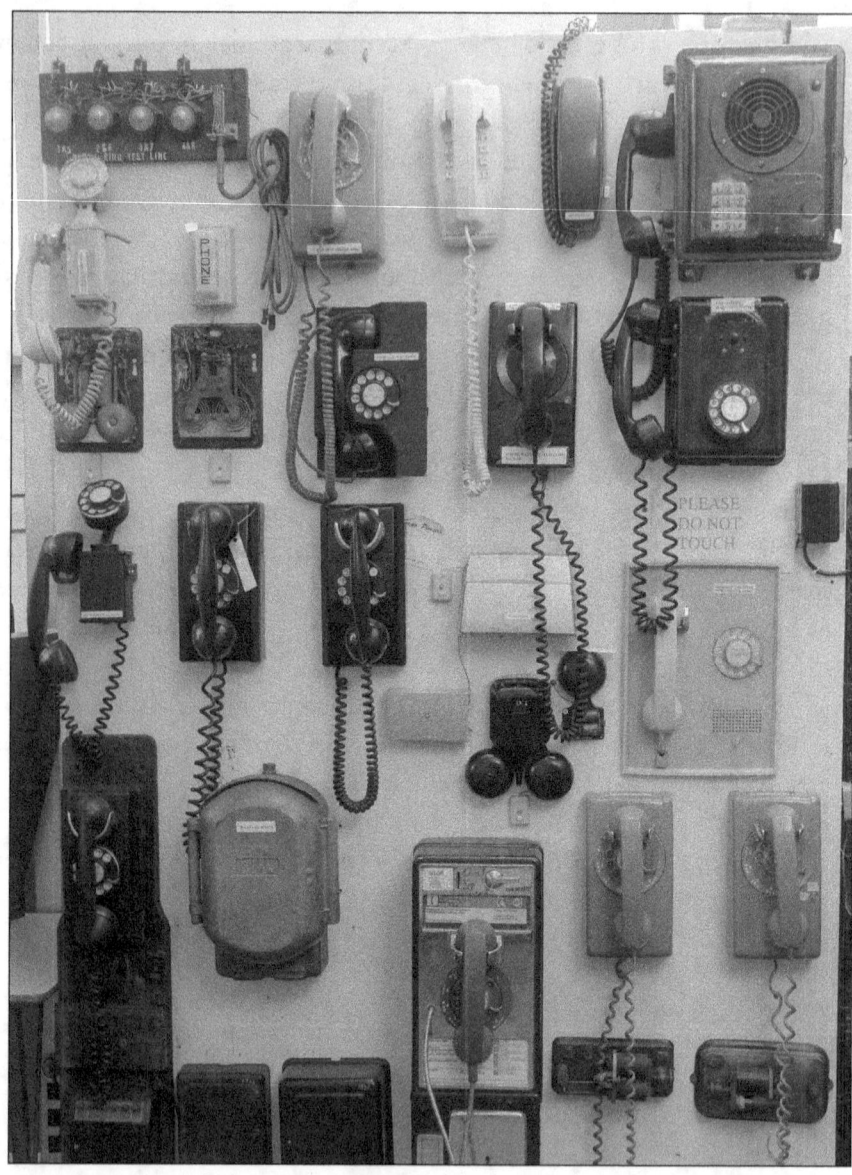

Remember these things that once hung the walls of American homes, factories and businesses? Replaced by cellphones, these handset units were stashed away by telephone company employees who had the foresight to pull together artifacts of voice communication for a museum. The esoteric collection is housed in a telephone building in Fairmont and open only three hours a week and by appointment.

Chapter 6

'What Number, please?'

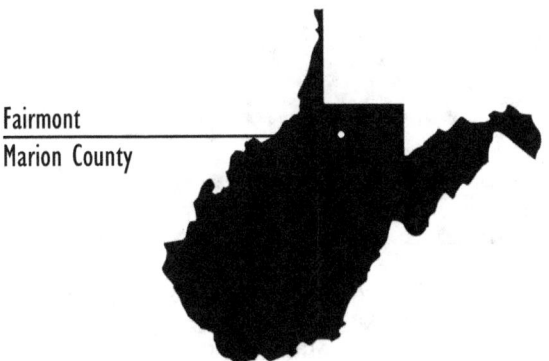

Fairmont
Marion County

Sue Merrill vividly remembers the personnel manager's comment from her first job interview with Chesapeake and Potomac Telephone in 1966.

"She asked me, 'Do you have children?' I said, 'Yes I have two sons.'

"'That's nice, but you realize the phone company is your first responsibility?'" Sue recalled during our interview in 2022.

Sue saw that company-first policy implemented many times during her 36-year career with "the phone company." Indeed, decades after retiring from Frontier, Sue was still giving several hours a week to the industry as she led tours of Fairmont's nonprofit Telephone Museum, located in Frontier's Monroe Street building.

The three-story, brick building houses digital equipment, and several employees still work out of the structure, which has "Bell Telephone" written on its alley-facing side. During my visit in 2022, Sue told me there was a time when hundreds of people worked in and out of this three-story building. Morgantown and Clarksburg, likewise, had hundreds of "telephone company" employees who labored around the clock to keep people, businesses and essential services connected.

Sue Merrill, who worked as a telephone company operator for several years, explains the steps involved in patching through a long-distance call using a switchboard in the Fairmont Telephone Museum. Looking on is Maddie Vanata, who frequents the museum with her grandfather and volunteer, Terry Patterson.

While cell phone towers and fiber-optic cables have replaced the switching center, operator boards and myriad-stranded cables that facilitated voice and data communications, that transition is incomplete in West Virginia. And that makes the Telephone Museum more than just a historical curiosity. Sue points out that there are many places in the mountainous terrain where cell phones have no service, leaving landlines as the only option.

For West Virginia residents beyond the age of 50, the museum is a place to once again dial up the technology and tools that connected them to a sweetheart in the next hamlet, reported a birth to kinfolks across the mountain or summoned rescuers to a mine explosion. For younger folks, this analog collection, dominated by the ubiquitous handset, is a journey through the rapid evolution of an invention hailed as one of the 19th century's most important.

The Fairmont collection exists because foresighted employees salvaged outdated equipment being discarded by their employers. These collectors met regularly for breakfast, over which they developed a plan for the growing but homeless collection. The group included Dave Curry, George Eddy,

Something rarely seen in the 21st century: retirees who spent all of their working years in one industry, with one company. Former employees of the Bell System hold a document given to employees at the time of the "Ma Bell" breakup. From left, Gary Elliott, Sue Merrill and Terry Patterson volunteer at Fairmont's Telephone Museum.

Ray Nichols, Gene Waggoner, and Vernon "Mutt" Whetzel, according to a brief history of the museum's founding.

The collection, much of it drawn from Morgantown and Fairmont operations, includes a two-person operator switchboard, private branch exchange (PBX), teletypewriter, diagnostic and lineman's equipment, transmission cables, pole insulators, telephone directories and a fiberglass telephone pole that was tested in The Mountain State. Stashed in a Bell Atlantic storeroom for two decades, the collection became a museum open to the public in 2005. The occupancy is tenuous; no formal written agreement between the museum and Frontier exists. A simple sign in the front window of what was once a business office identifies the museum, run by a small but very dedicated and knowledgeable volunteer staff. Tours are from 9 a.m. to noon on Thursdays, and by appointment.

While the equipment and memorabilia are in themselves fascinating, many of the artifacts would be little more than esoteric curiosities without the interpretation, context and anecdotes provided by these volunteer guides. Assisting Sue with the tours are C&P retirees Terry Patterson and Gary Elliott, who respectively had 40 and 37 years of service.

Both men went through the mandatory "climber's school" that the phone company required of its linemen. The self-insured company emphasized training in equipment, procedures and safety. The retirees say management stressed that employees were the face of the company and required them to adhere to high standards of appearance, conduct and professionalism.

"You were expected to start each day with clean clothes, even though you'd soon get dirty climbing poles," Gary said. "You were the company the public saw. You were expected to keep your hair cut. Then the Beatles came along, and by the 1970s, you could do whatever you wanted to."

Ironically, employees who were unseen by the public had the most rigid dress codes. When Sue started as a switchboard operator at Morgantown's C&P office, standard work attire was a dress, stockings and high-heel shoes. Skirt lines had to meet certain standards of length and were checked by supervisors. "And nobody ever saw us," she said.

Sue spent a little over four years as an operator, an assignment that became a lifelong career for many women because the telephone company provided medical insurance. "With women, there were very few jobs back then where you got benefits," she said.

The job paid about $60 a week, plus the benefits that made raising a family of five children less stressful for Sue. The hours were miserable, however, especially for rookie operators. New hires typically worked a split day of two four-hour shifts. They had no holidays or weekends off; only those with seniority could take their vacation time during the summer months.

Sue eventually tested for a job in the business office, where she worked a 7½-hours shift and had holidays and weekend off. But decades after the switchboards went dark, Sue could still walk a museum visitor through the many steps required to route a long-distance call through the board.

"People don't realize how involved being an operator was," she said.

When a weather emergency hit the area, operators instinctively knew to report for duty and expect to stay there for the emergency's duration. Sue recalled pushing snow with her vehicle's bumper to get to downtown Morgantown. When that didn't work, the company dispatched a service truck to fetch her.

"They got rooms at the Hotel Morgan and sent the girls down there

Gary Elliott, who worked for "the telephone company" for 37 years, explains analog switching equipment to a museum visitor from Florida. Gary started his career at Farmington, from where this equipment was salvaged by employees with an eye toward preservation.

to stay because they had to be at work," she said "That was very common for (employees) up in the mountains, like in Elkins. They had a standing agreement with the motel across the street from the office there; if a big snow came, they had six or eight rooms dedicated to the telephone people."

The museum preserves a complete switchboard from Morgantown, along with lists of emergency numbers, company codes, directories and reporting forms used by operators. Sue said an operator was expected to answer an incoming call within five seconds. In Morgantown, the volume was often heavy with the university, industries and hotels on the exchange.

"You had to be alert all of the time," Sue said. "I have seen this board lit up like a Christmas tree from one end to the other. And the supervisors are saying, 'Get that call, get that call!' Well, you are working as fast as you can, because (the supervisors) are observing you constantly." Their observations included listening in on the calls. "And believe me, if your tone wasn't right, you'd hear about it. You're supposed to have a voice with a smile, is what they would tell us," Sue said.

The operator physically routed calls using cords plugged into the various jacks on the board. The task of repairing and maintaining all this equipment fell upon technicians like Gary Elliott. The Farmington resident was hired in 1964. Like most male employees, he started at the top and worked his way down the telephone pole.

"It made you a telephone person," Gary said. The poles were typically 28 to 30 feet tall, and the company had only one lift truck at Fairmont, so linemen climbed. The museum includes a display of a lineman's safety equipment and tools, which were carried in a canvas bag.

While that equipment is vaguely familiar to anyone who's admired the courage of a lineman hanging from a pole in the middle of a snowstorm, the switching and trouble-shooting gear from central office is baffling. During the tour, Gary dialed his old four-digit number assigned to his childhood home in Farmington, 2-7-2-7. Relays clicked and a phone rang a split second later. Gary explained that Farmington was an early adopter of automatic switching equipment because the region had so many coal mines with phones for reporting emergencies. When a few seconds could make the difference between life or death, automated equipment was more efficient and reliable than a human operator.

Even more efficient ways of connecting and transmitting calls replaced the clunky electro-mechanical equipment and copper cable. Fairmont went digital circa 1994. Central office employees had to learn a whole new technology, even as linemen adapted to the challenges of repairing fiber-optic cable systems. Gary said he preferred working on the old analog equipment; there was something magical about it, just as there was pride in being the link that connected people across town or the state.

"We were there to work, to help the customer," Terry Patterson said. "We were trained to give service."

Terry spent his entire career as a lineman; centralized positions came with job insecurity. Terry said that as technology progressed and management looked for cost-cutting opportunities, central-office operations were consolidated into multi-county sites, then out-of-state centers. Operators were especially vulnerable to consolidations and the transition to electro-mechanical switching technology.

"But if you worked outside, you had a little bit more security there," Terry said. That security came at the cost of working in horrible weather. Linemen were expected to quickly trace and repair breaks in the lines caused by downed trees, ice or bored folks with a rifle.

"They'd shoot the cables," Terry said. "They'd go out deer hunting, get frustrated and they'd look up there at a big terminal on a cable . . . yeah, there was vandalism. But not as bad as today. You know, people respected stuff then. You know, it's not like it is now. It makes me sick."

The challenges of maintaining lines in a rural setting created tension between linemen assigned to those areas and their supervisors, who increasingly were based in urban areas far from West Virginia.

"I worked in Salem, and they used to try to say, 'Well, you should be able to get six troubles a day or seven troubles a day. People in Pittsburgh, people in Baltimore, don't have any trouble getting seven.' I said, 'Well, yeah. They parked their truck and walked to three of them. I fix a trouble, and then my next trouble is 22 miles down the road.' You just couldn't pound that into their heads. You know what I mean? When you don't know anything about the job, you make stupid decisions. I mean, if you don't have a background, I don't care what anybody said," Terry said.

His comments reflect the frustration felt by veteran employees following the crash of Ma Bell's vertical monopoly and the loss of local control within the new companies. But the pride that came with being a "telephone company person" remained and is evident as these retirees lead visitors through a century of telecommunications artifacts. Their anecdotes and knowledge animate this sterile collection of dials, switches, cables, relays and telephones for any visitor willing to pick up a handset and listen.

Sue told me that most museum visitors are not former telephone company employees but folks who are curious about the past and its technologies. She said schools occasionally bring entire classes to the museum, where youngsters step inside a payphone booth, watch Sue patch a call through and learn about the engineering and safety issues unique to coal-mine phones. Rows and rows of both residential and business phones are displayed; one of them is sure to dial up a memory or two of those happy times chatting through a landline-telephone connection.

Like Gary told me, "This is history."

Fairmont's Telephone Museum, 214 Monroe St., is open 9 a.m. to noon on Thursdays, and by appointment at other times. Call Sue Merrill to schedule: (304) 983-2463. Admission is by donation, which goes toward maintaining the collection.

John and Glinda Bowman lived in this townhouse on Centre Market in Wheeling. Authors, antiques dealers and enthusiastic supporters of the community and its history, the Bowmans were the kind of people that makes West Virginia a special place to live and visit. Photo from 2011.

Chapter 7

Wandering Centre Market

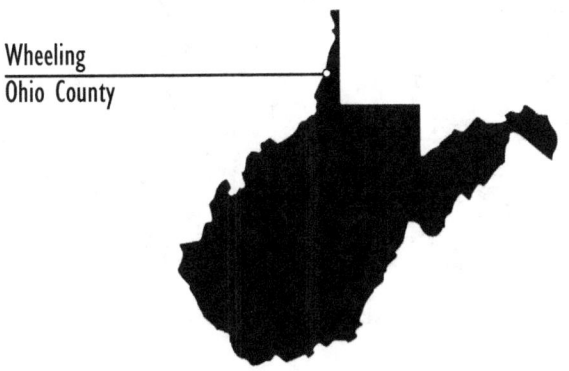

Wheeling
Ohio County

Whenever my wife and I visit the City of Wheeling, we make it a point to walk around Centre Market and explore the antique shops and architecture of this historic commercial area, established in 1853. The market house, whose tenants include Coleman's Fish Market, dominates the district, which is flanked by townhouses and shops on Market Street.

Years ago, one of those storefronts was home to Yocum's Antiques, owned by the late Bob Yocum of Glen Dale. Housed in a former five-and-dime store's building, the antique business had been there for decades when I caught up with Bob on a March day in 2011. The entire 90-feet length of the building was stuffed with merchandise stacked 4 to 6 feet high and 10 feet wide on both sides of a narrow path through the store.

It was downright dangerous to poke about the stacks, so you had to tell Bob what you were looking for. He would try to remember where he last saw it and paw around that area until he found it.

"One woman said she wanted a pair of Paden City glass horses, but I couldn't find the other one to save my neck," Bob told me during one of my visits to the shop. I am sure Bob had some items in there that would have been of interest to me, but I was wandering the city by myself and

Bob Yocum's place on Centre Market was a picker's dream and commercial-insurance agent's nightmare.

didn't want to have to explain to my wife how I ended up in the hospital trying to get to something we didn't need.

When I visited the city a couple of years later, Bob's jumble of merchandise was gone, and a much more upscale shop had replaced it.

He died at the age of 89 in a nursing home on April 20, 2021.

Family-owned, century business

Coleman's Fish Market wins Centre Market's longevity prize. In its third generation of family ownership, Coleman's is the Northern Panhandle's largest wholesale fish distributor, although most visitors know it for the famous fish sandwich on white bread.

It all started in 1914, when John and Nellie Coleman, who had a farm in Hannibal, Ohio, walked away from their poultry and eggs business and heeded the advice of veteran fishmonger Sam Hurdle of Wheeling.

"The old man was getting out of the fish business, and he told my grandfather, 'If you don't like selling chickens, you ought to try selling fish,'" third-generation owner Joe Coleman told me back in 2010. Joe was

Joe Coleman holds one of his eatery's famous fish sandwiches served on white bread.

3 years old when his grandfather died and referenced stories that his late father, Robert, had shared with him.

Hurdle's place was at the south end of the market house where Coleman's is located, but John Coleman's fish market made the rounds before landing in the market house in the early 1920s. There was no need for such a large space, at least not initially. Joe said his grandfather's business in those early days consisted of a 150-pound barrel of whole fish brought in over the National Road from Baltimore.

For several years, John and Nellie rented narrow storefronts along the market square, and at one point lived above the market in a small apartment. John named his business Union Fish Market, capitalizing upon the New York fish market's moniker. To this day, the parent company's name remains Union Fish.

Joe said his grandfather was doing both retail and wholesale fish sales when he moved his business into the market house, long associated with food purveyors. Originally open on the sides, the market buildings were hubs of commerce, where everything from live chickens and eggs to fish and fruit were sold.

"In those days, there were no supermarkets," Joe said. "This would have been the Walmart of the day."

The market-house tradition gave way to mom-and-pop corner grocery stores, which were put out of business by supermarkets, most of which were smaller than today's "convenience store." Coleman's survived by adapting to and evolving alongside the times and trends.

Joe said that when his father came back from serving with the Marines in World War II, he began experimenting with sandwiches that could be prepared and sold at the retail location in the market building. Blue pike or "Jack fish" was abundant, cheap and readily available from Lake Erie fisheries 150 miles north of Wheeling. It was this species that Robert Coleman created his first fish sandwich, which sold for a nickel back in 1940.

"I found some old invoices where my dad could buy the fish plus delivery for 3 cents a pound," Joe said

To Joe's knowledge, the sandwich has always been made with white bread. The breading, developed by Robert Coleman, greatly contributes to the uniqueness of the Coleman Fish Sandwich. Joe keeps the recipe under lock, and one of his myriad duties has been to make up this mixture in 100-pound batches.

Robert was thrust into the business when his father suffered a heart attack at the age of 62. Nellie stayed on with the business and helped her son make the transition from soldier to fishmonger. "My dad, he carried on the business and it grew," Joe told me.

Years later, Joe had the same baptism by fire into the family business. Joe was aboard a Navy nuclear-submarine tender, getting some sleep before embarking on a tour of Europe with his wife, when a knock on his door changed the course of his trip, life and Wheeling's culinary history.

The visitor was a chaplain, who informed Joe on that fateful night in 1973 that his father had suffered a heart attack. The next day in Rome, Italy, Joe met up with his wife, Renie. Instead of touring Europe, they caught a flight back to the United States to be at his ailing father's bedside.

His father suffered a fatal heart attack three months later. Management of the family business fell upon Joe. "I came in and basically, I said, 'I'm your new boss. Tell me what to do,'" Joe said.

A hands-on owner, Joe Coleman pitched in and fried the fish during busy times at Centre Market. Long lines were common during Lent.

"I wanted to be an architect or engineer," Joe said. Rather than work in the family business, he had spent the summers of his youth building houses with his future father-in-law and working for the West Virginia Road Commission on highway maintenance and construction. He enlisted in the Navy, and for the next five years worked on the reactors of nuclear submarines. As he was approaching the end of a six-year commitment, his father asked him to consider running the business for a year. If he didn't like it, he'd be free to go back to engineering school and complete his education. Joe was just four months away from starting that arrangement when the chaplain knocked on his door. He never returned to the submarine business.

Coleman's celebrated its 100th anniversary in June 2024. The business is owned by Joe Coleman and his sister, Mary Rich. Jodi Carder, Joe's daughter is office manager. It offers hand-filleted fish sandwiches ($7.45 in early 2025), chicken sandwiches, fries, soups and beverages. No tartar sauce comes with the sandwich (and it really does not require it), but packets can be purchased separately. A special-order line offers items that take longer, and for those who prefer to cook at home, the deli's fish cases offer a wide range of fresh seafood from alligator tail to squid. Coleman's is closed on Sundays; visit the website for hours, options and current pricing: colemansfishmkt.com.

The author who modeled his subjects

Across the square from Coleman's, at 2220 Market Street, was the townhouse residence of John Russell and Glinda Jo (Sanford) Bowman, whom I first met in 2009. Their narrow abode was just down the street from the Paradox Book Store (see "Wheeling's Paradox" in Volume 3 of this series), whose shelves I enjoy browsing.

The first floor of John's and Glinda's two-story home had a large front window that displayed the wares of their "Antiques Parlor" business. I enjoyed shopping there for esoteric items of local historical interest, but most of all, I enjoyed their friendship. They were kind people, treating me to lunch at Coleman's on my first visit, and dedicated ambassadors for Wheeling and its heritage. Both were authors and understood the agony of creating of a book. No wonder they were "my kind of people."

Glinda was a historian who researched and collected miniature perfume bottles. She wrote two books on the esoteric subject. I had no idea that such bottles existed until I met her. (The books, *Miniature Perfume Bottles* and *More Miniature Perfume Bottles*, are published by Schiffer Book for Collectors.)

John was an expert on Wheeling steamboat history. He wrote at least five books on the subject, as well as books about the Wheeling Stoogie and Centre Market. Finding his books is more challenging than those by Glinda, which are on amazon. A starting point is White's Clock Shop, 2265 Market St., Wheeling (whiteswatchandclock.com).

When I first visited John in 2009, he'd just finished his first book, *Wheeling, The Birthplace of the American Steamboat*. It was published in 2008 with support from the Wheeling National Heritage Area Corporation. His second book, *A Pictorial History of Wheeling and Ohio River Steamboats*, was self-published in 2009.

"This was the birthplace of the steamboat, but there was no written history of it," John said. "It was a much-needed subject for a book," Glinda said.

John, a native of Wellsburg on the Ohio River, found no evidence of shipbuilders or river men in his ancestry, but was fascinated with the subject. And although he grew up near Wheeling, the "Birthplace of the American Steamboat," John retained only a vague childhood memory of his subject matter.

John and Glinda Bowman loved Wheeling and enjoyed showing visitors the attractions at Centre Market, where they lived in a townhouse. John's knowledge of the city and its history was phenomenal and is preserved on the Archiving Wheeling website, a project of the Ohio County Public Library and heritage partners. Visit it at archivingwheeling.org.

"Living in Wellsburg, we shopped in Wheeling, and when we came down the river to the south end of Warwood (north of Wheeling), there was a coal mine with a tipple. And at that tipple, there were always two or three old steamboats sitting there in the water. That was the only thing I remembered about seeing steamboats as a child," he said.

John served in the U.S. Air Force and trained for a gunner's job, but when the military eliminated the aircraft he'd trained on, John switched his specialty to pest control, as in termites, rats and fleas. That education gave him the foundation for 40 years of selling pest-control products on the road. He worked in the Southwest, typically driving 250 miles a day doing commission sales.

"I drove 1,237,000 miles (during my career)," John said.

John and Glinda eventually moved back to the Northern Panhandle to be closer to his aging parents. They purchased a mini-farm thinking it

The historian and model maker at work in his basement. John Bowman spent dozens of hours building a single section of his Ohio River steamboat models.

would be a great lifestyle of freedom, but John quickly discovered that the time tax of maintaining the property far outweighed its alleged benefits.

"Cutting those three acres of grass became my life," John said. "We decided that maybe we didn't need that for the rest of our lives." That's how they ended up with their Market Street townhouse and "not a blade of grass to mow."

With property chores at a minimum, John had time to pursue researching and writing about Wheeling's steamboat history. One of the second-floor rooms was dedicated to John's library and study, where he stored his collection of photos and documents about the Ohio River's steamboat industry. Although John never owned or operated a pleasure craft, let alone a steamboat, his years of study enabled him to talk on the subject like an experienced riverboat captain.

"I studied all the terms of building a boat and studied the pictures," John said. "I have 80 books (about boats), and I've read them all."

It was a photo from his Wheeling newspaper, *The Intelligencer*, that piqued this interest in steamboats. The clipping, from the late 1950s, shows Glinda's late father, John Sanford, with his back to the camera as was welding on a barge. The caption suggested the work harked back to a

The *City of Wheeling*, one of the many models John Bowman crafted using historical photos of the long-gone vessels.

time when Wheeling was a center of steamboat construction and suggested the time was right for revival.

The clipping also sparked conversation about Glinda's recollections of her father's occupation. A Mississippi native, Glinda grew up in river towns as the family followed the breadwinner's assignments. In 1955, they moved from Louisville to Wheeling.

Glinda said her father's job involved welding under water. When John first heard this, he thought she was taking advantage of his shipbuilding naivete. But the story piqued his interest and set the course of his retirement.

He discovered the first successful steamboat on the Ohio River was built in Wheeling just two years after Robert Fulton and Robert Livingston launched a trio of steamboats on the Ohio River at Pittsburgh. In practice, early river steamboats like the *Comet*, launched from Brownsville, Pa., in 1814, had issues that limited their practicality. His research revealed that the first successful and practical river steamboat was *Washington*, launched at Wheeling, May 12, 1816. He said that event licensed the city to lay claim to the title "birthplace of the American steamboat," a moniker first pinned on the city by author Garnett Laidlaw Eskew in *The Pageant of the Packets*.

John said that steamboat hulls were frequently built elsewhere on the

John and Glinda Bowman had a small antique shop in the street-level floor of their Centre Market townhouse. He displayed his models in the shop.

river, where there was a more abundant supply of hardwood, then towed to Wheeling for completion. His research identified 225 steamboats that were either built in their entirety or completed in Wheeling between 1815 and 1900.

During this steamboat era, Wheeling daily received a boat loaded with in-season vegetables from Marietta, Ohio, which was known for its tomatoes. It is estimated that 1,200 steamboats were on the Mississippi and its tributaries by the mid-1840s, and there was seldom a shortage of investors willing to put up $15,000 to $20,000 to add another vessel to the Ohio. By 1855, these palatial "Floating White Palaces" were transporting 3 million people annually, creating the steamboat's Gilded Age.

These observations come from John's first book. While writing that book was something John had planned to do in his retirement, modeling the boats he'd researched was coincidental. It came about from a $10 purchase.

John said a man who sold him some books suggested he also buy a steamboat-model kit. John really wasn't interested in the offer, but he bought it all the same and stashed it in a closet. After he retired in 2006, John soon

John collected artwork of the boats that once worked on the river just a few blocks from their residence in Wheeling.

discovered that he couldn't spend all day reading and researching, no matter how enticing that mirage seemed to him while living the life of a salesman. He retrieved the model kit and started building what he soon discovered was, at best, a mediocre representation of an American steamboat.

"I thought, 'I can do better than this,'" John said. "I could do something that would be authentic to Wheeling."

He chose the *City of Wheeling* as his first project. The 109-foot-long steamboat was the last to be completed at Wheeling. Built for Capt. Thaddeus S. Thomas and Charles (C.Y.) Higgs by William Henry and Marshall Mozena, it was the largest steamboat built by the Mozena Boat Works. Interior cabin carpentry was completed in 1900, and the steamboat first ran out of Wheeling in 1903. It was soon sold to another owner who operated it on the lower Mississippi for about a year. Re-sold and re-named *Harry Lee*, it ran out of Memphis, Tennessee, until 1911, when it sank. It was raised, only to burn at Memphis on March 19, 1914.

Without having the actual boat for reference, John relied upon two photographs taken in September 1900 as the *City of Wheeling* docked at a wharf not far from his house. The views, one at street level and one from an upper-story window, provided John with the scale and perspective he needed. He selected a scale of 3/16-inch per foot, a standard among model makers.

With only one kit model to his credit, much of John's first effort with transferring the drawing to balsa was trial-and-error. Harking back to his days as a salesman, when he had to document every expenditure and sales call, John kept meticulous notes on each aspect of building the model: materials and techniques used, the amount of time spent on each phase and mistakes made in the process. He also retained mistakes for reference.

John said the most challenging and time-consuming aspect of building the models was creating the articulating paddle wheel. A typical steamship had a 24 paddles or buckets on its wheel. Each paddle had to be modeled from balsa and painted, and required 120 wood supports, which John made from square toothpicks her painstakingly painted.

Even after building 15 models, John said paddle-wheeler boats were still the most challenging. His approach was to assemble the paddle wheel first, then lay the hull and install the engines and coal bunker. The bulkheads and superstructure came last.

John spent 80 hours building just the paddle wheel and hull for the *Sidney*, the only Wheeling steamship that was painted a color other than white. He listened to opera and other classical music while he worked on his models in the basement. His workspace was boxed in by his collection of nearly two dozen machinist toolboxes. John preferred them to mechanic's toolboxes because they have small compartments for the tools of his craft—knives, files, scissors, pliers and small saws. His power tools were a band saw, jigsaw, hand-powered grinder and a small drill press for drilling out cylinders to create smokestacks.

His workshop companion was Blackie, a cat who kept watch from the top of the custom-built case John constructed for each model. Occasionally, Blackie left the perch to inspect John's progress and give a meow of approval or disapproval. Glinda also gave feedback.

"If something doesn't look right, I'll tell him," she said.

While John did not model cabin interiors, he equipped each one with a pot-bellied stove, telegraph and wheel fashioned from common household articles and painstakingly painted.

John Bowman's models, with details often made from discarded household items, are in the museums of Ohio River towns and private collections. The Ohio County Library in Wheeling displays his models, as well.

He created his models long before 3-D printing made a model-maker's job much easier. John used a stem cover from an automobile tire to create a searchlight fixture and the top of a pushpin for the lens. Black rubber bands from a beautician's shop became weld points in the smokestacks. Brass B-B's topped off poles, and the vessel's whistles were fashioned from copper wire. John even raided Glinda's jewelry boxes for loose pearls and other small jewelry pieces he incorporated into the models.

"That's what fascinates me about the models," Glinda told me. "He has to be creative about what he uses."

John printed flags for his models using an ink-jet printer, paying special attention to the number of stars on Old Glory at the time of the ship's launch. Most of his models also sported a Mail Pouch thermometer or

John spent a day bending the wire for the boat owner's Mozena Boat Works logo suspended between the *City of Wheeling's* smokestacks. Several of his models are displayed in The Ohio County Public Library, 52 16th St., Wheeling.

advertising sign. Wheeling was home to the famous tobacco company, which boldly advertised on steamboats and barns alike.

"Every boat that ported here at Wheeling was furnished by Mail Pouch with signs to put on the boat," John said "They'd get a lot of exposure all up and down the river from that."

John spent hours crafting a single detail, like the company logo displayed on *City of Wheeling*. It took a day of bending and re-bending a single strand of wire to create the distinctive "M" of the Mozena Boat Works logo suspended between smokestacks.

Construction of the *City of Wheeling* and its display case required 200 hours. A model of the *Homer Smith* held the record—349 hours. The model was a commission from Point Pleasant residents Lynn Durst and Nancy Jewell, granddaughters of the ship's namesake.

John modeled more than a dozen steamboats, one boat club (a rowing-style boat popular on the river after the Civil War), four wharf boats (floating commission warehouses), four coal barges, one shanty boat (houseboat) and a dish boat. The latter was used to peddle wares along the river. There were also patent medicine and photography boats that worked the rivers and provided a residence for their practitioners/owners.

He preferred to work on a model in blocks of eight to nine hours a day. John surrounded his workspace with photographs of the ship under construction to ensure the details were always before him and that his model would authentically represent the subject.

"There is absolutely nothing left (of the old Wheeling steamships) that I can refer to," John said "I have to have pictures of it. I'm not going to build anything for which I don't have a picture to go by."

John's primary sources of photographs were his own collection; that of the late Herb Bierkortte, a Wheeling photographer/collector; the Inland Library at the Public Library of Cincinnati and Hamilton County, which has the largest public collection of riverboat photography and reference material; and the Fred McCabe/Liberty Marine Photos collection. John dedicated his second book, a visual amplification of the first volume, to McCabe, of Hannibal, Ohio.

John Bowman was recognized as an expert on the topic of Wheeling's steamboat history and was frequently a speaker on the subject at historical gatherings in river towns. His models are in both private collections and those of the Point Pleasant River Museum and Monroe County (Ohio) River Museum. The Ohio County Library in Wheeling has several of his models, as well. His Wheeling history articles may be accessed online through the library's Archiving Wheeling blog (archivingwheeling.org/blog/author/john-bowman), one of the most attractive and informative regional-history sites on the Internet.

In 2009 John received the West Virginia History Hero Award. The Wheeling Area Historical Society, of which John was an active member, nominated him.

All this came from a man whose first attempt at making a model ended in disaster. John told me that when he was a child, his mother purchased a balsa-wood model airplane kit for him to build. John took it to his bedroom and went to work; the first task was cutting out the parts with a razor blade.

"I spread it out on the bed and ended up cutting up my bedspread," John said. "She threw away my model kit and took the razor blade away from me, and I got a new bedspread, instead."

John Bowman died May 18, 2023. Glinda died January 8, 2025.

Steve Smith, a Roane County native, was inducted into the West Virginia Music Hall of Fame at the Sagebrush Round-Up in 2024. A McHenry, Md., resident, Steve drops in on the Roundup when he has a free Saturday night and joins the house band on the historical stage on Bunner Ridge.

Chapter 8

Saturday Nights on Bunner Ridge

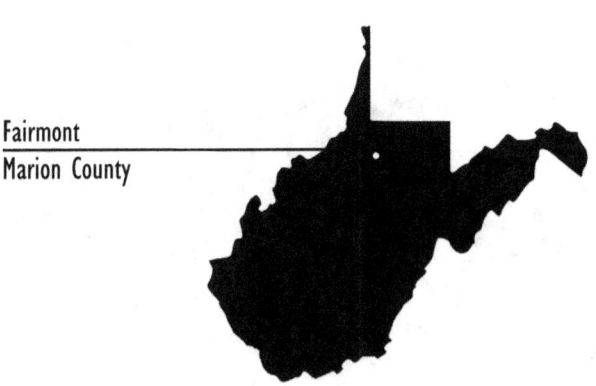

Fairmont
Marion County

It is 6 p.m. Saturday in Marion County. The sun is setting and out on Bunner Ridge, eight miles east of Interstate 79's Exit 139, a red velvet curtain is rising on the Sagebrush Round-Up.

A single slice of butterscotch pie lingers on the counter of the music hall's restaurant. Guests who paid their $8 admission early and bought the $15 dinner share their medical-procedure stories around folding tables near the main entrance to this 17,000-square-foot building, once part of an auto assembly plant. They lean across scraps of country-fried steak and cup their ears toward their neighbor as the energy emitted from the hall's massive speakers soars above 100 decibels. The Round-Up is no place to visit your neighbors after 6 p.m.

The friends ramble, shuffle and bounce to the beat as they make their way toward the folding, upholstered seats immediately below the stage. Spotlights in primary colors play across the performance area. Dressed in snazzy outfits and swinging guitars that shower the audience with sparkles,

The Stagecoach house band back in 2003: Standing, left to right, Sam Manno, Rex Ward, Jim Clise, Lawrence Tolley and Bill Janoske; Seated, Lisa Janoske, Darrell Carpenter and Donald Hayhurst.

the six-member band belts out a modern country song that wafts across Bunner Ridge like a 2 a.m. fire siren.

The musicians are Bill and Lisa Janoske, Brandon Howdershelt, Skip Lamm, Leo McMillen, and Dana Murphy. They call themselves The Round-Up Band. Bill Janoske is on lead guitar, and his wife, Lisa, handles bass guitar, tambourine, mandolin, vocals and background vocals. She's also secretary to the board of directors, and Bill is treasurer.

Brandon Howdershelt is the president, the youngest one the Round-Up has ever had. He plays rhythm guitar, lead guitar, drums and bass guitar. He sings vocals and background vocals, too. His guitar teacher introduced him to the Sagebrush Round-Up when he was 10 years old, and he's been coming ever since—20 years in 2024.

"I really enjoy the classic country music, the atmosphere and the people here. And I just enjoy coming every week to entertain the crowd," Brandon said.

He and the other five members open the show and play several sets throughout the evening. If single acts need a backup, the band is there for them, as well.

This Saturday night in April 2024 is about 14 years short of a century since the Fairmont-area tradition got its start on December 10, 1938. The original Sagebrush Roundup ("Roundup" was written as one word back then) debuted that night to live and radio audiences from the stage of the Fairmont Armory on Jackson Street. WMMN, Fairmont's local radio station, attempted to build a Saturday evening audience with a show modeled after the popular Wheeling Jamboree broadcast on WWVA. Stocked with talent from WMMN's live, weekday radio broadcasts, the one-hour program showcased some of the best musical talent in Appalachia: Grandpa (Marshall Louis) Jones, Little Jimmy Dickens, Cowboy Loye (Donald Pack), Uncle Rufe (Armstrong), the "Old Pardner" Murrell Poor and his Tradin' Post Gang, Curley Mitchell and his Ploughboys, the Buskirk Family, Tex Mitchell and the Rhythm Rangers, and "Little" John Graham and his wife, Cherokee Sue.

"We played the Roundup practically every Saturday night," John Graham told me back in 2003. "We'd usually play a fiddle tune, sing a song, maybe five or six songs."

The 8 p.m. broadcast was but an hour long, but the musicians continued to entertain the live audience late into the evening. "They moved the chairs out, and they would square dance in there," recalled Bob Cunningham, who attended the original Roundup shows as a young man.

"You'd have so many people who would come out to watch, there would not be anywhere for them to sit," recalled Bill Murray, who played and sang with the Mountain State Melody Boys. "The audience would stand outside and watch through the windows."

Most contemporary Round-Up audience members will not know this, but the Bunner Ridge stage pays homage to the original show in several ways. A 10-by-30-foot section of the old armory's floor is incorporated into the contemporary Round-Up's 60-foot-long stage. Décor on the stage—a lighted railroad cross-buck and country-store porch—hark back to the rustic appearance of the original Roundup stage.

"I saw Grandpa Jones bake biscuits on that stage," said Rex "no relation to Montgomery" Ward during my interviews with band members back in 2003. Rex, in his 80s, was a house band member. "This, to me, is seventh heaven," he said. "It is on par with the 'Grand Ole Opry.' There is so much history on this stage, you wouldn't believe it."

Virgil Anderson sits amid sponsor signs while waiting for the Sagebrush Round-Up show to start on an August evening in 2003. Sponsorships have helped keep the Round-Up going and growing.

Rex played stage left, in the shadow of the railroad crossing sign whose lights were activated whenever a vocalist sang a railroading song. The lights honored the late Casey Reese, who sang many railroad songs on that stage before he rode the glory train home in 2000. The country store backdrop was a nod to the porch on which Paul and Donald Hayhurst played with their Hard Cider Band.

"They just played square dances. They were back-porch entertainers," Paul told me in 2003. His father, Blaine, and his uncle Glenn played in the Hard Cider Band along with Virgil Toothman, Vernon Heiskell and Oscar Butcher. They used to play all the old fiddle tunes: 'Mississippi Sawyer,' 'Soldier's Joy,' 'Ragtime Annie,' 'Redwing.'

"Mom said that I'd lay in the cradle and cry from the noise, in tune with them, I guess," Paul said.

In 2003, old-timers like Rex Ward and Bill Eisentrout were still attending the Round-Up gatherings, where they loved to share its history. They could talk to you about Grandpa (Marshall Louis) Jones, who graduated from the Roundup stage to the Grand Ole Opry's, and Little Jimmy Dickens,

Country Music Association of W.Va. President Paul Hayhurst (left) and Secretary Jim Thornburg were instrumental in bringing the former auto plant building to Bunners Ridge to serve as the home of Sagebrush Round-Up and the association's museum and hall of fame. Photo from August 2003.

the Raleigh County native who stood 4 feet 11 inches but dwarfed many Sagebrush Roundup acts in fame.

"As a boy about 11 years old, it was a thrill for me to go to the Roundup," recalled Bill Eisentrout, who was serving as treasurer of the Country Music Association of W.Va. in 2003. "Little Jimmy wasn't much bigger than I was."

World War II, gasoline rationing and Saturday night overtime in the mines and factories that fed the Allies' war effort diminished attendance at WMMN's live shows. The Roundup held its final show October 2, 1948.

Fairmont's tradition of live music retreated to front porches and family gatherings until the early 1980s, when jam sessions came to the Winfield Community Building. Those sessions grew into regular Saturday night shows that drew many of the former Roundup performers and audience members to Bunner Ridge.

Buddy Priest, one of the "cans" in the West Virginia Six Pack Band, told me in 2003 that these small gatherings were the phoenix that rose from the ashes of mid-20th century cultural fires.

"The jam sessions started in the early 1980s as a place for the older people to go on Saturday nights that was not a bar atmosphere and where anybody who could play could be a part of," Buddy told me. Other musicians and groups who took part in these revivals included The Pioneers, Paul Crane, the Vandergrift Brothers and Stormy Young.

The musicians held their first spring festival at the park in 1981. Although the event drew no more than 50 spectators, subsequent festivals drew hundreds, and the event was expanded to three days. Concurrently, the Saturday-night gatherings were seeing audiences of up to 700 and dozens of entertainers, some of them former Roundup performers.

This renewed interest led to a formal organization in 1984. Originally known as the Winfield District Country Music Association, the non-profit group in 1991 changed its name to the Country Music Association of West Virginia to more accurately reflect its mission. Currently known as the West Virginia Music Hall of Fame and Museum, Inc., the group's mission includes providing "a suitable environment for displaying memorabilia and other artifacts related to the musical heritage of this area . . . and for musicians and fans to meet and enjoy country music and fellowship."

Board members and a hall of fame member of the West Virginia Music Hall of Fame and Museum gather around the "largest guitar east of the Mississippi" in the auditorium in 2024. From left to right in the front are: Leo McMillen (inductee), Debbie Hutson (hall of fame committee member), John Keefover (board member) Bill Janoske (treasurer), Lisa Janoske (secretary), Dave Haun (vice-president) Brandon Howdershelt (president), Donnie Leonard (board member). In the back are board members Rick Musgrove, Chris Johnson and Bob Johnson.

A big deal

That "suitable environment" is the 17-by-100-foot steel-frame building that once was part of the Volkswagen manufacturing facility in New Stanton, Pa. In the summer of 1993, volunteers erected the building on land donated by Jack "Hardrock" Bunner. Round-Up musicians and audience members alike supported the project with personal loans and donations so the seasonal outdoor shows would have an indoor, year-round venue.

As with any venture of that magnitude, improvements to the structure have been ongoing in the ensuing years. Recent updates/improvements include new restrooms, a dance floor, new heating and air conditioning units, LED stage lighting and enhanced sound reinforcement.

"I think one of the reasons that we're around is that we have a very nice building," Lisa Janoske said. The venue is set up to seat 460 patrons, who

The West Virginia Music Hall of Fame and Museum holds an annual induction ceremony for those entering the hall. Larry Reed was inducted in 2024.

can choose from folding chairs at tables in the far back, rows of folding chairs in the middle or 270 upholstered theater-style folding seats in the front and VIP sections.

It took volunteers three days to disassemble the rows of upholstered seats and load them into a big rig. "They came from a church in Philadelphia," Brandon said. "And three months to put them back up."

The work was done during the COVID-19 pandemic, which forced a suspension of live performances beginning in March 2020. Bill Janoske said the association weathered the financial storm thanks to its savings account, a state grant and ongoing support from individuals and businesses. Live country music, with proper social distancing protocols, returned as soon as restrictions were relaxed.

"We can't say enough about the donors and sponsors that helped us through that. We really didn't have to dip into our savings very much, if any, to keep the (utilities) on in the building because of all the people who donated and just love the place as much as we do," Bill Janoske said.

Drawing upon their library of recorded shows, the directors kept the Round-Up alive on home screens thanks to streaming. As in the early 1940s,

The West Virginia Music Hall of Fame and Museum provides exhibits focused on WMMN, West Virginia country artists, coal mining, and much more.

when AM radio brought the Roundup into isolated homes, live streaming continues to provide a front seat at the performances.

"We stream on social media through Facebook, TikTok and YouTube Live," Bill said. "We do that every Saturday, except when we do the Nashville shows. (Radio broadcasts) are no longer an option for us because of the cost.... The only (country music show) still broadcast on the radio nowadays is WSM in Nashville. It's the only one left, but at one time, every radio station had their live country music show."

Those days are recalled in the Music Hall of Fame Museum. Memorabilia from the show's WMMN days and the musicians who performed on it fill several rooms in the well-lighted, spacious exhibit area. Radio sets dating back to the 1920s, the guitar once strummed by Cowboy Loye and the microphones that converted those notes into electrical signals are displayed. Hundreds of photographs, autographs and other paper memorabilia provide a newsreel of that era when families gathered around the Philco after a long week of work on the farm or in the coal mines. One display pays homage to the latter occupation, which once fueled the Fairmont area's economy.

Equally well documented is the modern-era Round-Up story. Hundreds

The West Virginia Music Hall of Fame occupies several walls in the museum at the Sagebrush Round-Up facility in Fairmont. The museum is open during the shows, held most Saturday nights late February through December.

of photographs and dozens of autographed posters from the Nashville stars who played the association's venues cover the walls. Bill said the directors typically book two "national acts" out of Nashville annually—in 2024 they did three shows: The Davisson Brothers Family Band, Ben Haggard and the Strangers, and Bellamy Brothers.

"They will probably fill the place," Bill predicted, noting that early ticket sales for Haggard, son of Merle, pointed to a sold-out show. These events provide greater exposure for the venue, whose "regular" crowd comes from a radius of approximately 50 miles. The stage draws its performers from a much wider circle, thanks to a musician-friendly atmosphere.

"Sagebrush is cool," said Steve Smith, a Roane County native and string musician who lives in McHenry, Md., and drives over to perform at the Round-Up.

"We draw bands from Charleston, all over the state," Bill Janoske said. "They come here to play, and they are top-notch. There are even out-of-state bands that come from Pennsylvania, Maryland and Ohio."

Band members receive very little compensation, "gas money" Bill said,

The house band performs under the large red curtain of the Sagebrush Round-Up stage following the hall of fame induction ceremony in 2024.

but they still come because the venue is first and foremost about the music, heritage and camaraderie.

"We always have a crowd that loves music," Steve Smith said. "That's important."

Bill said the venue's large stage and appreciative, focused audience draw talent.

"It's not a bar. I hear a lot of (musicians) say, 'You go to a bar, and you are the secondary attraction. The band is there, but, they can only play until the fight breaks out,'" Bill said. "Here, we have a lot of bands compliment the audience because the audience came to see the band. They didn't come for some other reason, although this is a very social venue. A lot of people come week after week to see their friends."

And eat. The Round-Up offers a full-course, eat-in dinner prior to the show, as well as a concession stand with snacks and soft drinks during the performance. But no alcohol.

"We are family friendly venue," Bill said. "No smoking, no alcohol. We have grandparents that bring their grandkids, and parents that bring their kids. And those kids come back. It's an older crowd, and the musicians don't have to deal with that bar scene."

This musician-friendly atmosphere helps the board fulfill the organization's mission to "find, cultivate, educate and encourage new talent." An open stage prior to the main show most Saturdays is the talent farm. "So, anyone can sign up for our open stage and sing a couple of songs with the house band," Lisa Janoske said. "And then, if they are really good and win over the crowd, we usually book them for a future evening show."

Bill said the Round-Up has helped make the Fairmont area a "magnet" for talent that would otherwise have a difficult time finding a regular performance venue. The Janoskes travel from Garrett County, Md., to play in the house band. Some of those musicians also play in other bands, and if they can't make their Round-Up engagement, Lisa and Bill know they can call upon others to slide into the vacancy.

"If somebody were to cancel tonight, I could go out in the audience and find a top-notch band member in a heartbeat," Bill said. "Fairmont in general is just amazing, all the musicians that are located in this little area.".

"I have my band here tonight," Steve Smith said. "But sometimes I'll use the Round-Up Band, as well. It's an advantage, I think as a performer, that if you can't put a band together, you can still slide in here and be part of another group. Sometimes, I sneak in, if that makes any sense, because most of the time when I go somewhere it is because I'm always asked to play. But the Sagebrush gives me the liberty to just sit in the audience and listen, too. It's kind of cool to be able to do that."

While musicians visit and perform as their schedules allow, many of those who come to listen have a standing date.

"I love country music, and I love coming here," said Dorothy Maio, whose friend, Ed King, brings her to the show almost every Saturday night. Look for them at the back of the room.

Dorothy is in her late 80s, and Round-Up board members admit that the mostly over-50 audience presents a challenge to the tradition's longevity. The house band has adapted by transitioning its repertoire into the 21st century and being realistic about what attracts a younger crowd. One outcome is that the Round-Up dropped its tradition of doing an all-bluegrass night in those months with a fifth Saturday.

"Over time, bluegrass kind of faded . . . we just were not getting the crowds," Bill Janoske said. "It is mainly classic country. That is our draw . . . we play classic country here."

While country music continues to evolve, the group's West Virginia Country Music Hall of Fame has fulfilled the group's mandate to recognize

Hall of Fame inductee Albert Anderson is surrounded by family for photographs on his big night at the Sagebrush Round-Up's induction in 2024.

the state's country music talent. (The West Virginia Country Music Hall of Fame is not to be confused with the Charleston-based West Virginia Music Hall of Fame.) Back in the spring of 2011, Bill and Helen Hutson were working in the group's archives when they came across documentation concerning this component of the association. Three individuals—Floyd J. Priest, Paul C. Crane and Edwin "Bud" VanGilder—were named to the hall in 1987, but formal recognition and ongoing additions were absent.

The Hutsons petitioned the board to revive the formal induction event and recognition. In 2012, six individuals were inducted in a ceremony prior to the show, which featured the new inductees' talents. Since then, the hall of fame has taken over an entire wall of the museum, where a plaque and photo of each member are displayed.

Lisa said any person can nominate an individual or group for inclusion through a written request. Nominations also come from Hall of Fame Committee members and organization directors. The committee reviews the nominations and reaches out to the nominee for additional information before presenting their findings to the board of directors for final selection.

"There are different criteria that we look for when they return that application," Lisa Janoske explained. There are categories for performers, non-performers and Nashville acts, but in all cases, longevity in their art is a priority—at least 30 years.

Those in the latter category include Hawkshaw Hawkins, Little Jimmy Dickens and Kathy Mattea. At the 2024 induction ceremony, Little Roy & Lizzy Long and Kevin & Debbie Williamson were brought into the Nashville fold, while Albert Anderson, Jack & Cindy Falbo, Samuel Manno, Larry Reed, Steve Smith and Esther Wolfe received their plaques as Sagebrush Round-Up performers and supporters.

Steve Smith, who also is a member of the Wheeling Jamboree Hall of Fame, said it was an honor to be included in the Round-Up's Hall.

"You know, West Virginia always seems to be looked down upon, right? So, it's an honor for me to be inducted into the West Virginia Country Music Hall of Fame for the fact that it shows West Virginia has talent, and its people have ability, and that music here is just as good as it is anywhere else," Steve said.

The entire world can be the judge of that, thanks to the Round-Up's streaming of the Saturday night gatherings on Bunner Ridge.

"I think it helps us," Bill Janoske said of the social media presence. "You'd be surprised. We get them from Arizona, California, Florida, all over the United States watching our live feed. I think people watch the live feed and then say, 'I want to go there in person.' And we do get a lot of that. They come and say they've seen us (on social media)."

Volunteer Bob Johnson said these long-distance travelers can camp out on the Sagebrush grounds in their motor home or travel trailer. The campground offers 30-amp electrical service at each site, a dump station and water source for filling tanks. The amenity is especially popular with those who attend outdoor events held on the 68-acre campus. They include an annual car show, flea market and Fourth-of-July concert with fireworks.

But most of all, folks come for the camaraderie, music, heritage and memories of a tradition that was just too good to fade away.

The Sagebrush Round-Up is Saturday evenings mid-February through December. Special events and performances are held throughout the year. For current information, visit their Facebook page.

Bill Murray on the Sagebrush stage in 2003. He and Granny Blosser did an hour-long gospel show on the fourth Saturday of the month.

Sagebrush original: Bill Murray

The late Ortha Lorn (Bill) Murray (1915-2013) was the last of the original Sagebrush Roundup radio broadcast members still performing at the Round-Up in 2003, when I first visited the venue.

He often performed with Granny Blosser (another Sagebrush Roundup legend) and the Stagecoach Band in an hour-long gospel show held the fourth Saturday of the month.

Bill grew up in the Dellslow area of Monongalia County and was introduced to the guitar at the age of 9. A fiddle-playing neighbor, "Dad" Grant Fisher, was his mentor. "I just picked it up and took off with it," Bill told me. "Fisher and I got together, and I learned to play the guitar."

Bill was the youngest of 12 children in the Arthur and Elizabeth Murray family. His father was a coal miner who lost his life when Bill was just 3 years old.

"There was no welfare back then, and my mom had to raise us, working for 50 cents a day," Bill said. He went to work and used his earnings to buy a $6 Regal guitar from a mail-order catalog.

"We picked blackberries, huckleberries," Bill said. A gallon sold for 10 to 15 cents. "That was the way we had to make a living back then."

Grant Fisher invited Bill to join his new band, the Mountain State Melody Boys, in the early 1930s. Other members included Bob Thomas on mandolin, Flip Cow on guitar, George Leach on banjo and Gordan Bishop on bass, except he couldn't afford a bass and made do with a jug.

"We all stuck together. It was like a family. It was just the same as a family," Bill told me. "There was no drinking, and no smoking, allowed."

Their first gig was on a Saturday night program broadcast over WMMN in Fairmont. There was no compensation, and none of the band members had a vehicle. A friend, Phil Noose, hauled them to Fairmont.

"Phil had an old Chrysler, and we'd all pitch in enough money to buy the gas to take us up there," Bill said. Gas was 9 cents a gallon.

The payoff was to pick up a job playing for a reunion or other event resulting from their radio publicity. "We got paid, maybe, $1.50 apiece," said Bill, recalling what performers earned back then.

Their act was heavy on gospel, bluegrass and "old-time fiddle and banjo picking."

"We just mixed it up," Bill recalled. They played at the Sagebrush Roundup, but Bill could not recall being compensated. He recalled the attention he received from the audience as nice but unfruitful.

"The girls would wait for you outside, and when you came out, they'd want you to go for a little ride, but you didn't have a car," he said.

Going professional was never an option. "As a young boy coming up as I was—your dad being dead and no one else to feed the family—you had to go to work," Bill said. He started out as a water boy on a road gang, did some carpentry, blacksmithing, welding and barbering, then got a job in the coal mines. He spent 60 years in the industry, all of them above ground in the equipment maintenance and repair shop.

The Mountain State Melody Boys stayed together until 1946, when the members' personal commitments overwhelmed their free time. In the early 1960s, Bill put away his guitar and focused on making a living. Thirty-five years later, following the death of his first wife, Rachel, in 1999, he picked up his guitar and started playing again.

"It's just an enjoyment that brings back memories when I go to Bunner Ridge to play," he said.

John Graham and his wife, Harriet "Cherokee" Sue (Dieckerhoff) were country music performers on Fairmont's WMMN Sagebrush Roundup show. *Photo from the late John Graham's collection.*

Sagebrush original: "Little" John Graham

June 22, 1941, was a sweltering day in Buckhannon's Green Valley Park. Several of the 14,000 people who came to the park that afternoon fainted from the heat while waiting for the 4 p.m. wedding ceremony of "Little" John Graham and Harriet "Cherokee Sue" Dieckerhoff.

For several weeks prior to the wedding, WMMN, the Fairmont radio station where John and Sue were country music performers and disc jockeys, promoted the wedding as an entertainment attraction. Recognizing an opportunity to make some money for both WMMN and the couple, the station pulled together a show from its roster of performers, charged an admission and claimed one-third of the take for itself.

"Sue and I was pretty popular, especially Sue," John told me during an interview in 2003. "The price was 20 cents a person to get in. Sue and I got $702.53 that day. We went down the next day and bought a new Chevrolet for $900. And boy, it was one of the best ones, too."

In addition to the cash, John and Sue were supplied with just about anything a newly-wed couple needed, thanks to the generosity of the many sponsors who advertised on WMMN. "We had everything given to us, everything except the rings," John said. "I could have had the rings, too, but I said, 'No, I'm buying the rings.' I paid $80 for the set of rings, and that was a pretty fair set of rings back in 1941. But all our clothes and everything else were given to us."

The couple set up housekeeping on Jackson Street in Fairmont, a short distance from the armory and radio station where they worked. John had a solo morning show, as well as a 4 p.m. show with Sue. They also played the Sagebrush Roundup live-audience radio show.

John, a vocalist and guitar player, began his rise to radio fame just a few hundred yards south of the Mason-Dixon line on a mountaintop farm in northern Monongalia County. The mail came out of Brave, Pa., but the family farm was a mile up a mud road into West Virginia from Brave.

Born February 10, 1920, John was the fourth child of John and Eva Graham. He was the only one of the couple's seven children who showed any inclination toward music.

"I sang," he said. "Mother would send me to the basement. My gosh, she'd get tired of hearing me sing. I'd go down there anyway, because it would ring better; you could hear it a little better in the basement."

John learned about music by associating with other musicians in the community. "I'd see a guitar and see other people playing, and I'd say, 'How about you showing me that chord?' I was very eager (to learn)."

"Big John Stockdale," a neighbor who played the violin and guitar, took a special interest in John. Three years older than his neighbor, Big John became "Little" John's mentor.

John Graham holds a calendar from the days he was a "Jubilee Boy" with the group headed up by Radio Dot. Photo from 2003.

"I remember it so well, he saw my dad and said, 'Can your son come up and play music with me? We'll play music, listen to the Grand Ole Opry and I'll bring him back Sunday,'" John told me. "Dad said, 'If John wants to, he can go.'

"So, he comes down on a horse, and I got my guitar and got on the back of that horse and went up there, and we played music that night. And he brought me back the next day."

John was 16 when he and Stockdale first got together. John received his guitar from his father, who gave it to him as payment for painting the fence around their property.

It was Dorothy Henderson, "Radio Dot," who brought Graham and Stockdale down from the mountain and into Waynesburg, Pa., to "practice, practice and practice." Freddie Wells, another Brave musician, completed the quartet with his banjo playing.

The group called itself "Big John, Little John, Freddie and Radio Dot," although "Little" John Graham was actually taller than "Big John" Stockdale. John Graham said it was Dot's idea to call him "Little John," and although he objected, the name stuck.

Hymns and story songs were the group's mainstay. "The songs they sing today, a lot of them don't say anything and you can't understand the words," John lamented. "But I sang hymns and story-like songs, that's what most people did back then."

When the quartet, "Radio Dot and Her Jubilee Boys," was ready for the big time, Dorothy took them to WMMN for an audition. The station was a haven for live country performers and had a large audience that extended up the northern panhandle and as far east as Winchester, Va. Several legendary performers paused before the WMMN microphones on their road to the big time, including Buddy Starcher, the legendary Nicholas County guitar man and vocalist, and Grandpa Jones, who spent two years polishing his comic and vocal talents at WMMN. Even Herb Porter, the reporter remembered for his live coverage of the Hindenburg crash ("Oh, the humanity . . . ") worked at WMMN.

"We just loved what we were doing," John recalled. "We went over to Fairmont, to the radio station, to audition, and (Howard Hopkins) "Foxy" Wolfe, the program director, said, 'Well, we don't have any time right now, but we'll call you when we get some time.' "Cowboy Loye was there, and he was buying an hour and 15 minutes on there every day. He was almost the boss in 1937, a man that would buy an hour and 15 minutes. Cowboy said, 'You got time, put them on.' And we went on. That's the way it was."

"Cowboy Loye" Pack came to WMMN from WWVA in 1937. Extremely popular with radio audiences, Loye paid for his time on the radio by selling

John Graham at his home in Bridgeport, August 16, 2003.

a line of products he licensed. These included Cowboy Loye guitars, which he sold over the air for $15 each, shipping included. Loye also peddled Blue Bonnet Mineral Crystals, a laxative product. Strangely enough, Pack's female vocal group—Sylvia, Lillie and Florence Curry of Hundred—was named "The Blue Bonnet Girls."

John believes it was Dorothy Henderson's friendship with Pack that landed them the job on WMMN. Cowboy Loye and Radio Dot briefly worked together at WWVA.

For John, the youngest member of the group, the decision to go on the air meant dropping out of school at the age of 17. "I left 10th grade in high school," he said. "My daddy didn't want me to do that at all. I said, 'Dad, I want to make a buck.' I don't know if it would have been better if I'd gotten the other two years of high school or not."

John got a boost to his career from his uncle, Frank Hastings, who bought him a new L-5 Gibson guitar when he learned his nephew was playing on the radio. "Uncle Frank Hastings: He was a man who was very conservative and had lots of money. He used to send me five dollars in the mail when I was living over there in Fairmont. That came in pretty handy," John said.

John moved to Fairmont, where he got a room on Jackson Street for $2 a week. "I could eat for a quarter, and for 35 cents, I could get a good meal," he said. John got his material by listening to new releases on the jukeboxes that blared in virtually every restaurant and bar.

"I'd go in a beer joint somewhere and I'd put a nickel in. Boy, did I hate to let go of that nickel!" John said. "And I'd get the song by listening to it. I could get the tune the first time, but I'd have to put another nickel in to get the words. I'd write every third line of the song because you couldn't keep up with the song. Then you'd have to skip a line to get the next third line. That's the way I'd do it. Cost me 20 cents, sometimes more, to get a song."

John went on the air with Radio Dot in August 1937. There was no salary; the money was made through public inquiry accounts—listener responses to the advertising pitches that performers worked into their shows. The station paid a stipend for every inquiry generated by their mention of a product or service on the air.

Having at least one musician who also had the gift of gab and a persuasive radio voice was essential to group's survival. Dot was that person. "She didn't play an instrument," John said. "But she was a good singer and announcer."

Initially, Radio Dot promised to split the group's earnings four ways. John said Dorothy also provided transportation to their gigs throughout the state. These ranged from as far south as Webster Springs, east to Winchester, Va, and all along the Ohio River. "We never played beer joints," John said. "We played theaters, we played high schools, we played reunions, we played churches. But we would never play beer joints." In keeping with her desire to present a respectable group, Dot insisted that the men in the band wear a suit and tie to performances.

The performers were on the road most every night, and it was from these engagements that the band generated most of its income. "She bought a Chrysler Imperial built with little jump seats in the back," he said. "Well, shoot, that was a $2,300 car in about 1938. That was a really expensive car. That's what we traveled in. We put our instruments in the back, and we had a PA system, just a little thing that would fit inside the two speakers, and one microphone. That's all. One microphone, that's all you'd take in. We could get practically everything in the trunk."

The financial arrangement was for the members to share evenly in the receipts. But in the second year, it seemed as if Dot was doing better than the other members.

"Twenty dollars a week, that's what Dot paid us. We played shows all over, and they were charging 25 cents at the door then," John said. "We were having big crowds, but she'd put us on a $20-a-week salary. That's why I quit her."

By this time, John had established a friendship with Murrell Poor, "The Old Pardner," who had come to WMMN in 1937. "I was telling Murrell about Dot not splitting even with us boys, and he said, 'You want a job?' And I said, 'Yes!' I quit Dot that night, and she offered me $35 a week to stay. But I said, 'Dot, you did me wrong once, you're not going to do it again,'" John said.

Murrell made a spot for John in his Tradin' Post Gang, and life went on pretty much as it had when John was a member of Radio Dot's group, except John made more money because Murrell paid a percentage of the profits. The Old Pardner was immensely popular with WMMN audiences. "Murrell was one of the best announcers on WMMN," John said.

John's time with Murrell was short. Around 11 p.m. May 29, 1939, The Tradin' Post Gang was returning from a job in Mill Creek when their car went out of control on the highway between Philippi and Fairmont. Jimmy Smith, the group's steel guitar player, was driving. Murrell was in the front passenger's seat, his window rolled down. John, Howard "Big-Eared" Zip Bennix, the group's tenor banjo player, and Zip's girlfriend, May, were in the back seat.

Decades later, John shared vivid memories of that night. "We went over this hill and started down another one, and Murrell shouted, 'Watch out!' (Jimmy Smith) had fallen asleep, run off the road. He zipped her back on the road, and we zigzagged down the hill, and with each zip he'd get a little quicker, and over we turned."

Murrell's head was smashed against the pavement as the car rolled over, fracturing the Old Pardner's skull. "We were there at 1 o'clock in the morning, and old Jimmy was running around the car crying, 'It's my fault, it's my fault!'" recalled John, who had kicked out a back door to get out of the vehicle.

Murrell was taken to a Philippi hospital, where he lingered until his death June 1, 1939.

His calling hours and funeral were legendary. According to the *Fairmont Times* of June 5, 1939, 10,000 people packed the funeral home, National Guard Armory and an adjacent block of Jackson Street for the services. The funeral director, R.C. Jones, stated that it was double or triple the size of the largest funeral he'd previously seen in the city.

The Tradin' Post Gang broke up after Murrell's death. John found work in a new group, "Budge and Fudge" the Mayses brothers from Buddy Starcher's hometown of Sutton. Starcher had given Paul the name of "Fudge" to rhyme with his brother's actual name. The fourth member of the group was "Cherokee Sue," an import from Warren, Ohio.

John said his future wife had come down from Warren with her sisters and their manager, Joe Edison, and landed a job on WMMN. Sue developed a following among the youngsters, who were fascinated with her Native American heritage. She had coal-black hair and was one-quarter Cherokee. An athletic woman especially fond of swimming, horseback riding, boating and motorcycle racing, Sue arrived in Fairmont in the fall of 1940. She was a vocalist with a special knack for announcing and selling products.

"I just fell in love with her," said John, who was two years her senior. "That's just the way it was. I'd seen prettier girls, but none nicer than Sue." Eight months after meeting, John and Sue were wed at the Green Valley Park ceremony in Buckhannon. John said neither he nor Sue had any money, and they were in full agreement with the station making a publicity stunt out of their wedding.

"I went in and told Foxy Wolfe that we wanted to get married and to let us get married on the (Sagebrush Roundup) stage," John said. "And he asked me, 'What are you trying to do, capitalize on your wedding?' And I said, 'Put it anyway you want, but we don't have a thing, and we're going to get married.'"

John said all of the WMMN acts were there—Budge and Fudge, the Buskirk Family and Hank the Cowhand. Cowboy Loye was deceased by then, having died in 1940 at the Cleveland Clinic.

The Rev. F.L. Radcliff of the United Brethren Church of Adrian performed the half-hour ceremony. Norma Francis Armstrong, known to WMMN radio audiences as Uncle Rufe's wife "Petunia," was matron of honor. Sue's sister Mary was bridesmaid. Best man was Paul Mayse. WMMN

John Graham continued to sing at the weekly gatherings of performers at Rick Cottrill's house in Clarksburg. Photo from November 2003.

kiddy club program stars little Joan and Gladys Clonch of Clarksburg were Sue's train bearers.

Following their wedding, John worked with Sue on her program, "Cherokee Sue and Little John," and with several other WMMN performers, including Starcher. A draft notice in 1942 sent John packing for the European Theater. John still remembers the day he left Sue behind at the bus station in Fairmont.

"She was acting pretty good, then I looked back and saw her crying," John said. "That was the thing. People holler about not wanting to go to the service, but the thing that bothered me was leaving Sue. I was for my country as much as any person, but I didn't want to leave Sue."

Sue visited John while he was serving at a post on the Mojave Desert, and from that visit came their son, John, in 1944. A daughter, Susan, was born to them in 1948. John served in a field ordinance company during the war. His captain encouraged him and other musically inclined soldiers in the company to sing and play their instruments as a morale booster. He traveled through France with his trusty Martin guitar, which he sold to a fellow soldier for $55 while waiting to board the boat to come back to the United States.

Back in Fairmont, Sue and John resumed their careers on WMMN, staying there until the summer of 1947, when WPDX, a new Clarksburg station, went on the air. The 1,000-watt, clear-channel station presented a serious challenge to WMMN and attracted many of that station's top talent. "We were on the inaugural broadcast, the first day it went on the air August 18, 1947," John said. Budge and Fudge joined the couple on WPDX, and the group became known as the West Virginia Hillfolks. John had a 15-minute solo program, Sue did a one-hour disc jockey show, and they did a 15-minute hymn program together at 4 p.m. John said Sue was his ticket to get on the air.

"They wouldn't have hired me by myself," John said. "I went along with Sue. Sue was a saleswoman on top of it, and I wasn't. Sue would say, 'Now we're going to talk about (a product). You want to get up and talk about it?' And it just wouldn't come out right, and I'd end up saying, 'Sue, you do it.' We sold everything. She had Coco-Wheats, she had White Cross Insurance. She would get a dollar if the station got a card in (from a listener), she would get a dollar, and the station would get five dollars. She had a beauty shop that advertised. My gosh, she had a dozen different sponsors." On one unusually good day, the station received 5,000 letters, each one containing a box-top and quarter in response to a Coco-Wheats belt-buckle offer.

Demand for live shows dropped off during the 1950s as recorded music replaced live performers and the melancholy story songs gave way to rockabilly. Sue continued to work as a disc jockey and did some early television work on Clarksburg's WBOY. Garden Fresh Markets sponsored her show. "It was just a show where she played music on TV," John recalled. "She would come in and give a commercial. She did that about a year, then she got sick and had to pull out. I'll never forget it. She was down to St. Mary's Hospital, and they called me and said, 'We think Sue is pregnant.' Then we come home a day or two, and they wanted Sue to come back. They said, 'No, Sue's not pregnant. She has an ovarian tumor.'"

Sue died in 1967 and is buried in Floral Hills Memory Gardens, Quiet Dell, just below the grave of Budge Mayse, who had died in February of that year. "When I got married to Sue, I was doing what I wanted to do," John told me. "I never made very good money in country music, but I enjoyed it. That was the main thing."

John Graham with his song-writer friend Dorsey Wiseman at the 2004 Singing in the Hills gathering in Mabie.

John put his guitar away after Sue got sick and eventually went into the plumbing business. Years later, he did some performing around the area, including at Singing in the Hills with its founder and his friend, Dorsey Wiseman.

John Graham died November 30, 2008, at 88.

A photograph of Dorsey Wiseman rests against the platform of where Singing in the Hills artists raise their voices in praise. From left are Dustin Lambert, Carolyn Connor and Jimmy Howson. Photo is from the 2024 event.

Chapter 9

Singing in the Hills

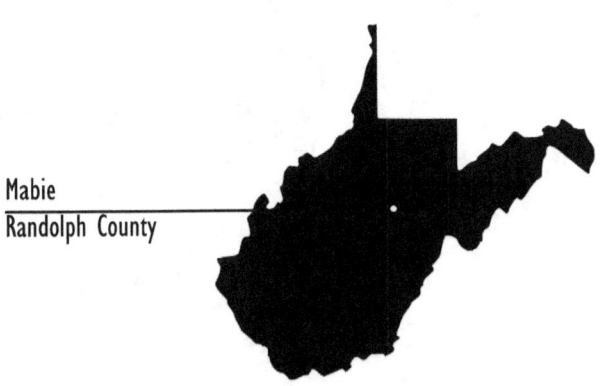

Mabie
Randolph County

If the trees and clouds on Rich Mountain could pluck guitars and the birds and breezes sing, their music would sound like "Singing in the Hills."

The two-day gospel music event is a decades-old tradition on the grounds of the Harrison Community Church in Mabie, Randolph County. Vocalists and musicians come from throughout West Virginia and neighboring states to perform and encourage the listeners who are drawn from an even larger geographic area. Held the second full weekend in August, the event sprawls across the church grounds, with the musicians on a platform—not a stage—in a pavilion that seats more than 100.

On the floor at the front of that platform is a black-and-white photo of man standing at a microphone. His jaw is deformed; skin taunt; expression pained but sincere, determined. The man was Dorsey Wiseman. Depending on who you ask, he is at least partially credited with being the sing's founder. And, for those who knew him and preserve the tradition, he is at least partially the reason it is still going strong long after his death.

The Wiseman presence pervades this wide spot known as Mabie. Dorsey Wiseman's grandmother once tended her vegetable garden where the

Dustin Lambert (left) said he was called into a music ministry during a Singing in the Hills event. He credits the late Dorsey Wiseman for helping him in that work. Dustin's repertoire includes songs Dorsey wrote. Photo from 2004.

church stands; the Wiseman family donated the land so the community could have a place of worship. Across the street is the house where Dorsey grew up and, after a period of working in northeast Ohio, returned to as an adult with his wife, Tippy.

Both Dorsey and Tippy are deceased. Family and veteran musicians alike remember them fondly as people who brought this gospel music festival to the Wiseman homestead.

"This meant the world to him," said Elizabeth Currence, a granddaughter whom Dorsey and Tippy raised. "He absolutely loved it. All year long he was planning and talking to singers and singing groups to come in for (the event)."

Elizabeth said Singing in the Hills is part of Dorsey Wiseman's legacy, a legacy that included song writing, performance and Christian testimony.

"Uncle Dorsey always was big into music," said Joey Simmons, Dorsey's nephew who lives down the road from the church. "He liked being in the

Dorsey Wiseman walks the grounds of Harrison Community Church across the street from his Mabie home, October 2003. Dorsey said God told him to have the annual gospel music gathering on these church grounds.

limelight, and he just wanted to start a gospel sing. He started inviting groups, and it just grew into what it is today."

"Dorsey, he gets all the credit for starting it, but actually it was my mom (Lena Simmons) and my aunt June and my Aunt Margaret and Dorsey, they all started it together," Joey said. The three sisters and Dorsey recorded an album entitled "The Wisemans" in the 1970s while living in Ohio. Two of Dorsey's original songs were included on the album, released by Marbone records.

Dorsey credited his mother for the siblings' interest in music and performance skills.

"My mother would set a broom in front of us like a microphone stand, and that's how we got started," Dorsey told me in an interview back in 2003. Dorsey's mother loved music and played the piano for her church.

"Everybody on the mountain here played music of some kind. You just watched it and learned," he said. Dorsey bought a guitar while in high school and began performing solo and group gigs in churches, schools and on WDNE radio in Elkins. He and several other soldier-musicians formed a group while serving at Fort Knox in the 1950s. Returning to civilian

Dorsey Wiseman's kin still make music at the annual event and run the concession stand. From left are Joey Simmons, Patricia Wilson and Donna Thomas.

life in West Virginia, Dorsey teamed up with Jimmie and Loren "Lodi" Currence of Cassity for a twice-weekly bluegrass show on a Clarksburg television station.

He wrote songs, as well, with personal experiences often inspiring the lyrics. But when it came to his gospel tunes, Dorsey described himself as "just a penman," with God telling him "what he wanted me write."

His gospel hymns have been recorded by Carolyn Connor, also a songwriter, and his "Beacon Light" song is usually performed by at least one vocalist during Singing in the Hills. The beacon is a reference to a light tower on Rich Mountain that was visible from the front porch of the Wiseman home. His father instructed Dorsey to look for the landmark if he ever got lost while hunting in the woods.

"That has lived true for me and others by following that light," Dorsey said, explaining how the Rich Mountain beacon was a metaphor for the light from "Mount Calvary."

Descendants of Dorsey and Tippy Wiseman take to the platform to sing a modern Christian song during Singing in the Hills 2024, which was the 50th anniversary of the August gathering.

Like many Appalachian young couples in post-World War II America, Dorsey and Tippy migrated to industrial Ohio for work and better wages. They also frequently returned to their home places in the mountains. It was on one of those trips back to Mabie that Dorsey received the inspiration for Singing in the Hills. Dorsey told me that he was sitting in the church pavilion when, "God told me to have it. He put it in my heart to have a sing there. God said, 'Here is where I want you to start it.'"

Joey said 1975 was the first year for the event, which was initially held in the church but moved to the pavilion after a couple of years. Joey, 15, was living in Ohio with his Aunt Margaret. "Dorsey got it planned, and we all packed up and left Ohio and came down here, and he had his thing," Joey said. "I don't even remember who the singers were, but I was here. I don't think I ever missed one."

Several years into the event, the paths of Dorsey and Carolyn Connor and her husband, Don, crossed in Ohio. "We were singing in Ohio, our family was traveling, and we met Dorsey up around Akron, Canton,"

Battling bone cancer and no longer able to sing, Dorsey Wiseman still worshiped during the Singing in the Hills event, 2004.

Carolyn told me in 2024. "So, when he moved this way, he started inviting us to the sing."

Carolyn said both the performers and attendees started "coming in droves."

"We've had several hundred people on top of this mountain," she said. "It just kept growing every year; he brought more groups in, groups from all over the United States. So many people looked forward to it every year, and it just kept growing."

"I got people coming from Kentucky. I got them from down in North Carolina, Georgia. You name it," Dorsey told me in 2003. "You name it. We gather in here and sing it."

Back when Dorsey was running the event, it stretched from Friday evening to Sunday afternoon. The music went late into the night; many of the folks camped on the grounds. Carolyn said the event amounted to a family reunion with music and Christian fellowship. "They looked forward to getting together that time of the year and just having a gospel sing and fellowship," she said.

No one anticipated this gathering more than Dorsey Wiseman, however.

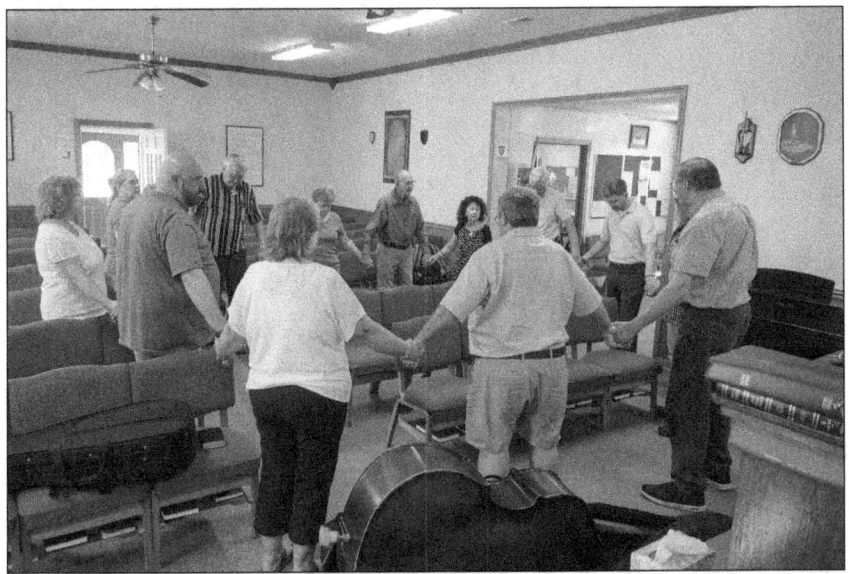

Musicians and vocalists involved in Singing in the Hills gather for prayer in Harrison Community Church prior to starting the 50th gathering, August 2024.

Dorsey was diagnosed with bone cancer in late 1996 and battled it for over a decade. As the disease, multiple surgeries, and chemotherapy took their toll on Dorsey's energies and body, the prospect of living one more year to attend Singing in the Hills kept him going.

Wearing a ball cap with "Borrowed Time" and a cross embroidered on it, Dorsey shared his faith with attendees as he told stories of God's protection through the prior year and how he'd ministered to other cancer patients in the Cleveland Clinic cancer ward.

"The Lord's never called me to preach," Dorsey told me in 2003. "He never gave that call to me. I'm calling this proclaiming, a testifier of what God can do. And a singer. I promote gospel music."

While his proclaiming flourished, his music suffered—the chemotherapy damaged the nerves in his fingers to the point he could no longer pluck his guitar. It also destroyed his hearing. But not his humor. When he lost a portion of his jaw to cancer, doctors removed part of a leg bone to replace the diseased section. "They wrote on my hospital chart that I have a deformed jaw," he said. "But I don't have a deformed jaw, I have reformed jaw. I used to put my foot in my mouth, now I got my who leg in there."

Friends of Dorsey Wiseman and musical guests respond to the music during the 2004 Singing in the Hills event.

Dorsey died at the Cleveland Clinic in Ohio on July 26, 2007, just three weeks shy of the 33rd Singing in the Hills.

"Dorsey was in the hospital at the time (of planning the 2007 event), and he talked to his wife and talked to me and Don, and he asked us if we would keep it going if something happened to him," Carolyn said. "We comforted him and told him yes, we'd do our best to keep it the same. And that's been in our hearts. There was a sense of urgency about continuing this after Dorsey passed."

Carolyn faced that same sense of urgency after her husband died and when the COVID-19 pandemic made an in-person assembly risky. Refusing to miss a beat, Carolyn organized a virtual Singing in the Hills.

"We asked each of our groups to submit a video clip of them singing, and we put a little video together and released it on our Facebook page," she said. "We had a great response from that. And you know, honestly, that's when we thought, 'Wow, you know we can continue this, people are interested in continuing this.' We decided to bring it back in person."

The format has remained unchanged since those early years when Dorsey called upon his extensive network of acquaintances to stop by and sing on Rich Mountain for at least 20 minutes. Carolyn Connor said the programming is "led by the Spirit."

Elizabeth Currence was raised by her grandparents, Dorsey and Tippy Wiseman, and recalls coming to Singing in the Hills since childhood. "This meant the world to him," she said. Photo from 2024 event.

"We don't have a program, so when we invite a group of singers or a soloist to the platform, it really is what you feel. We may start by saying, 'Give it 20 minutes; if you feel like the Spirit's moving, keep going. But otherwise, there's never been a competition among singers to outdo the others. With that atmosphere it makes it very simple for us to just allow our singers to do what they do best—sing," Carolyn said.

Dustin Lambert assists Carolyn with organizing the event and scheduling the artists. The task is made even more daunting by the minimal compensation plan: a freewill offering divided among the musicians. At best, that amounts to gas money.

Dustin serves as master of ceremonies for the event and, along with Carolyn, steps up to the microphone and sings during breaks between artists. The event and format are very familiar to him; Dustin has been attending since he was a baby (1988). The Pocahontas County native was introduced to the sing by his grandfather, who "got very acquainted with

Brother Dorsey, and it just kind of blossomed into a family affair for us," Dustin said.

"We'd bring our blankets over and our pillows over and drape them over the chairs. People knew that's where we were going to be for the duration of the sing, and you would find four little bodies in the front row," he recalled. "We couldn't wait to get to the mountain to see (Carolyn) and the rest of the groups that Dorsey had invited to the sing."

Dustin learned dozens of gospel songs and eventually found his place on the platform, as well.

"Really, my calling in gospel music, it started here in the mountains," he said. "In 2006, my sister and I felt a strong calling to enter the ministry together. My sister was just 11 years old when we entered the ministry."

His sister left the duo after she married, but Dustin has continued as a soloist, doing an average of 100 venues a year throughout West Virginia and neighboring states. He also has a full-time job as coordinator of the West Virginia Department of Education's Governor's Schools. Both Carolyn Connor and Dorsey helped him develop his ministry.

"Dorsey not only recruited singers, but he truly inspired those who wanted to be part of the gospel music family," Dustin said. "I found at a very early age that Dorsey was somebody I could look to for guidance ... it really does take a special anointing to do what we do here on that little platform down there. It's not a stage, it's not some place where we perform. Dorsey was very keenly aware of the impact of that platform and how it changed people.

"Dorsey was real, absolutely and completely real," Dustin added. "He spoke words of wisdom to you both spiritually and musically. It was just a wonderful relationship that we had with Dorsey, and we miss him dearly. It's different without a great songwriter."

Many of those who attend this gathering are unaware of the man and legacy behind the tradition. Nevertheless, they come year after year for the music, camaraderie and blessings.

"I honestly believe what makes this gospel sing more unique than others is the sense of family and home that you get from being a part of it, said vocalist Jimmy Howson, who started coming to the sing after Dorsey had passed away. He has not missed one since—13 years in 2024.

"A lot of these folks we only get to see once a year, so, in a sense, it's like a big family reunion," he said in describing what makes it special. "Having the sing in the mountains of West Virginia makes it even more special."

Jimmy also mentions "food" as a reason that the event is a "highlight" of his year. Joey Simmons knows all about that aspect—he is one of the volunteers who prepare and serve meals and snacks in a concession trailer on the grounds. The venue is famous for providing value. An adult dinner that included dessert and beverage was priced at under $5 a head in 2024. The pricing amazed visitors.

"I was sitting down there talking to a feller and there's another guy sitting, eating at one of them tables," Joey said. "And he said, 'I got a question for you . . . How do y'all make any money with no more than what you charge down there?' And I looked at him, and I told him, 'We don't. Our goal is to keep everybody happy and get enough money back to do it again next year. We ain't out to make money. We don't give the money to fund something. But the way we got it figured, if you keep people fed, keep them happy and they don't have to go home and get dinner or nothing, they will stick around. And you'll get people that'll come early in the morning and not leave until they shut (the sing) down at night."

Food, music, camaraderie, mountains, traditions, family—these are all verifiable reasons for Singing in the Hills outlasting its founder. But Joey said it keeps going "because the good Lord wants it to." Elizabeth Currence said it is part of her grandfather's legacy.

"Just his words and his songs and his music, just throughout everywhere, not just here on top of this hill," she said. "I don't think it would be the same if it were held anyplace else."

Dorsey Wiseman's story of his courageous battle with bone cancer is in *More Wandering Back-Roads West Virginia Volume 2*.

Singing in the Hills has a Facebook page on which dates of future gatherings and other news are announced.

Doug Evans checks the whirling machinery's operation in the Evans Mill, Hazelton, October 2012. The mill processed the flour used at the Preston County Buckwheat Festival's breakfasts and dinners for many years.

Chapter 10

The Buckwheat Stopped Here

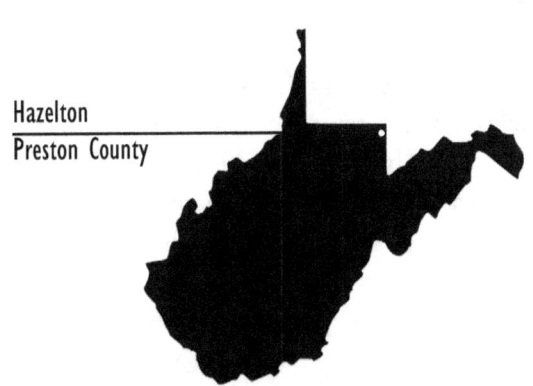

For a few brief moments on a perfect October day in 2012, it was as if John G. Evans was once again a lad looking out the window of his grandfather's Preston County gristmill.

Sitting at the desk of Hazelton Milling Co., John could see a line, albeit short, of customers for the mill's buckwheat flour, hulls and bran. The spurt of business reminded him of those halcyon autumns of long ago, when his grandfather was the miller and his father the apprentice to a business that has since largely faded from Preston County.

"There used to be one of these on every stream," John told me, naming Muddy Creek, Clifton Mills and Bruceton Mills as examples of communities built around the town's gristmill. "Back then, the farmer didn't travel very far with his horse to go to the mill. The farmers used to bring their grain here in wagons. I'd see them lined up and down the road, waiting their turn. There would 10, 12, 15 of them waiting to get in."

After over seven decades of living and working around the family mill, John knew when the cacophony of slapping, whirling, grinding and chugging signaled a healthy state of things just beyond the door of his office.

The sounds of the machinery, belts, stones, blowers and gears laboring against the buckwheat were as familiar to his ears as the voice of his wife, who according to John made his buckwheat cakes just the way he liked them: thin and brown.

Do not err by calling those earthly flavored creations "pancakes." The faux pas for that would be akin to calling Champagne "white wine" while sipping it on native terroir.

"Pancakes, that a bad word," John corrected me, his reprimand tempered with a smile.

While its name suggests a grain akin to wheat or rye, the botanical fact is that buckwheat is a fruit whose family members include sorrels and rhubarb. Technically, buckwheat is therefore a cereal impostor, a pseudo-cereal. Encased in a hard hull, the buckwheat germ, or groat, is triangular shaped, like a beech nut, which is the source of buckwheat's original name, "beech wheat."

Although buckwheat is rich in amino acids and other essential nutrients, its popularity is much greater in China and Russia than in the United States. That is changing, however, thanks to the gluten-free nature of the product, which fits well into the diet of those with celiac disease.

Buckwheat was first planted on Preston County's hillsides and valleys in the summer of 1859, the year an early-June frost wiped out their traditional grain crops. Preston County farmers responded by replacing the lost crops with buckwheat, which can be planted as late as July for an October harvest. In the ensuing years, farmers made the crop a mainstay due to the insurance it provided and flexibility of planting and harvest. The *Preston County Journal* reported in late June 1884 that Portland District farmers had finished their buckwheat planting slightly earlier than usual because frost came early the prior autumn. The plantings were the "largest of that grain sown in this section this year than ever before," with 10 to 12 acres being the average size of the planting on each farm.

Buckwheat plantings are relatively rare in Preston County these days; it is more likely to be planted as a cover crop than for harvest. Nevertheless, servings of buckwheat cakes are as plentiful as curvy roads in this north-central county that has held its annual Buckwheat Festival since 1938. The agricultural fair is a big deal, and thousands of buckwheat cakes and sausage patties are served during the four-day celebration. This reverence for

John Evans carried on the milling tradition established by his grandfather at the family's mill in Hazelton. Photo from October 2012.

buckwheat continues in fire stations, church dining rooms and community centers that hold buckwheat-breakfast fundraisers from fall to spring.

The flour that went into the thousands of pancakes served at the festival and these fundraisers was most likely ground at the Evans Mill. John told me that the festival alone used about three tons of buckwheat flour from the family's Hazelton mill. Most folks who slathered butter and poured syrup on the thin cakes probably didn't know that a mill in the county's northeast corner had processed the buckwheat into flour.

"I don't know of any mill in West Virginia that is still doing this, although there are some mills up in New York State that still do it," John told me in 2012. The lone exception at that time was probably Reed's Mill in Monroe County (see *Wandering Back-Roads West Virginia Volume 1*), which has since had to abandon the stone wheels for grinding.

Packaged under the Star Mills label, as it was for more than 100 years, the flour and self-rising buckwheat cake mix produced at Hazelton were sold and shipped throughout the United States. Although the product was sold year-around, or until supplies were exhausted, the mill operated

The Hazelton Mill in Hazelton, Preston County. Built near a stream and at one time powered by water, it had been converted to more reliable power sources by 2012, when this photo was made.

September through December, during the peak months of harvesting and processing the crop.

"It's a seasonal thing. Beginning with September, the first job is to supply the Buckwheat Festival," said Tonia Hall, a mill employee.

The festival and Evans family ownership of the mill roughly paralleled each other. John D. Evans was a full-time miller who ran the nearby Clifton Mills prior to purchasing the Hazelton mill in the 1930s. John's father, Dayton Evans, took over the mill from his father and worked in the coal mines to support his family of eight children. John was just 9 years old when his father became the miller in 1945.

"It had been shut down for a few years," John said. "He bought it and started it back up. I suppose it had been shut down because of the (war) economy."

John took over the mill from his father in 1963. His daughter, Victoria Evans Lewis, became the owner in 2012, but John remained the hands-on overseer and lived just a few houses down the street from the mill. His son, Doug, was the miller and maintenance man responsible for keeping the machinery running at peak efficiency. Most of the major pieces of equipment were over a century old; the equipment that gave them the

Interior of the Hazelton Mill, 2012.

most trouble were often the modern items, such as the hand-held sewing machines used to close the bags of hulls, bran and flour with a white string.

The relative simplicity of the vintage equipment allowed John and Doug to make repairs with prosaic materials and a little ingenuity. One of the canvas conveyor belts showed evidence of multiple repairs and splices as it made the monotonous journey between the first floor and attic.

"If you were that old, you would have some of them, too," John said, pointing to the belt' patchwork.

The mill building is from 1914, but John said there were predecessors at this site going back to the 1700s. Waterpower dictated the location. Mill Creek, a relatively feeble stream that wanders about moss-covered rocks in a narrow passage behind the mill, once delivered sufficient flow to run the machinery.

"The mill had an 18-foot over-shot wheel," John said. "The mill ran by waterpower. They always built the mill along the creek where they had waterpower."

John never saw the mill operate on waterpower, but he recalls playing on the wheel, which was removed in the early 1950s.

"We weren't allowed (to play on it), but we did," he said. "Me and my only brother (Harry Wayne "Buckwheat"), we'd get in that wheel (like a hamster in a wheel), and we'd get it going."

When John was born in 1936, the mill was on its third power source. Mill Creek's flow became unreliable after the big timber was cut out and the mountains could no longer gradually surrender their aquatic resources to the streams. In 1917, according to the date on the concrete chimney that stood across the street from the mill, a boiler house was built and its product, steam, was piped under the road to drive the machinery.

John said steam was a "good bit before my time," but he recalled a time when the mill was powered by a straight-eight Studebaker engine for several years. His father soon switched it to a diesel engine, which John upgraded to a 100 horse-power model in 1963. The engine powered the drive shafts that ran the cutters, burr stones and conveyor belts. Electric motors powered the sifters and cleaners.

"The mill (power source) used to run those too, but I decided to convert them to electric," John said

There was a time when the mill would grind just about any kind of grain on a "toll basis"—the mill kept a percentage of the grain as payment. "If they brought in 50 pounds of grain, we might keep 10 to 15 pounds, and then we'd sell the flour," John said.

The operation became exclusively buckwheat in 1964. John said a state tax of 75 cents per bushel of grain drove the decision to specialize in buckwheat. Further, the number of farmers growing grains for processing into flour was decreasing. Over the next four decades, many of the community mills like the one at Hazelton closed forever.

As to why Hazelton survived as a one-trick pony, John quoted his wife's observation about him.

"She said I don't have blood in my veins, I have buckwheat flour in them. I just enjoy it," he said.

Despite having a festival dedicated to it, Preston County farmers stopped raising buckwheat. That necessitated importing it from out of state to keep their millstones churning out the staple. John said there was a two-year period when he sourced his buckwheat from a Kansas supplier. He finds no regional difference in the quality or taste.

"Buckwheat is buckwheat, I don't care where it is grown," John said. "There is no difference in quality."

John Evans and his son, Doug, were running the Hazelton Mill in 2012. It operated during the last several months of the year, when buckwheat was available from regional growers.

The milling process is another matter. A nearly lost art, milling is to grain what pressing is to winemakers. Done properly, the full nutritional value and flavor profiles are recovered for further exploitation in the finished product.

Locked up in his safe, John kept his grandfather's milling manual that provided a written reference to the occupation. In practice, the millers' experience sifted down through four generations guided their craft.

The process began with delivery of the grain, which was stored in metal silos behind the mill. The mill could purchase grain already cleaned and dried to the optimum moisture content, but more often than not, Hazelton Mill performed those initial steps.

The grain came directly from the field to the mill by truck. Using a combination of air blowing across the grain and screens, the mill's cleaner removed chaff, stones and pebbles.

The grain's moisture content had to be in the optimum range, 11 to 12 percent, for grinding. If the grain was excessively moist, John passed on it. Otherwise, the grain went into the mill dryer to bring it to an optimum

Buckwheat hulls were bagged and sold as animal bedding.

level. Propane fired the dryer; the moisture content determined the length of drying. John said it typically required about 1½ hours to dry 300 bushels. The dryer enabled the mill to operate efficiently and independently of other processing facilities. John added drying equipment in the late 1960s; prior to that, the grain had to be trucked to a facility in Somerset, Pa.

Once the buckwheat had reached its proper moisture content, the mill's steel rollers cracked the hard hulls and released the buckwheat groats. The rollers were on the first floor; a system of wooden cups attached to a canvas conveyor belt delivered the cracked buckwheat to sifting machinery on the third floor. The groats returned to the first floor, where they were fed into a pair of horizontal millstones, 60 inches in diameter and housed in a wooden box called the hub.

These stones were imported from France in the mid-1850s. "They were the Cadillac of burr stones," Doug said. The stones were not specific to buckwheat milling; the same stones processed corn and wheat, as well.

The bottom stone, or bed, did not rotate. The top stone, the runner, spun above the bed; a fraction of an inch separated the stones. Buckwheat was fed into the center of these stones; furrows in their faces provided a conduit for the groats to move between them from the inside out. The edges of the furrows acted as scissors, reducing the hard fruits to flour and bran.

There was both science and art at work when earth's fruit encountered these stones. Every few minutes, John or Doug pulled a sample of flour from the stones and rubbed it between their fingers. "We're looking for the quality of the flour, how fine it is," John explained.

John believed that the stones imparted a subtle but unique characteristic to the mill's flour.

"There is something about that stone that makes the flour so much better," John claimed.

The stones eventually developed a glaze on them and required "facing." An overhead wood derrick was used to lift the stone from the hub and give the miller access to the glazed furrows. Re-facing was done with a hammer and metal, chisel-like tools developed specifically for the purpose. John, who learned the skill from his grandfather and taught Doug, used both antique and modern tools. It was a hazardous job because of the specks of stone or metal that could fly off and become lodged in an eye or pierce the face. In the old days, men who made a living dressing millstones often grew a beard to protect their faces.

"You have to wear goggles and gloves," John said. "It takes a good while to do the job. You do that in the summer."

John said the mill's stones were original and, thanks to diligent, skillful re-facing, they served their family well. The mill owned replacement stones, also of mid-1850s vintage, just in case. "At one time, the mill used three stones, so I have a couple of extra sets," John said.

The flour and bran spun off by the millstones traveled upstairs to another sifter, where the components were separated. The bran was pulled off and bagged; the flour went into a bin.

The hulls were sold as animal bedding and upholstery filler. The bran, with a protein content of 29 percent, was purchased by regional farmers as a additive for livestock feed. Doug said some of their flour customers also purchased bran as a fiber supplement that restored some of the nutrition lost in the milling process.

A room separate from the mill housed the bagging operations. Chemical ingredients were added to the flour to make the mill's brand of a self-rising mix. The formula passed unchanged through four generations of mill

Bagging was the last step in the buckwheat flour production process. The mill also mixed and packaged a ready-to-use buckwheat cake product.

ownership. The mix was a convenient way for buckwheat cake lovers to make the treat without going through the work and wait of creating a "sour batter."

The flour, bagged in quantities of 2, 5 and 10 pounds, bore a classic buckwheat cake recipe on the bag.

"They've used that recipe for generations," John said.

The bagging room employed several area women who worked as a team to fill a bag, sew a line of thread across the top and pack them in boxes for shipping. In 2012, the employees were Brandy Loughry, Alicia Murphy, Shannon Baker and Pam Rosenberger.

John Evans takes a break from his work at the family's Hazelton Mill, which in 2012 was the last commercial buckwheat mill operating in a section of West Virginia known for its Buckwheat Festival and culinary tradition.

As with the Evans family members, most of the employees had a taste for buckwheat.

Alicia said her favorite buckwheat dish was waffles made with the self-rising mix. She made them with slightly less water than that suggested for the buckwheat cakes recipe. Alica liked to top off the waffle with an over-easy egg and let the yolk explore the depressions.

"I'm getting hungry for buckwheat cakes, now," she told John as they took a break in the mill office. "John, why don't you go up to the house and make some buckwheat cakes for us?"

John reminded them that their break time was nearly over and there would be no buckwheat cakes for lunch, at least not today. Besides, the walk-in traffic was far too brisk on this perfect autumn day to indulge in satisfying the miller's appetite for his product.

A Hudson resident, Everett Kidwell, placed his order, a 50-pound case of flour.

"I'm going to eat it," Everett said. "First thing I'm going to do is take

A customer stops by to place his annual order for buckwheat flour fresh from the grinding stones of Hazelton Mill in Preston County. John Evans was taking care of business this day in October 2012.

it home and put it in a freezer. I eat a good bit of (buckwheat cakes). I bought a special freezer to put the buckwheat in."

John collected the money and thanked Everett for his patronage, then returned to monitoring the music of milling. There was a particular comfort in the earthy song of the runner whirling above the bed; the spinning stones seemed so fitting to the chore, so emblematic of the overarching cycle of planting, growing and milling. John Evans, the miller with buckwheat in his blood, was as much a part of that circuitous journey as the falling leaves outside his window, the drive shafts and stones revolving in his mill. There was hope in all that revolving. And hope is always a good business in which to be, no matter how many revolutions one's life has completed.

"My daughter said I have to stick around for at least another 25 years," John said with a grin.

John died shortly after our interview in 2012. Two years later, the milling operation closed.

Hunter Thomas, a Preston County commissioner, started Heritage Milling to preserve an agricultural and culinary tradition in West Virginia. His mill is located between Hazelton and Cuzzart.

Buckwheat-milling tradition revived

Preston County native Hunter Thomas grew up on a farm where buckwheat was grown, then milled at the Evans family's mill. He grew up eating buckwheat cakes several times a week, and Hunter was King Buckwheat for the 2019 Buckwheat Festival. He was destined to revive the cultivation and milling of buckwheat in his native county.

"Ever since high school, I knew that I wanted to open up a flour mill and bring the heritage of milling buckwheat back to Preston County," he said. He raised a new mill building on Cuzzart Road, a short distance from the shuttered Evans Mill, and produced his first Heritage Milling buckwheat flour in 2025.

While his milling equipment is powered by electricity and of modern vintage, vertical stones grind the buckwheat, which is grown on his parents' farm and leased fields. About 100 acres were planted in 2025 to meet anticipated demand for his specialty buckwheat flour.

Involved in every step of the process, Hunter spent months tweaking the flour's consistency and composition so it contains just enough hull and bran particles to impart that "old-fashioned buckwheat-flour color and make a good buckwheat cake." The result is a nutty, coffee-like tasting flour specifically crafted for making thin, crispy buckwheat cakes in the Preston County tradition.

Heritage Milling products are sold through retailers in and around Preston County. For updates on those locations, visit the Heritage Milling WV Facebook page.

Janie Morgan stands at the entrance to her family's Organ Cave near Ronceverte, Greenbrier County, in 2007. A section of the cave is open to the public for tours, but much of it remains unexplored.

Chapter 11

Organ Cave Speaks for Itself

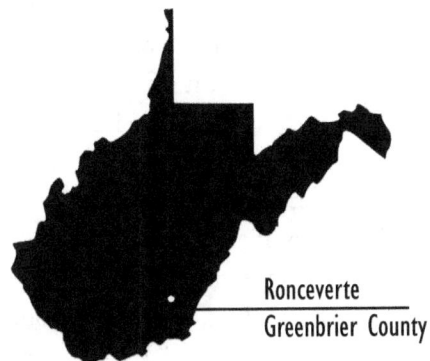

Ronceverte
Greenbrier County

Greenbrier County has nearly 1,200 known limestone caves, yet native Janie Morgan spent the first 45 years of her life without stepping inside one. But when Organ Cave went to auction in September 1997, Janie and her husband, Sam, became the owners of an underground property that had lost face with its namesake community.

"When the cave came up for sale, we started asking people in the community about it, and they laughed at us. The cave had never been kept up as far as the buildings or anything. It was in a pretty sorry state," Janie told me in 2007.

The stairs that descended 100 feet to the mouth of the cave were rickety and dangerous; the cave had become a giant neighborhood garbage pit. A dilapidated mobile home served as the gift shop, and a gutted trailer housed the restrooms, which lacked sufficient water flow to flush the toilets.

"There wasn't a whole lot of interest in it," she said. "At the auction, there were an undertaker, a retired man and a lot of cavers who'd pooled their money to buy it."

Sam reminded Janie that livestock, not bats and stalagmites, were their forte. But the price of livestock was tumbling, and the couple needed another revenue stream. Further, a serious medical condition had forced Janie to re-evaluate her life; the cave seemed a good fit for her.

When the auctioneer's hammer dropped, Sam and Janie had bought Organ Cave.

"We are livestock dealers, so we are used to purchasing things on the spur of the moment," Janie said as we visited in the attraction's log-cabin style gift shop. "I didn't walk through (the cave) until after I purchased it. I knew of its history, and I did not want to see it destroyed. I did not want to see someone buy it and close it off."

Sam, who suffered from osteoporosis and could not tolerate the cave's dank environment, gave Janie full authority over the purchase. More than a decade after taking her first walk through it, Janie spoke of Organ Cave as a living organism, a fascinating world within a world where she went to escape the cares of life above ground and, ironically, grow closer to God.

"When you are underground, you forget about this world up here," Janie told me. "It's rather amazing. It's like two worlds in one, another world within this world. There are only two places remaining on Earth that we have not completely explored: our oceans and our caves."

Spelunkers began mapping Organ Cave's myriad passages in 1948. When combined and reconciled, the explorations of some 400 men and women collectively documented about 45 miles of passages. However, some 200 of the "leads" that branch off these passages had remained unexplored in 2007.

"We don't know how large the cave is, and it is doubtful it will ever be known, said Janie, who did her fair share of exploration. "You could probably spend the rest of your lifetime exploring it, and I don't think you could ever accomplish it all."

The second-largest commercial cave east of the Mississippi, Organ Cave was named for the 40-foot-tall calcite formation that resembles an array of organ ranks. The formation is about a half mile from the entrance and toward the end of the commercial segment. At one time, in an era before West Virginia's strict cave law prohibited misuse of these treasures, musically inclined visitors played this formation with rubber mallets—the various "pipes" produced different tones when struck.

There are accounts of at least two wedding ceremonies that were held in front of this organ. In the early 1900s, the organ was pure white, like the cave's nearby "Christmas tree" calcite formation. However, due to repeated contamination from human touch and natural sources, the formation turned tan.

Janie said her research showed that the last time someone coaxed music from the organ formation was 1976, when a woman tapped out "Silent Night" on the ancient deposits.

Historical cave

European pioneers first became aware of the cave in 1704, although the discovery of "Irish Monk" symbols on rocks therein suggested a European visitation prior to Columbus's "discovery" of the New World. Harvard biologist Barry Fell attributed a controversial petroglyph on a Wyoming County rock wall to Irish monks who came to America between the 6th and 8th centuries; most archaeologists, however, attribute them to Native Americans.

Janie said Organ Cave's walls and ceilings have deposits of nodule chert, a fossilized coral also known as flint. The cave was likely a source of this material for the Neolithic Native Americans, who fashioned arrowheads, knives and fire-producing tools from it. These artifacts were found in the cave and on the grounds surrounding it. Additional petroglyphs of an unknown origin were discovered on walls and ceilings, as well.

The first of several historic events that cemented Organ Cave's place in American history occurred in the late 1700s, when the bones of a giant, three-toed sloth were found in a cave believed to be Organ. Thomas Jefferson learned of this discovery and made a written record of finding fossil remains of a prehistoric animal in a limestone cave on "Frederic Cromer's place beyond the Blue Ridge Mountains on the west side of the Greenbrier River."

Jefferson presented these bones to the Philosophical Society in Philadelphia. In 1799, Casper Wistar described the bones as those of an extinct ground sloth and named this creature *Megalonyx Jeffersonnii* in honor of the president.

"It turns out, Thomas Jefferson was our nation's first paleontologist," said Janie, who produced copies of the documentation proving Jefferson's

The commercial tour takes cave visitors through the area where saltpeter was processed by Confederate soldiers and farmers.

association. "At first, they didn't know what it was. They thought it was a giant lion or an elephant."

These sloth bones were the first of their kind to be discovered on the North American continent and are considered the largest of such remains found in the United States. In 2008, the West Virginia legislature designated *Megalonyx Jeffersonnii* as the official state fossil.

Janie obtained a casting of a sloth's bone for display in the gift shop. During the cave tour, guides pointed out the spot where the bones allegedly were found more than 200 years ago.

There are historical references to the cave providing a source of saltpeter, an ingredient in gunpowder, during the War of 1812. Cave explorers discovered wooden sleds that were attributed to this activity, according to Blanche Humphreys' 1928 history of the cave's hometown near Ronceverte. 'Also known as potassium nitrate, saltpeter is a component of guano, the excrement bats deposit in caves.

Commercial use of the cave began in 1822, when stagecoaches running between resorts at White Sulphur Springs and Salt Sulphur Springs stopped at the cave to change horses and give passengers a break from the grueling

Wooden hoppers used in processing saltpeter for ammunition were left behind by Confederates when they abandoned the region. The soil in Organ Cave was rich in nitrates from the guano of bats. Saltpeter was extracted from this soil and used to produce gunpowder for the Confederate Army until 1863.

ride. The stagecoach switchback was still visible as it descended the hill behind the gift shop.

Known as "John Roger's Stage Coach Stop," the cave provided weary travelers with a cool respite from the heat and humidity. "They charged them 10 cents to tour the cave," Janie said. "They used candles, but only one out of every three persons got a candle."

Organ Cave was opened to the public in 1835, making it one of the earliest commercial cave tours in the United States. One of the many legends connected to the cave's commercial history places Mrs. Robert E. Lee as a frequent visitor, as well as her youngest son, Robert E. During the tour, guides pause at a rock bearing an inscription attributed to this son.

History favored the cave again during the Civil War, when it and several other limestone caves in Greenbrier County were used as sources of saltpeter for the Confederate Army. Janie said up to 75 percent of the Confederacy's saltpeter supply came from Organ Cave. More than 1,000 soldiers, as well as farmers from the area, labored in this wartime industry.

A solution channel, cut through the soft limestone by the underground river, left a narrow ledge above the stream. It was along this ledge soldiers lugged their bags loaded with 100 to 150 pounds of nitrate-rich soils and rock to a processing room. Upon reaching the entrance to a second cut through the limestone, the soldier had to give a password and torch signal to proceed.

Beyond this point stretched a curving channel that provided acoustic isolation for the covert activity. It was in this area that the nitrates were washed out of the rich clay/mineral mixture and concentrated. This work was accomplished in rectangular wooden hoppers 6 feet wide and about chest high. Made of oak, locust and cucumber lumber, the hoppers were assembled with just two nails. The raw material was placed in a hopper and water poured over it. A trough collected this slurry, and the process was repeated until the nitrate concentration was sufficient to float an egg. Outside the cave, the concentrate was mixed with wood ash to produce saltpeter. From Organ Cave, the chemical was shipped to Atlanta for ammunition production.

The process was simple, but the work was difficult, monotonous and performed in damp, dark, dangerous, noxious conditions. Janie pointed out that most of the workers toiled without the benefit of shoes and wore whatever rags they could find to protect their feet from this inhospitable environment.

Janie saw documentation of at least one officer dying in the cave during the Civil War. Given the unhealthy conditions, there were likely other casualties who possibly left behind a ghost to haunt the darkness. She said some cave guides have quit because of what they saw or sensed while in that grotto. Likewise, photographers occasionally reported inexplicable ghostly blurs in their images.

These experiences were foreign to Janie, however. "I am at complete peace in that cave," she said.

The saltpeter operation ended in 1863, when pressure from advancing Union armies forced Confederates to abandon the work. When the army left, they didn't bother to destroy the hoppers. Of the 52 hoppers left behind in Organ Cave, 37 remained more than a century later.

"It is the largest collection of Civil War hoppers in the United States," Janie said. "When a man (Terrace Moore, chief of Park Planning & Special Studies) and his associate from the National Park Service came here and looked at them, he (remarked that) he'd never seen such a mining setup for saltpeter as there is in this cave. They were totally amazed by it."

Tour guides ignored the saltpeter story when commercial tours resumed after the Civil War. It was not until the 1930s that this story of the cave's human history came to light. Fortunately, prior owners had not disturbed the artifacts, which are tangible links to an aspect of warfare ignored by many history books.

In the early 1900s, the availability of electric lighting opened new opportunities for the commercialization of limestone caves. James H. Boone, a Daniel Boone descendant and Sam Morgan's third great-grandfather, installed a Delco generator and 72 storage batteries in a shed on the hill above the cave. He strung several miles of electrical wiring in the cave, which had electrical service before utility lines reached homes in the area.

A couple by the last name of Carter purchased the cave in 1926, and it eventually passed to a son-in-law, George Shiveley, who ran it as a cash cow. Many residents of Organ Cave, the town, worked as guides.

The cave and its picnic grounds were popular community gathering spots. In the 1940s and 1950s, public dances were held in the cave's commodious main room near the entrance, which also provided the perfect dark venue for slide shows.

Shiveley displayed little regard for the cave's uniqueness or history; he even trivialized it by placing Disney cartoon figures in the area known as the Christmas tree. "Tour guides were not taught anything about its geology, history, anything like that," Janie said. "It was just a look-and-see tour."

Janie was determined to restore the cave's integrity. The couple built a new staircase, cleaned out the decades of trash and installed a new lighting and electrical system.

"(The wiring) had been patched to keep it going, there were bare wires throughout the cave just hanging around," she said. "You'd hear this electrical sparking noise when you turned on the power."

They chose a low-voltage system and just enough lamps to illuminate the commercial passage and accent features such as the hoppers, the Confederate sentry, formations and chasms. Lights are activated only when a tour is present to reduce the growth of light-loving algae. Kerosene lanterns were used wherever possible.

"We decided we wanted it to look like it was stepping back to the 1800s," she said. "That's when all the history is in this cave."

Under Janie's and Sam's ownership, the commercial tour covered 2.2

The cave's namesake "organ" formation is on the tour. At one time, visitors were allowed to play "music" on the formation by tapping it with a hammer.

miles. Guides were required to learn 11 pages of cave history and trivia before leading tours. And guides had to find their way out of a section in the dark should a power failure occur.

Extended expeditions were offered in sections that required crawling, climbing and the use of basic caving gear. The expeditions included the Waterfall Room, which has three waterfalls that drop 90 feet, and the Mini Cliff Hanger, navigation of which involved boulder climbing in areas with steep drops.

The cave continued to yield artifacts to these explorers. Caribou teeth were discovered in the 1950s, and in the spring of 2000, spelunker Robert Godshall came across a caribou antler. A wooden ladle associated with saltpeter production during the War of 1812 was uncovered.

In an average year, the cave hosted several thousand commercial tour visitors and hundreds of extended-tour explorers. A few of the latter went to great heights and depths to leave their initials. "RHH" is inscribed in a rock 50-feet above the floor—Robert Handley crawled through a tiny hole in the ceiling to leave that mark. Bud Rutherford, a Charleston resident who mapped much of the cave, asked to be interred therein. In 1999, his ashes were scattered according to his wishes.

The cave also attracted scientists who came to study the geology, biology, archeology, paleontology and ecology of this environment. At least nine species of bats—three endangered, two rare—were identified therein.

A group of scientists and cavers took Janie and Sam out to dinner shortly after the couple purchased the cave.

"They were afraid of what we planned to do with it," Janie said. "They offered their expertise, and I took them up on it. They took me through the cave and showed me things, pointed things out to me. The more I learned about it, I found out that the world down under is a completely other world and fascinating at that."

Janie's passion for Organ Cave drove her to pursue National Historic Landmark designation for it from the Department of the Interior/National Park Service. It also has National Natural Landmark designation and is on the West Virginia Civil War Trails circuit.

"If you want to see history and you want to see a real cave, it is here," Janie said. "You can't deny it. It speaks for itself."

Janie Morgan died August 21, 2016. Sam died December 1, 2017. Family members continue to own the cave and told the author they intend to keep it open for tours.

Visit the attraction's website at organcave.com for more information.

The City of Sistersville II awaits a tow at Fly, Ohio, on the Ohio River, September 2024. Its namesake city is across the river in West Virginia. The ferry is the only one operating between Ohio and West Virginia on the Ohio River.

Chapter 12.

Last Ferry to Fly

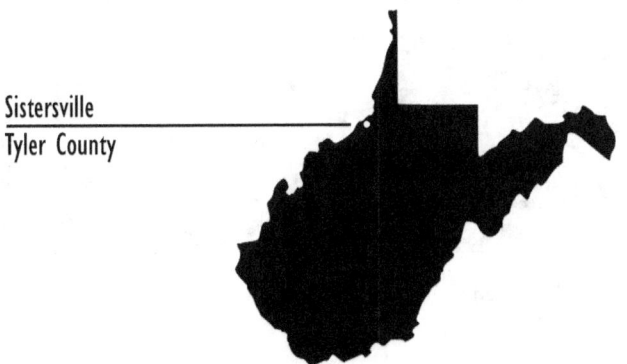

Sistersville
Tyler County

The Ohio River town of Sistersville does not have "public transportation," per se. But it does have the only public ferry service on the 277-mile stretch of the Ohio River along West Virginia's border.

A tradition dating back to the early 19th century, the Sistersville Ferry is rich in lore about the boats and men who piloted them. On a late-September day when a calm Ohio River reflected the cerulean sky, I made several crossings between Fly, Ohio, and Sistersville with Herman "Bo" Hausen and Tom Meek in the pilothouse. It was Bo's last season on the job, and he had spent the summer training Tom for the responsibility. Tom was handling the 17-ton gross weight ferry and its 63-ton barge like a pro, which gave Bo the freedom to chat with me as he relaxed in a folder chair within sight of the pilothouse.

"Tom is doing a good job," Bo told me. "When he first started, I was (in the pilothouse) all the time because he was just learning. But now, he's doing so well, I can just relax. I get bored."

Among Bo's reasons for sticking with the seasonal job and the boredom of making the same, five-minute trip over and over, was to be part of a story

Captain Herman "Bo" Hausen (left) trained Tom Meek to take over command of The City of Sistersville II in 2024.

that began with the General Assembly of the Commonwealth of Virginia on January 28, 1817. That's when the ferry franchise was awarded to John McCoy. He, his wife and heirs ran McCoy Ferry until 1894, when it was sold to another private owner.

Back then, a horse on a treadmill powered the ferry. The 1890s oil-and-gas boom in Ohio River counties ushered in a new era of prosperity and the ferry's capabilities and motive power were upgraded accordingly. As motorized land vehicles proliferated in the early 20th century, so did bridges that diminished the need for river ferries. By the late 1980s, Sistersville was the lone Ohio-West Virginia ferry.

Sistersville's unique survival was formally recognized while the ferry was under Bo's command. The West Virginia Senate passed a resolution on March 28, 2017, marking the ferry's 200 years of service and its distinction of being the only ferry operating on the upper 427-miles of the Ohio River. Other bullet points included being the river's only crossing owned and operated by a West Virginia municipality and the state's oldest transportation service still in operation.

Its longevity can be partially attributed to Tyler County being the only

Captain Herman "Bo" Hausen relaxes on the deck of the Sistersville Ferry while waiting for the next tow, September 2024.

West Virginia river county without a bridge to Ohio. Sistersville residents must travel north to New Martinsburg or south to St. Mary's to cross the river. The distance between the two bridge-enhanced towns is about 29 miles.

The commute mattered more back when many Tyler County residents crossed the river to work in Ohio mines and industries, particularly the former Ormet Aluminum Plant in Hannibal. Once employing up to 2,000 workers, it was shuttered in 2014. Bo said he still gets a few Sistersville residents who take the ferry to their Ohio jobs, like Michael McKinney, chauffeured by Sistersville resident Amy Deen. Michael made the passage while seated inside a SUV while Amy enjoyed a cigarette and the river breeze on deck. She said the gasoline burned by taking one of the bridge routes costs more than the $5 fare for a vehicle and its passengers. Even with the ferry, Michael had a 20-minute commute from the dock at Fly.

"A lot of the reason why we take it is to keep (the ferry) going," she said. That's a sentiment also expressed by Steve Hadley. He and his wife, Janet, were driving to a popular eatery in New Matamoras and decided to drop $10 for the two ferry crossings rather than use the St. Mary's bridge.

A grandfather and his granddaughter have lunch in the Riverview Restaurant at Fly, Ohio, the Sistersville Ferry's other port. The restaurant's windows provide a view of the West Virginia shoreline and ferry's movements.

"I don't really care about the money," Steve said. A Sistersville resident, Steve has been using the ferry for decades; he can recall when the vehicle fare was $1.50. At more than three times that, the fiver was still a bargain.

"Five bucks in gas, it goes like that," Steve said, snapping his fingers.

As Sistersville residents, Steve and Janet consider it a civic responsibility to keep the ferry tradition alive, even though its scope has been pared back significantly over the decades.

"It used to be year-around and go all night, all three shifts," Steve said. "I used to work in the coal mine up the river, and I'd take the ferryboat. I'd work in Ohio and take the ferry boat sometimes, even at midnights."

In 2024, the ferry service operated 10 a.m. to 6 p.m., Thursday through Sunday, May to September. Bo and the ferry board developed the lean schedule after poring over years of use statistics and receipts.

"We used to run from April to the end of November. And at the end of the year, we were always in the red, so it wasn't sustaining itself," Bo said. "So, we had to figure out what we could do to keep money in the bank, to keep it running and do maintenance, all that. That's how we came up with Thursday through Sunday, the busiest days of the week."

Fly, Ohio, was once an important jumping off point for ferry passengers who worked at several large industries in the region. These days, it is mostly tourists taking the ferry as part of a two-state road trip.

Bo said tourism and pleasure travel keep the ferry afloat financially.

"There's only a couple of people who work on that side and live here, and vice versa," Bo told me. "In the summertime, it is actually a lot of tourism, just for the experience. People from three hours away will drive here just to ride across on the ferry and back."

Sitting in a window-front booth in the Riverview Restaurant at Fly, a grandfather and his granddaughter observed this activity while sipping iced soft drinks from tan plastic glasses and waiting for their sandwiches. Featuring fish sourced from Coleman's in Wheeling, some 45 miles north of this point, the eatery caters mostly to locals. It and a gas station/convenience store comprise the wide spot's commercial district, most likely the only reason someone from Sistersville would have business in Fly. Occasionally, a pedestrian will cross as part of an exercise regimen.

The captain will run the ferry across the river for that single pedestrian waiting on the other side. Bo said the vessel will use 25 gallons of fuel a day whether it is idling at the landing or running against the current, so he likes to keep it in service. And driving the ferry is a lot more interesting than just sitting along the shore waiting for the next vehicle or motorcyclist to show up.

Some of the ferry's business comes from former Sistersville natives who include a river crossing as part of a homecoming pilgrimage. The ferry itself is peripheral to their memories. What they remember most are the captains like Gilbert "Dib" Harmon, who owned the ferry from 1964 to 1977. He continued to operate it after the City of Sistersville purchased it and restored operation in 1981. Dib's colorful stories of dealing with ornery passengers, operating around the clock and calendar, and transporting "baby cases" from Ohio to West Virginia are legendary.

The latter is a reference to Dib's pregnant passengers on their way to a hospital. Dib was proud of the fact he'd never had to deliver the mother *and* her baby while making the passage.

Bo never met Dib, but the barge attached to the *City of Sistersville II* is named in Harmon's honor. Like his distant predecessor, Bo is known by his nickname. "My father, he was Bo,' and when I was younger, I was Bo's Bo," Bo said. "I asked him how he got the nickname, and he said he didn't know. He just had it when he grew up."

The right man for the job

A New Jersey native, Bo adopted West Virginia by way of his wife, Sue, who returned to her hometown of St. Mary's after Bo retired from his 30-year Coast Guard career.

"I moved to St. Mary's, which is about a half-hour south of here," Bo said. "My wife and I were on a motorcycle ride coming up through Ohio. And my wife said, 'Let's take the ferry back across.' I said, 'O.K., what ferry?' I didn't know there was a ferry here."

Bo's daughter, who was a reporter for the Sistersville newspaper, told him the captain's position was open. "So, I got my resume together and a couple of papers, attended a meeting, and I was working the next day," Bo said.

Bo came well qualified with an offshore captain's license. Bo said his Coast Guard search-and-rescue training, which involved towing disabled boats alongside the rescue craft, gave him tugboat experience. After one month of training under an experienced captain, Bo was in charge.

"It was like five years before the Coast Guard inspector noticed that

The Sistersville Ferry arrives at its dock in West Virginia. The deck can accommodate up to 10 passenger vehicles at a time.

I didn't have the appropriate (rivers system) license," Bo said. "So, they said, 'OK, you've been running this boat for this many years without any incidents ... (we're) going to grandfather you in,' and it was OK."

Bo said the biggest challenge to learning how to pilot the ferry involved the steering sticks and rudder arrangement. The ferry has two sets of steering sticks—one for steering while moving forward, the other when operating the astern propulsion that increases maneuverability

"It's got steering sticks instead of a steering wheel, and its rudders in front of the propellers and rudders in back of the propellers for more maneuverability," Bo said. "That I wasn't used to, and I just had to get used to it ... like everything else, if you train on it, you'll get it."

Bo took an interest in the boat's mechanics, as well, delivering extra value to the city.

"I just keep the ferry running," Bo said. "I try to treat it like it's my own vessel, because if it breaks, I've got to fix it. I'm not a mechanic, but I can read a book, and I work on all my own vehicles and always have since I was a kid. So, I don't want it to break, otherwise I've got to fix it."

Captain Bo was a 30-year Coast Guard veteran when he took the ferry job. He said his experience with search and rescue operations prepared him for the unique challenges of operating a side-tow ferry.

His many roles were noted upon Bo's retirement. Ferry Board President Gary Bowden, quoted in the *Tyler Star News,* said that "if the Sistersville Ferry had a heart, it would be Bo Hause."

"He didn't just operate the ferry, he treated it like his child. He was its chief mechanic, and would even lower himself into its dark, grimy bilge to check for leaks. In the off-season he would babysit, always checking to make sure it was tied securely and the Ferry's diesel engines were running properly," Bowden added. "The ferry runs the river six months a year, but Captain Bo ran the ferry every single day."

Bo said that his priority always has been the safety of the passengers, crew and boat whenever he ran. The unique arrangement of the barge running alongside the boat required paying special attention to the river's mood.

"If the river is too rough, we can't run because the barge will bang up against the boat," Bo said. "And it will break the ledge that holds us together when we're moving slow. High winds going up the river are pretty much the only reason we cannot run, unless the river is too high or too low; the landing on the Ohio side cannot accommodate (either) river stage."

One of the most harrowing experiences in his 12-year career was piloting the ferry during a summer flood.

"I was dodging hay bales, tires, refrigerators. I mean, the river was really high, and it got to the point where I had to stop running because I couldn't land on the other side because the river was too high on that side," Bo said.

"We're in a drought now, but if it rains and the river starts coming up or starts flooding... it could be a current of 5 or 10 miles an hour," he added. "Trying to get across—the current flows north to south—we may be steering straight across but the current will push us. So, when we're coming in, we got to go downstream a little bit and turn up into the landing."

A microburst storm during his last season on the river made for a scary closing chapter to his career.

"All of sudden, I saw it on my radar screen," Bo said. "I saw that the storm was coming because I can see rain on the radar. And I had a couple of passengers on deck. It started pouring all of a sudden—sideways rain, thunder, lightning and probably 50- to 60-mile-per-hour winds. And I couldn't see out the windows. So, I had to navigate across using my radar.

"And then, when I got across to the other side, I told my deckhand, 'Alright, put some ropes on, let's get tied up.' And (the deckhand) said, 'I'm not going out there.' It scared him to death. So, the (passengers) on deck got out and actually put the ropes on."

That crossing was the rare memorable one. Bo said he's had days where he made upwards of 90 trips across the river. A smooth crossing that does not require waiting for a barge or other traffic takes just five minutes. It is repetitious work for both Bo and his only crew member, a deckhand, who secures the gates, takes the fare and holds passengers to the safety rules.

Finding deckhands is almost as challenging as hiring a pilot; Bo had more than a half-dozen in his time on the ferry. The work is monotonous and performed in all manner of weather, but the summer heat is the worst.

"My wife was actually one of my deckhands for two years," Bo said. "But it got to the point where she couldn't take the heat. It gets very hot out here ... this deck, if you didn't have a good pair of shoes, gets so hot the shoes would wear out from melting."

Bo said the factors that made for a good day of work were pleasant weather and strong ridership.

"Having a lot of people come aboard and having a nice day put me in a

Tourists account for much of the ferry traffic. This group of motorcyclists was touring Ohio and West Virginia.

good mood," Bo said. "(Drivers and their passengers) will get out of their cars, talk to each other. People meet each other that way, they'll make acquaintances while they are going across the river."

Bo has a special affinity for the children for whom the ferry ride was something special. He added to the thrill by occasionally inviting a child to ride with him in the pilothouse.

"I've never met a person I didn't like," Bo said. "Some more than others, sure. I've watched families grow. I let the kids come up to the pilothouse when they come on board. This one particular family, (the daughter) was in a car seat, and I still remember her sticking her little arm out the window with a five-dollar bill and saying, 'Here you go!' And now she is a teenager dating."

All has not been smiles and good vibes, however. The pay is considerably less than what Bo could have made working for one of the towboat operators on this river. Every summer weekend has been booked for Bo and his wife since he took the job. Rainy days are miserably boring.

Throughout his service on the ferry, Bo was hounded with back pain resulting from his military assignments. Several years into the captain's job,

The ferry yields at the Fly dock to a passing towboat and its line of barges. The City of Sistersville is in the background.

he obtained his CDL and tried driving a trash truck instead of piloting. But he discovered that was equally brutal on his back, and Bo returned to the ferry, whose operation had been suspended for lack of a captain.

"And people kept asking me to come back, because they couldn't find a replacement pilot," Bo said. "It's hard to find a pilot in this area . . . so, I came back."

When Bo announced his plan to retire at the end of the 2024 season, a replacement was literally on deck, where Tom Meek was working as a deckhand. As with Bo, Tom is not a native West Virginian, is a veteran and was introduced to the ferry by his wife.

"We live on the Ohio side back there in the hills, on the inside of that ridge right there," Tom said, pointing to the northwest as he stood on the ferry deck. "We just came through here one day, saw there was a ferry, jumped on it, and rode it two, three, four times. And eventually I came to work on it."

A California native, Tom's military service included serving as an Army Ranger. After his military years, Tom went to work for a sheriff's department outside Savannah, Ga. Seven years later, he returned to California

The City of Sistersville II's 2024 crew consisted of (from left) Captain Bo Hause, deckhand Joseph Throckmorton, and Tom Meek, who was training to take command of the ferry in 2025.

and worked in a police department for nearly two decades before retiring to Montana. After two years of "not doing anything" in Montana, he got the itch to get back into law enforcement in Georgia. He met his wife, a native of Dayton, Ohio, during his second stint there. After they married, they relocated closer to her parents, which led them to Sardis, Ohio.

"Quite frankly, my wife and I both just got tired of sitting around," Tom said. "She was a retired police officer, too, just watching the snow fall. I turned in the application (to the ferry board) to work on the deck. And the deckhand came in and found himself a better career move. He quit (on the day Tom applied), and that day I came to work."

During Bo's time as captain, the board expanded the ferry's scope of operation to include evening charter cruises booked through the Sistersville Ferry office. The cruises have ranged from live-music venues to historical-themed jaunts. Bo said the ferry is also called upon to do off-season assignments.

"There's an annual old farm tractor parade," Bo said. "I'm not sure where they start from in Ohio, but they would take the ferry and go up Route 2 on the West Virginia side. It's a parade of 15 to 20 tractors... and a couple of custom-built vehicles. So, when they loaded up, they didn't just want to go across the river. I took them south to New Matamoras, Ohio, because they wanted to take a ferry ride with all the tractors. So, it took about an hour and we drove down the Ohio River with a barge full of tractors. Then they got off and did a different route for the parade."

Bo also ferried a horse-and-buggy with its Amish driver. "He came up from Amish country, a couple of hours away by car," Bo said. "He had to hold on to the horse because (the animal) got a little upset when we got under way. The horse was not used to it, of course. And (the Amish passenger) cleaned up the mess."

The barge's 72-foot-long deck can accommodate one tractor-trailer rig, six large pickup trucks, or up to 10 small cars. Bo said that on a typical weekday, the ferry will transport three dozen or so cars during the eight hours of operation. "But last week, on either a Friday or Saturday, I had 81 cars in one day," Bo said.

Increasingly, folks take the ferry for the same reasons they opt for a back road with a covered bridge or little town with a diner—the rare opportunity to patronize history with a practical purpose and swap tales with a future legend.

"The ferry is history," Bo said. "It's been here for over 200 years. And I like the fact that I'm being a part of history. You know, maybe people will remember me. They'll talk about me in the days to come and say, 'Yeah, I remember when Captain Bo let us up in the pilothouse and drive.'"

For operating times and days of the Sistersville Ferry, check the website at https://sistersvilleferry.org.

North of Albright on Route 26, the Virginia Furnace stands as a relic of the 1850s and Preston County's short-lived iron industry. It and the Henry Clay iron furnace in Coopers Rock State Forest provide the best surviving examples of iron production infrastructure in Virginia's western lands.

Chapter 13

Virginia Furnace

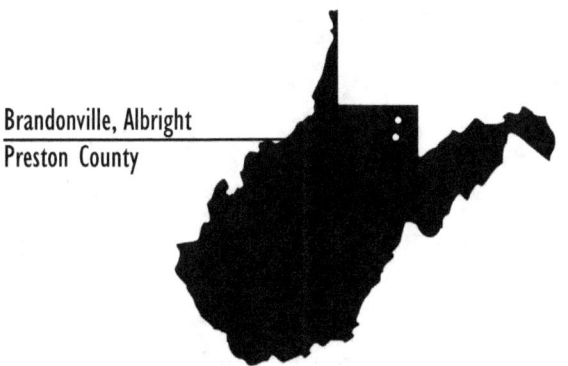

Brandonville, Albright
Preston County

A few miles south of the Pennsylvania/West Virginia border, Route 26 passes through Brandonville, a wide spot marked by two early 19th-century red-brick buildings and a companion two-story stone house. One of the brick structures bears a sign, "Hyde House," the other, "Hagans Store." The latter is a remnant of what was once a chain of frontier-era stores that doubled as banks and purchasing agents for farm goods and services in both north-central West Virginia and southwest Pennsylvania.

Brandonville was a flourishing community in the first half of the 1800s due to three roads that terminated or passed through the settlement: the Brandonville Pike to Terra Alta, the Brandonville-Evansville Pike to Albright, and the Brandonville-Morgantown Road, which was eventually extended to the Ohio River. The name comes from Col. Jonathan Brandon, who built the town's first house. Harrison Hagans, one of three brothers who came to town in 1818, opened his first store in a back room of Brandon's house and eventually built the extant structure that housed the store operated by his son, H. C. Hagans. More merchants followed, as did business ventures overseen by Harrison Hagans.

The store founded by Harrison Hagans and his stone house still stand in Brandonville along Route 26, Preston County.

Continue south on Route 26 toward Albright, and the curving, steep highway eventually follows Muddy Creek as an aqueous third lane for several miles. The creek dashes and slips over orange-stained rocks on its way to the Cheat River and at one point encounters a series of falls that make for a lovely setting, despite the discoloration caused by acid mine drainage.

Rising just above the road grade is the stony tip of Virginia Furnace, a well-preserved iron furnace dating from 1854. This pyramidal furnace, Hagans' Store and the stone house at Brandonville are cousins in a family of ventures that created economic growth in the early days of Preston County, when it was still part of Virginia.

Levi Kennet built the stack for Harrison Hagans, who was always looking for ways to grow the fledgling area's economy through exploitation of its location and natural resources—specifically iron ore, waterpower, limestone and timber. Situated below Muddy Creek's waterfall, the furnace once drew upon the stream's energy to power the blowers necessary for achieving the stack's interior temperature of 3,000 degrees. The cut-stone pyramid rises about 25 feet to road level and is partially open at the top. The road-level access facilitated loading the raw materials from above.

Limestone was plentiful near the surface of these mountains. Iron ore came from the hillsides surrounding the furnace. Charcoal, the fuel of choice for these operations, was produced by burning the stately hardwood trees that grew on these mountainsides. Thousands of acres of forest were thereby destroyed producing the pig iron. The efficiency of the furnace determined how much timber was required to produce the requisite amount of charcoal, which was made by heating the wood in a low-oxygen environment. Author Gordon G. Whitney estimated that at least 50 acres of woodlands were necessary to produce enough charcoal for a furnace whose output was 100 to 400 tons of iron annually.

The molten iron was drawn out at the bottom of the furnace and routed into ditches dug into the ground. These crude molds, or "pigs," were fed from a long ditch, the "sow," that led from the furnace. The product thus produced was called "pig iron," which, when economically and logistically feasible, was transported to urban markets like Wheeling and Pittsburgh.

Virginia Furnace was not Hagans' first investment in the iron industry. Morton's *History of Preston County* states that the Greenville Furnace was built in 1818 on Laurel Run, east of the Cheat River and about five miles from the Mason-Dixon line. Walter "Wat" Carlile, "a man of no education, but of good business qualifications, without capital, but endowed with powers of wonderful perseverance," envisioned the doomed endeavor and raised capital for it using a barrel of "watered whiskey," box of home grown tobacco and a counterfeit note for $10. Amazingly, this under-capitalized effort plodded along for several years until Hagans took control in 1837 and gave it a fresh infusion of capital.

Hagans used his New England connections to raise the money that was absent in the fledgling Preston County community. With Hagans as president, The Greenville Furnace and Mining Company contracted for the materials necessary to manufacture pig iron. In November 1836, Hagans contracted with James Gibson to cut more than 1,000 cords of wood and "cole" it into charcoal for the furnace (by one researcher's estimate, an acre of timber yielded about 30 cords of wood). Jonas Shaw agreed to provide Gibson with all the wood he needed that year for $5! The ore, obtained from the Rock Ore Bank, was contracted at $2.25 per ton. Robert Patterson got the contract for the limestone in 1837. He agreed to provide whatever was needed during the entire year for $27.50. The prices speak to

The remains of other old iron furnaces are found throughout West Virginia. Barbour County's 1848 Valley Furnace lasted only six years and was operated by C.W. Bryant and Isaac Marsh. About 9,000 pounds of iron were produced daily and had to be hauled 50 miles by a mule team to the Monongahela River near Fairmont.

the relative abundance of each natural resource and the related difficulties in harvesting and transporting them to the furnace.

Hauling the iron to market was virtually impossible on the mud pikes of that era, and a two-mile connecting railroad had to be constructed. The cost of getting the iron out of the mountains and to Pittsburgh further damaged the operation's chances of profitability. The iron nail in Greenville's coffin was the Panic of 1837 and the several years of economic depression that followed.

"The see-saw policy that has resulted of antagonistic policies has at one time encouraged, and at another time discouraged, enterprise in the manufacturing of iron, and financially ruined those engaged in it. These are the reasons why our rich ores have not been developed and turned into the channels of commerce," Hagans declared in 1865 as he looked back on the venture.

Hagans didn't give up, however. In 1847 he opened in Brandonville a foundry to manufacture his "Ten-Plate" Cooking Stove. The behemoth was

Muddy Falls powered the blowers that pumped air into Virginia Furnace. The orange color of the rocks are the result of mine acid drainage into the stream.

a wood burner (from start to finish, Hagans's industries were no friends of the forest), built of heavy iron. "Those who remember it say it had a three-leaf clover appearance," wrote Reardon S. Cuppett in his master's thesis, "Harrison Hagans and His Times." "The front had two wings and the back was rounded out to about one half the size of the front. Underneath was the firebox and spacious oven."

Again, getting these things to market made for a very marginal profit, if any.

In need of a local source of iron for his foundry, Hagans once again turned to making iron in 1852 with his Muddy Creek/Virginia Furnace venture. Operations at the stone furnace began in the fall of 1854, with George Maust as manager. A son of Christian Maust, originally from Maryland, George managed Greenville Furnace and sold Brandonville cooking stoves throughout the region. He also possessed legal knowledge and argued cases before the magistrate. Interestingly, Harrison Hagans was a district justice.

The weekly output of this 24-hour-per-day operation was between 40 and 50 tons of foundry iron. But economical transportation of the output remained a problem, and the furnace struggled throughout the 1850s.

The Civil War brought an influx of business as the conflict created

Above: A log of the days employees worked at Virginia Furnace. At right, a page from the ledger showing food purchases at the operation. From the Harrison Hagans collection at the West Virginia and Regional History Center at WVU.

increased demand for iron artillery products. For a brief period, there was even a post office at Muddy Creek's furnace.

The ledgers and other records of the company are in the West Virginia and Regional History Center at WVU, Morgantown. According to those fragile documents, the furnace generated considerable economic activity in the neighborhood, with Hagans operating a store near the site.

"Harrison Hagans was always looking for opportunities," noted Preston County historian Janice Cale Sisler. "There were boarding houses, cooks and washer women at Greenville and Muddy Creek, as nearly as I can tell. There were also stores, as the records seem to indicate. A. C. Leach was often the teamster who delivered supplies from Brandonville."

After Maust's tenure as manager, a man named Lloyd ran the furnace. S.B. Patterson, who re-named it the "Josephine Furnace," was its last manager. The furnace went cold under his watch in 1880, according to historian Morton. Ancillary equipment and structures disintegrated, but the stone pyramid survived and became a landmark.

Virginia/Josephine Furnace eventually received its due honor from the community in 1966, when the Daughters of the American Revolution dedicated a roadside park above the old furnace on Route 26. The Muddy Creek Furnace property belongs to the Preston County Historical Society; the Kingwood Lion's Club maintains the site and roadside park.

The furnace is a popular stopover spot for history and waterfall fans, alike. Personally, I see it as a memorial to an ancient forest forever lost.

Sept 10	To Butter at Cranes 1.	60
11	5¼ lb Beef 5	27
	Apples 12	12
"	1 ½ lb Rice 20	15
"	1 lb Sugar 10	10
12	¼ Tea	25
"	1 lb Sugar 10	10
"	2 lbs Rice C 10 = 20	20
13	8¼ lbs Beef C 5 = 41	41
"	2 lbs Rice C 10 = 20	20
14	81 lb Flour C 5 = 405	4.05
"	Meal 23	46
"	½ Bu Apples 13 = 6	6
"	¼ B Peaches 10	10
"	Bill at Cranes 65	65
"	71 lbs Beef C 5 = 3.55	3.55
15	Per Alpheus Sypolt 56	56
"	⅛ Molasses C 50	6
"	Batting at Saml Cranes 13	13
	9½ lbs Flour C 5 = 48	48
	106 lbs Flour C 5 = 530	5.30
	1 B Apples 13	13
18	⅛ Gal Molasses	6
"	1 lb Sugar 10	10
14	Butter at Cranes 4½ lbs 12 = 56	56
15	do do 4½ = 54	54
19	106 lbs Beef C 5	5.30
"	1.88 for Elisha Liston	1.88
"	½ Gal Molasses C 50	25
"	12½ lbs Beef C 5 = 61	61
20	paying Box	69
"	40 cts for Alpheus Sypolt	40
21	1 lb Sugar 10	10
"	11¾ lbs Flour C 5 = 59	59
"	101 lbs Flour C 5	5.05
22	1½ Gal Molasses C 62	94

The Bruceton Mills dam in 1982. The quaint buildings are gone, but the dam remains 150 years after construction.

Emanuel Beeghley's dam

Bruceton Mills is located off Route 26 near Brandonville and along Big Sandy Creek, which provided waterpower for early industries. In the 1870s, the creek was harnessed with a 20-foot-tall dam built for Emanuel B. Beeghley, a businessman and miller.

Originally known as Milford, the town's name was changed to Bruceton in the late 1840s. The impetus was construction of the town's second mill by John Hoffman, who re-named Milford in honor of his step-father, Bruce, a descendant of Robert Bruce, King of Scotland.

A news brief in the *Preston County Journal* of September 22, 1881, stated that "Emanuel B. is protecting his mill by building a stone wall along the creek." The mill was evidently very successful; Emanuel and his wife wintered in Florida, and he contracted with farmers in both Preston County and Fayette County, Pa., for wheat that he milled and sold. The mill also sawed lumber, and Beeghley had a kiln for reducing limestone to lime, which the farmers used to sweeten their fields.

"After many changes, Mr. Beeghley now owns the mill, and it is in the charge of S. W. Fearer, an experienced miller," wrote S. T. Wiley in his 1882 *History of Preston County*. "He is assisted by Peter Nedrow,

The Bruceton Mills dam in 2022. Fire destroyed the mill in 1952.

whose father was killed by a log falling at a 'raising,' and was said to be the strongest man in the county."

Beeghley was always at the mercy of the Big Sandy's seasonal water flows. Due to low water levels in July 1884, he resorted to using steam power to run the mill's machinery. During a flood in August 1888, the Big Sandy rose to 5 feet in the street and a foot in the mill. Emanuel lost several hundred pounds of flour, a large quantity of lumber and five large hogs in the flood.

In a *Preston County Journal* article of March 13, 1884, an uncredited writer claimed that the Big Sandy at the dam was "a beautiful sheet of water, over a hundred feet wide and from five to fifteen feet in depth for over a mile, with delightful woods on both banks. Skiffs, in ordinary stages of water, can go to Clifton, three miles above, making this one of the most beautiful courses for rowing imaginable. The stream has been stocked with bass, and in a few years will be one of the best streams for fishing in the State."

The stone structure and its stream's reputation for fishing and rowing are unchanged. There is almost always an angler or two working the pool below the dam, and in the warmer months, kayak users enjoy the "beautiful sheet of water" for their recreation.

The doors of the Pleasant District Holiness Association Tabernacle open for one week during August, when campers come to the Valley Point landmark for training, worship and fellowship.

Chapter 14

'Oh, Glorious Times!'

Valley Point
Preston County

Traveling south on Route 26 from Bruceton Mills to the Virginia Furnace, the motorist may notice a large frame building in a depression with the words "GOD IS LOVE" painted in big letters over a set of doors. The tabernacle and rows of cabins surrounding it hark back to the 1930s, when spiritual fire moved worshipers to clap, sing, dance, shout, get on their knees and get right with God.

Once a year, this otherwise dormant property still undergoes a revival as devotees of the Holiness movement congregate on the campground to learn and worship in the Pleasant District Holiness Association Tabernacle.

Twenty-four feet to the peak, the tabernacle is a huge, open sanctuary built to accommodate the presence of God himself. The 44-by-82-foot frame building was constructed circa 1940 using native timber harvested from the property. Some of the main beams are 10 inches square.

"I'm amazed at the amount of work that went into that," said Robert Gray, a Virginia resident and camp association board member who has attended the annual gatherings for decades. Robert also has worked on many projects around the camp, including replacing the original dirt floor

The Pleasant District Holiness Association's Tabernacle was built circa 1940.

with concrete. He recalled a time when, prior to the concrete improvement, straw was spread on the earthen floor to make kneeling more comfortable. Modern worshipers bring a pillow with them to provide a layer of protection between their knees and the rough concrete when they knell to pray.

Camp is held the second full week of August; the dates, set by the board of directors, are posted on a sign along Route 26, at the entrance to the camp. Guests who come for the entire week can apply for lodging in either the dormitory or one of a dozen 400-foot-square cabins that flank the tabernacle. Most are single-unit accommodations, with a porch, front living room and two bedrooms in the back. There are no restrooms, showers or kitchens in these cabins; a separate facility below the buildings provides those amenities.

The dormitory is above the kitchen/cafeteria and offers rooms in either a men's or women's section. Common restrooms and showers are in the building. Robert stays in room number one of this complex, and like him, many of the frequent campers have permanently adopted one of these rooms as their "own" for the week.

Among Robert's tasks during camp week is ringing the large bell whose seven peels call worshipers to the tabernacle thrice daily.

Vernon Pierce has been coming to the Pleasant District Holiness Association's meetings for seven decades. He said "glorious times" have been experienced there.

"See these people around here? Have you noticed how happy they are?" Robert asked me as we watched Bible-clutching folks stroll from their cabins, dorm rooms and campers to the tabernacle on an August morning in 2023. Robert, a soft-spoken yet energetic man in his late 70s, brimmed with anticipation and happiness, as well. Equally excited was the Rev. John MacDonald, who wore a crisp white shirt, black trousers and black suit coat despite the August heat and humidity.

A Nebraska resident and full-time itinerant evangelist, the Rev. MacDonald was elected president of the camp board in 2021, after several years of service as a guest preacher. Both his grandfather and father have preached at Pleasant District, and his father, Charles, served as pastor of McConkey Church in Taylor County.

President MacDonald said camp experience mirrors the appointed times prescribed for the Israelites. Camp meetings have been held at Pleasant District since 1940, except for the two years when COVID-19 guidelines prevented large gatherings.

"We're following the pattern God has established," John McDonald said.

The Rev. John McDonald of Nebraska is the association's president. He presides over the week of activities at the camp.

"Oh, glorious times," said Vernon Pierce, who recalled the meetings that he and his son, Larry, have attended there. "Oh my, it was just like heaven on earth. Just wonderful. Maybe somebody gets up to testify or maybe it is a song being sung. I'll tell you what, it's almost like you got a hot seat. It's almost like you are sitting on a hot seat when the Lord comes."

Vernon began attending meetings at Pleasant District in the late 1950s, when Sam and Elizabeth Shaw were conducting Sunday "cottage prayer meetings" in the camp's dining hall. Vernon and Larry, who live west of Uniontown, Pa., recalled the treacherous journey on routes 40 and 26 to reach the year-around meetings.

"We had to go over Summit Mountain (Chestnut Ridge), toward Markleysburg," Vernon said. "Icy roads. We would go up on Sunday afternoon, and we'd make that trip and you'd be sliding all over (the road)."

The Shaws discontinued their meetings in the early 1960s, but the Pierce family maintained its association with Pleasant District by attending the week of summer camp. They brought their nieces and nephews and stayed in a cottage near the tabernacle.

"You had to pack your bedding, everything, just like you'd be camping out somewhere," Larry recalled. "Mom and Daddy would hang a sheet

The tabernacle at Pleasant District Holiness Camp takes advantage of natural "air conditioning" provided by the large shade trees and "windows" that capture whatever breeze may stirring about the camp. Shorts or other summer clothing that would provide a modicum of relief from hot weather are not allowed.

(across the middle of the front room), and Mom would have the girls on one side and Daddy would have the boys on the other."

The Pierces were Free Methodists at the time but now worship with the Allegheny Wesleyan Methodist holiness branch, which has a denomination camp at Stoneboro, Pa. But Larry and Vernon said the Pleasant District Association's camp felt more like home to them. More recently, they have elected to drive the 50 miles to Pleasant District on select evenings rather than camp there.

Vernon, 97 at the time of our interview in 2023, said he has received many blessings in that tabernacle.

"Oh my, yes! Our second home. We never wanted to miss camp because the Lord would just come in waves," Vernon said. "He blessed the people, blessed the church . . . And, oh, such preaching! Evangelists would take their text from behind the pulpit, and they would come down off that (stage) and just walk back and forth in front of the altar there. Oh, what preaching!"

Larry Pierce dances and runs up and down the tabernacle's aisles with joy during the singing of a hymn at the holiness association's meeting in 2023.

The Wesley tradition

Fifteen worshipers waited in their wooden pews for the evangelist and music director to open the morning session. All activity outside the tabernacle ceased; not a soul was wandering the grounds. That's a camp rule: "Everyone on the grounds is expected to attend all services except for possible medical situations."

Published in the camp brochure and posted in the buildings, the regulations ensure that the camp's mission to make and keep people right with God is achieved. Some of the rules seem archaic by modern standards—"no private visitation of the unmarried" and "all those spending night(s) must be modestly dressed," for example—but they are bedrock behaviors indicative of salvation and sanctification.

To the observant outsider, the most striking outward manifestations of these spiritual disciplines are the attire and lack of adornment among the ladies, who tuck their hair in a bun and wear skirts or dresses whose hemlines fall below the knees. Men dress plainly, as well; crisp, button-down

Worshipers bring pillows for the tabernacle services to make both sitting and knelling more comfortable during the lengthy gatherings.

shirts, trousers and impeccable grooming. No one wears shorts, bathing suits, halter tops or T-shirts at this summer camp. As camper Ardith Lewis points out, there's no such thing as "modest swim wear."

Robert Gray said the dress code, like everything else done at Pleasant District Holiness, is driven by the Bible. "In like manner also, that women adorn themselves in modest apparel, with shamefacedness and sobriety; not with broided hair, or gold, or pearls, or costly array." That is from the book of I Timothy 2:9, King James Version, the only translation permitted in the camp's pulpit. Further, the Bible must be read from a printed page, not a tablet or cell phone screen. Indeed, worshipers must disable their cell phones or leave them in their vehicles or dormitory rooms.

These practices, anachronistic to 21st-century standards, naturally emanate from folks who seek to please God, Robert said. Those who have been "sanctified holy" through a second work of grace at church or camp must put to death the sinful nature and behave accordingly.

"When you come to a camp and you get under the conviction . . . and when you find the Lord, then he comes and meets you in your heart, old things are passed away and all will become new," Robert said, quoting the

Bible. "We don't have the desire for the things of this world. We have a desire to please God. That's depicted in God's Word. So that's where the change comes from. It's not that these people are wearing any particular clothing because they feel they have to. It's because they want to."

While more liberal denominations might term these practices "legalistic," John MacDonald said they are indicators of "heart purity, the Holy Spirit abiding in the heart," the essence of holiness.

John Wesley, founder of Methodism, taught that a "second blessing" is required to remove what he called the "residue of sin within" that became part of the human condition with Adam's fall. Once experienced, this work of holiness imparts "perfect love" toward God and humanity.

"People would experience what we call 'conviction for God,'" Evangelist MacDonald explained. "It makes permanent changes in your life."

"My father used to say it this way: Things you used to love, you hate, and the things you used to hate, you love," Robert Gray said. "It's a complete reversal ... The heart changes, that's the forgiveness of sin, repentance and forgiveness of sin. And that's when the new life is created in you. Then, the heart cleansing. That's an inbred sin that we inherited from Adam ... we can't help the fact that we got that inbred sin. But we'd just like to get rid of that inbred sin through the process of sanctification, so there's not this half of us falling and being tempted. And, that's really what the second work of grace is about, getting rid of the old carnal nature."

It is an experience both sought and fostered at holiness camp meetings, where standard hymns like "He Abides" and "Glorious Freedom" are sung from tattered, red, paper-back hymnals and preaching goes on for an hour or more at the evangelist prods the saved toward "sanctification," a mysterious, elusive spiritual state conferred "instantaneously just as salvation, but lived out daily; progressive in its work, but instantaneous in its reception," said the Rev. Brian Bright, who was in charge of the music during the 2023 camp.

Holiness is preached at the camp's tabernacle gatherings, especially during the morning and afternoon sessions, where those who have not claimed this second work of grace are encouraged to seek and receive the blessing. During the evening sessions, the focus shifts to drawing sinners to the altar and getting them saved to the strains of "Just As I Am."

Campers are expected to attend each and every meeting held in the tabernacle during camp week. Women must wear dresses.

"When I see somebody come to the altar and get saved, that's the main thing, getting souls saved and keeping them saved. That's what camp is all about. There's been a whole lot of people saved in there," Robert said, motioning to the tabernacle.

Holiness denominations established camps like Pleasant District to ensure there would be venues where John Wesley's views on sanctification were preached and standards for holiness upheld. The camps are loosely associated, even in an era of social media, which makes it difficult to determine how many exist in West Virginia or the United States. The website campmeeting.us lists only Summersville Nazarene and Black Hills Free Methodist in Grafton in The Mountain State. Listings are voluntary, however. There are dozens of camps in the Central Appalachian region, and a dedicated seeker could attend a different one each week in the summer months. Sam and Cynda Gandee of Nevada, Ohio, live that lifestyle.

"It's more of a seasonal thing," Sam told me as he helped his wife make a peach cobbler in the camp kitchen. "A lot of these camps were not situated to deal with cold weather or anything like that."

Sam, president of the Venus camp, said they attend and serve at three or

Father and son Vernon and Larry Pierce drive from Uniontown, Pa., to attend a meeting during camp week at Pleasant District Holiness Association.

four camps annually. They own a camper and stay in that rather than camp accommodations. In 2023 they signed on as cooks at Pleasant District. The task involved planning and cooking breakfast, lunch and the evening meal for up to 100 persons for seven days.

Pleasant District's meal-preparation and lodging arrangements assume attendees will stay on the grounds throughout camp week and thereby have 24/7 access to the Spirit's work. With the permission of leadership, Pleasant District "regulars" can reserve the same cabin year after year. Such has been the case for Ardith Lewis' cabin No. 1, centrally located between a row of cabins, the tabernacle and restroom building. It is the cabin that her parents, Willard "Sam" and Velna Golden, occupied and where Ardith and her six children camped.

The front room of the cabin gives Ardith the space to peddle the craft items she makes and sells to help fund the camp—with the board's permission. "I made $437 for the camp (in 2022)," Ardith said. She deducts

Robert Gray has been coming to camp from his home in Virginia for decades. He has donated many days of labor to keeping the camp maintained and ready for the annual gathering.

nothing for the supplies that go into creating the crocheted angel wall hangings, Christmas ornaments, baby sweater sets, dolls and fancy towels. That's her contribution to preserving the holiness camping tradition in West Virginia.

Free-will offerings drive the camp's finances, whether they come from collections taken during each service or when meals are served. Giving to the camp is one of the posted tenets: "Support the camp in free-will offerings as God's blessings have been bestowed upon you; God loves a cheerful giver."

Evangelists, guest speakers and music ministers who provide leadership and ministry to the campers also work by donation, traveling to Preston County on faith that their expenses will be covered. Brian Bright and his wife, Pamela, come from Felton, Del., to serve. A full-time pastor, Rev. Bright said the camp board determines what financial renumeration will be offered, if any, for services they provide.

"There is no set fee, by any means," Rev. Bright said. "We wouldn't embrace that. Nor would we embrace an extravagant amount, either. It would have to be a very modest gift. It would not be accepted if it was not."

The Brights were doing double duty, serving as both song evangelists and children/youth workers. The duality of their work hinted at the challenge facing the camp when it comes to reaching youth. There were but four teens at camp in 2023. With the strict demands on dress, regular worship attendance and sacrifice, assemblies struggle to attract new converts who are unfamiliar the holiness concepts and culture. But Vernon Pierce said the standards can't be relaxed because they are integral to receiving the blessings of camp.

"You have to be obedient to God all the way, no sin whatsoever," he said.

Most overnight campers are retired seniors for whom camp week is a practice established in their childhoods and youth. Mayola Keller of Grafton was one of them.

"(Camp) means a lot to me," Mayola told me while waiting for a morning service to start. "I've gotten a lot of spiritual help here." She recalled the best memories of camp as those of the "oneness and fellowship, and the good preaching."

"I can't describe it," she said. "It's just like a second home, I guess."

Campers say the week-long, intensive experience of prayer, three services a day and fellowship over meals provides something the Sunday church service cannot provide. Larry Pierce said the familiarity and ritual of the Sunday service can lead to staleness. But, at camp, everything from the preaching to the relationships is on a deeper level. "So, we bear one another's burdens, we share our joys, and we share our sorrows," Robert Gray said. "There is a commonality here that most people don't understand."

For some, like Ardith Lewis, camp week is vacation, too. While she worshiped weekly in a holiness congregation, it was at camp she learned church etiquette as a young girl in the 1950s and 1960s.

"There were different things (the camp speakers) would explain from the Bible. Some people would get mad because the (preacher) was trying to help you; people don't want to give up stuff, so they get mad," Ardith said. "I mean, if it doesn't hit us once in a while with that sermon, what's the use to come?"

She recalled the Pleasant District camp meetings of the late 1950s, when she and her 10 siblings came with her parents after her father got off work.

"We'd have to sit in the back of the church. It was that full," Ardith said.

The large numbers, estimated at well over 125, were driven by cooperation

Ardith Lewis stands in front of her family's Cabin #1, August 2023. She is holding a few of the crafted items she makes and sells to support the camp, with permission from the board and only during breaks between tabernacle gatherings.

among the district's churches. "It used to be all the churches around would close their church down and come down here because (the camp) was non-denominational," Ardith said.

Robert described attendance as "light" in the years since the pandemic. That trend appears to track an overall decline in holiness congregations and attendance. Wesleyan Methodist Allegheny Conference congregation that Ardith worshiped with closed its building for lack of members

The volunteer board members who govern the camp are like bakers who keep the oven warm while they await the harvest. They believe that the remnant's spiritual health will ultimately determine the camp's future, which is in the hands of God. Their job is to be faithful, ready, for when the Spirit moves.

It all comes back to the paradox of holiness.

"If we don't keep the standards, you don't get the blessing. We have blessings in the service, and if we didn't keep the standards up, and the world takes over, there's no blessing. There's no God," Robert said.

The dates of the next camp meeting are posted on the association's sign along Route 26 at the camp drive.

The Rev. Winfield Scotty Mayle was predient of the Pleasant District Holiness Camp for 32 years. He and a member of his congregation, Ardith Lewis, await the start of services in August 2023, his last year to attend camp. He died December 12, 2023.

Rev. Mayle tended the holiness fires

The late Rev. Winfield Scotty Mayle served as president of the Pleasant District Holiness Camp Association for 32 years, an era when pews were often full and fervor for the holiness movement was still strong. The camp's board of directors honored the Bruceton Mills resident on August 7, 1999, at the close of his presidency.

A native of Moatsville, Barbour County, Winfield was born June 9, 1930. He grew up next door to a Holiness congregation that lost its building to the impounded waters of the Tygart Valley Dam in the mid-1930s. The pastor recalled those years as very difficult for his parents; his father had lost a leg to a gunshot wound before Winfield was born.

"Might have been '29, might have been '30," he said. "This guy comes by the house, I don't know whether he was jealous or what, and hollers for my dad. And he went out in the yard, and the man shot him in the leg. My dad lost his leg. They took him to this old doctor, Dr. Peck, I think it was, and he was going to take it off (closer to the knee), but my dad remembered that there was this man who got his arm caught in a mill of some kind, and they had to keep taking a little more of his arm off (most likely, due to infection). So, my dad knew that, and he said, 'Just take it off here,'" Rev. Mayle said, indicating the amputation was high above the knee. "And all the days of my life, he just had that stump."

The attacker's violence was due to his father's moonshine business. Rev. Mayle said it eventually got his father and the family's little grocery store in trouble with the law and led to a one-year sentence in an

Atlanta, Ga., prison for his father. Winfield was a little boy sleeping on the couch when the raid came down at dawn.

"They were FBI men," he recalled. "They couldn't get my dad for making whiskey because he couldn't get to the still with that one leg. But he sold (moonshiners) sugar, so much sugar that they knew he couldn't be making jelly. They got him for conspiracy, whatever that is."

His mother was the backbone of the family. "Mom didn't drink, or smoke, or nothing," he said. "She went to church in her later years, after my daddy died."

Winfield followed his mother's lead, was saved and trained for ministry in the holiness tradition. In 1955, he responded to a call from the Olive Hill congregation. "They needed a pastor, so I just stepped in," he said.

His last assignment was at the Woolen Mill Church near Lenox, Preston County. The church was affiliated with the Allegheny Conference of the Wesleyan Methodist Church.

When he responded to the congregation's call, membership stood at 12 or 13 souls, "but we ran (attendance) of 60, 70 sometimes," he said. When membership fell to just three faithful, the church building was mothballed and meetings were held in the house where Winfield lived with his son. Members continued to support him financially in keeping with Biblical instruction.

He said attendance numbers at camp meetings was the biggest difference between the way camp was at the beginning of his presidency in the 1960s and the state of things in 2023. Thumbing through a list of churches published by his denomination, he said most of the congregations were just "churches on paper" due to the dearth of pastors and members. The decline in Allegheny Conference congregations reflects Americans' waning interest in faith and morality, a trend that deeply concerned the soft-spoken pastor.

"We're coming closer and closer to something, aren't we?" he said. "I think we are. Everything seems to be pointing in that direction that we can't continue in. You and I never heard of what's going on today. You can't hardly walk out on the street without getting shot. You can't do it."

Words of experience, indeed, considering his late father's tragic story.

Charlie and Britney Hervey Farris are transforming a Brooke County farm that Hervey family members first worked in the 1770s. Their diverse operation ranges from maple syrup to strawberries; sweet corn to sorghum. Their children—Grady, 7, and Mylah, 5—assist them with farm. Photo from March 15, 2025.

Chapter 15

New Directions for an Old Farm

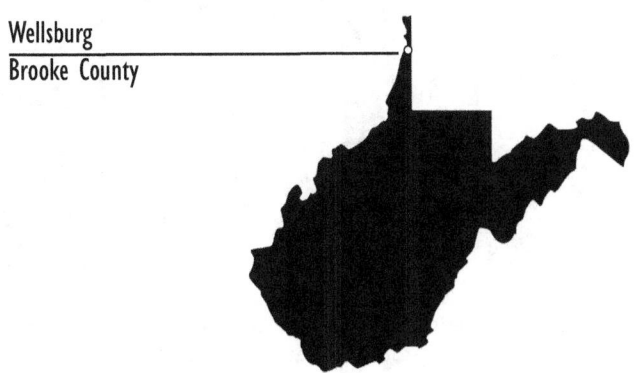

Wellsburg
Brooke County

Britney Hervey Farris believes West Virginia has more maple trees than Vermont, but New England gets all the attention for its maple syrup industry. A few days into collecting sap on the steep hillsides of the Hervey family's Brooke County farm, Britney's husband, Charlie, quickly figured out why making maple syrup on a commercial scale was slow to take root.

"You'd start climbing up the hill with a five-gallon bucket of sap in each hand," Charlie told me as we walked down a muddy road through a forest of predominately sugar maples. "You'd trip or slide in the mud and spill a bucket of that sap all over your pants. And it would be below freezing, and you'd be out there working in those wet clothes by lantern and headlamps."

Despite the misery and labor involved in collecting sap, Charlie said maple sugar production has an element of certainty that other farming ventures lack: There is always a harvest. It may come early, or may it come late. It may be heavy, or it may be scant. But there will be a harvest.

"The (harvest) season is different from year to year, but you know it always is going to come," said Charlie, who was grafted into the Hervey

Britney and Charlie Farris check their maple sap collection lines at their Family Roots Farm near Wellsburg. The farm produces maple syrup and sugar that have won many awards. They also grow strawberries and produce. Photo from 2015.

family in 2013 with his marriage to Britney, daughter of Fred and Cathy Hervey.

Despite the added physical challenges facing a West Virginia maple syrup producer, Britney and Charlie have excelled at their craft. The North American Maple Syrup Council in 2023 awarded the Herveys' maple sugar a first-place award, their second such honor in a decade.

Britney and Charlie started their niche agricultural business, Family Roots Farm, in 2013 using her parents' 40-acre tract at the end of Hervey Lane. Fred inherited the farm from his father, William Judson Hervey. Britney said Herveys have farmed on the mountaintops of Brooke County since 1770, but there was a break in the continuity of full-time farming two generations ago. Her great aunts, spinsters Mattie and Mamie Hervey, were the last to embrace the tradition; her grandfather and father made their livings working off the farm.

Being reared in the city of Wellsburg, Britney had no plans of being a farmer and earned her degree in athletic training. But during an internship, she realized her chosen career frequently would take her away from home. In 2012 she and her fiancé made the decision to move back to the family farm, build a house there, work in Brooke County and earn extra cash growing produce for farmer's markets.

"We both wanted to be as self-sufficient as possible," she said.

Their first crop was one acre of sweet corn, which sold well at Wellsburg markets. They plowed their profits back into the farm and built a storage shed for their equipment—a 1948 Cub tractor that Charlie's grandfather, Al Hanke, bought brand new and willed to his grandson.

That winter, the couple dabbled in maple syrup, tapping trees on an old sugar bush owned by Britney's aunt and uncle, Mary Kathryn and Alan DeGarmo. Fred, Cathy and Britney already had a rudimentary understanding of the process; for some 15 years they had tapped maples on the farm and made syrup for their own use.

Britney recalls making their first batch on her mother's kitchen stove—not a practical approach as the stream left a nasty stain on the ceiling. The next winter, they moved the operation outdoors and boiled the sap in a turkey cooker. From there, they expanded the operation to a homemade evaporator.

They tapped 100 trees in the winter of 2013 and produced their first quantity of syrup for the farm market. Their customers loved it, and the couple decided to invest more time and money in professional development and equipment. They learned about the chemistry of maple syrup and how to use that knowledge to produce a superior product. Much of their training came through the West Virginia University Extension Service, while the state's Department of Agriculture connected them to other producers.

Britney sharpened her business skills by attending Annie's Project seminars.

"That program really got us thinking outside the box," Britney said.

That included making value-added products, such as maple cotton candy and maple nuts. They also got into making granulated maple sugar with help from their friend, Gary Rush. A coal miner, Gary read all he could about the process of heating the maple syrup to 50 degrees above boiling and stirring it until it turns to a granulated product.

Under Gary's tutelage, they produced a vintage that won first place at the International Maple Conference, held at Seven Springs, Pa., in

The evaporator used to make maple syrup also works for boiling down the sorghum juice that Family Roots Farm added to its line in 2016.

October 2015. Ironically, they went to Seven Springs to learn and have their products critiqued, not endorsed. They walked away with a perfect score on their maple sugar.

A small patch of sweet corn and few gallons of maple syrup thus turned into a year-around farm operation in a matter of four years. Charlie was especially happy to see the maple syrup business prosper because the income allowed them to invest in a tube-collection system, ending those treks up slippery hillsides while carrying 70 pounds of sloshing sap by the light of a Full Hunger Moon. As the syrup aspect of the farm prospered, the couple invested in a computerized system to monitor levels in the storage tanks and sap lines.

Buoyed by their success and recognition, in late 2015 the couple hired an Amish carpentry crew to erect a multi-purpose sugar shack that doubles as a farm market in the summer and fall. Solar energy powers the shack. Also that year, the farm produced its first run of sorghum, once a staple sweetener for homesteaders.

Although more widely grown in the Southeast, sorghum is often offered as an alternative to maple syrup at pancake breakfasts in The Mountain State. And niche growers are picking up on its high value as a farm product and constructing events centered on its harvest and syrup production.

Britney Hervey Farris operates the corn binder that is pulled by a tractor driven by her father, Fred, during the 2016 sorghum harvest.

Sweet sorghum starts as a sap that is extracted from the canes of Sorghum bicolor (L.) Moench. Of African origin, the grass was introduced to the United States in 1853 by a U.S. patent officer. Because it is heat and drought resistant, sorghum was most suitable for planting in the southeastern United States. Tennessee and Kentucky are the nation's leading producers, according to the National Sweet Sorghum Producers and Processors Organization.

That organization, along with a handful of other growers in Ohio and West Virginia, helped Family Roots quickly ramp up production and get the product on their Sugar Shack's shelves. To generate consumer interest in the crop, they planted an acre of sorghum that was visible from the market entrance. As the tall, slender stalks grew to a height of 12 feet and brought forth seed heads and long, slender leaves, customers assumed that the farm was testing a new type of sweet corn.

"They'd say, 'That's a really nice field of corn you got growing there,'" Charlie said. "And then they'll ask, 'Where are the ears?' But the older people knew exactly what it was.'"

Neither Charlie nor Britney had experienced sorghum until 2013, when they encountered it at the Algonquin Mill Festival in Carroll County, where the Robert Rea family of Nettle Creek Farm in Salem, Ohio, was selling it.

Sorghum harvest requires many hands, young and old, to get the job done. From left to right are Britney Hervey Farris and Sean Tribett cleaning canes; Miriam Faulkner, Charlie Farris and Emily Tribett working the mill.

The encounter piqued Britney's interest, and she began researching the crop as an option for their farm. Because they were already producing maple syrup and owned an evaporator, making sorghum seemed like a safe bet. Further, consumers were looking for natural sweeteners, and the production process had agritourism potential. To introduce sorghum to the hills of Brooke County, the couple built a Sorghum Days event around the harvest. The first one was held in October 2016. Neighbors, family, customers and friends of all ages, participated. Re-invigorating a farm requires a community of believers willing to roll up their sleeves and pitch into the task.

"Being able to open our farm up to folks of all ages to learn the process of sorghum making and to see smiles on everyone's face as they take place in the harvest is rewarding," Britney said. "We have a love and passion for agriculture and truly enjoy sharing that with others."

The decision required investment in a cane press, a piece of steampunk that crushes the cane to release the light-green sap. The press is typically powered by a mule or horse walking in circles. A trough at the bottom of the roller array collects the juice, which is transferred to a larger container.

Because small farms abandoned the labor-intensive process decades ago,

Charlie Farris of Family Roots Farm feeds sorghum cane into the antique Western Case Mill No. 2 press, which extracts the sweet sap.

these antique mills languished in the corners of barns until the farmer got tired of pushing them around and sold them for scrap. The couople found their first press in Salem, Ohio. The Western Case Mill No. 2 seemed like a good deal at a price that was roughly a dollar a pound. Charlie said larger mills can weigh up to 1,000 pounds and cost thousands of dollars when restored and fully functional.

Charlie fitted the cane press to an angle-iron frame that distributed the weight and prevented it from tipping over in use. A locust branch that a previous owner had selected for its strength and curvature was used to link the press to a power source.

"It's a little bit hillbilly," Charlie said. "But it came with the press and it works."

The mill presents a substantial amount of resistance when loaded with cane, and while a strong man could power it for a short stretch, he would get a hard workout in the process. A garden tractor, while not as rustic or historically authentic as using a mule or horse, provided a suitable substitute for the purpose.

Roger Rothwell volunteered for the monotonous task of driving the

Roger Rothwell drives the tractor that powers the press that extracts sap from the sorghum cane during the 2016 Sorghum Days at Family Roots Farm.

tractor in a circle of about 25 feet diameter with the mill at the center. Roger is a family friend who worked on the Hervey dairy farm before it was closed.

"He's a really good family friend," said Britney, who credited both Gary Rush and Roger for lending their traditional skills, ingenuity and labor to reinventing the farm.

The mill was sited between the field of cane and evaporator for convenience and efficiency. The canes are fibrous and rigid; a machete is typically used to harvest them. Because of the danger inherent to machete use, Charlie and Britney sought a mechanized alternative and found it in another piece of steampunk, the corn binder.

Pulled by a horse or tractor, the binder grabs the stalk and holds it in place while an articulating blade cuts through it. The severed stalks are collected in a metal arc at the rear of the binder; an operator riding next to it discharges the bundle of stalks into the field when the holder is full.

During Sorghum Day, Roger Rothwell set a pace of slightly more than two revolutions per minute. One person fed the cane into the mill while a second pulled the crushed stalks from rollers and stacked them below

Charlie Farris and farm guests step gingerly as they take a tour of the farm during an open house celebrating the maple syrup crop for 2025.

the platform. Each person working around the mill soon learned to duck about every 30 seconds, when the long arm approached their noggins.

It was a learning experience for virtually every person who assisted with the various tasks. Few had tasted sorghum before Charlie and Britney introduced it to this ridge, and the experience of harvesting and processing it was even more foreign. Charlie said that, aside from the farmer who introduced them to the plant, "every other person I've talked to (who is producing it) is 55 years old or older."

It also appeared to be a new experience for the land.

"There is no record of sorghum making on the farm. (It was) previously a dairy farm, with a record of grains being grown during the 1800s," Britney said.

Britney is the educator; Charlie called her "the brains of the operation." She shares recipes and samples with the visitors and explains how molasses, often confused with sorghum, is a byproduct of making refined sugar rather than a primary product. Britney teaches their customers how to substitute sorghum for molasses or sugar and encourages them to try it on waffles and hot cakes.

Charlie and Britney Farris and Britney's parents, Fred and Kathy Hervey, display their farm's products and the awards that they received in 2015.

Sorghum prices roughly follows those of the farm's maple syrup. The labor-intensive process of making sorghum explains why it is more expensive than molasses. When consumers can witness all the risks, equipment, steps and work involved in producing these sweet products, they are more likely to view the asking price as more than fair,

Charlie points out that the farmer can determine, within a window of several weeks, when the sorghum processing will be done. With maple syrup, however, weather alone opens and closes the window, and the weather is usually pretty miserable at that. The downside is that weather and drought have a whole growing season to destroy a field of sorghum.

That happened to their 2023 and 2024 planting. The couple put sorghum production as developed and fine-tuned other uses for the land, such as growing strawberries. Initially approached as a pick-your-own operation, they have since scaled it back to supplying their market only. They expanded their vegetable production by adding high tunnels with automated openers, and are using pasture pigs to control waste on the farm and generate income from meat sales. And they fine-tuned their maple marketing to focus on their own market and use established retailers rather than traveling to numerous farmers' markets.

Charlie and Britney Farris include education as part of their farm's mission. Here, Charlie watches as a guest learns how to drill a tap hole in a maple log.

Being a farmer, wife and mother of two—Grady, 7, and Mylah, 5, in 2025—led Britney to develop hands-on science education units for conservation, maple syrup, horticulture and other fields that she teaches part-time at a private independent school. Their children help out on the farm, and their son conducted a fundraiser to build a kids' pedal-tractor pull at the county fair.

True to its name, Family Roots Farm is building a growing community rooted in the land, heritage and family. Their products are sweet, wholesome, traditional and nutritious. And they are making memories and perpetuating heritage in the process.

"Community remains extremely important to us," Britney said. "My parents, Fred and Cathy Hervey, remain an important piece of the puzzle for both the farm operations and making memories with their grandkids."

The farm and market are located at 245 Hervey Lane, Wellsburg. For upcoming events at the farm and to sign up for its newsletter, visit the website, familyrootsfarmwv.com, or their Facebook page.

A portrait of Dolley Madison's sister, Ruthie Payne, hangs above the piano in the room where Dolley Todd and James Madison were married at Harewood on September 15, 1794. The room had not been painted since then.

Chapter 16

Washingtons Slept Here

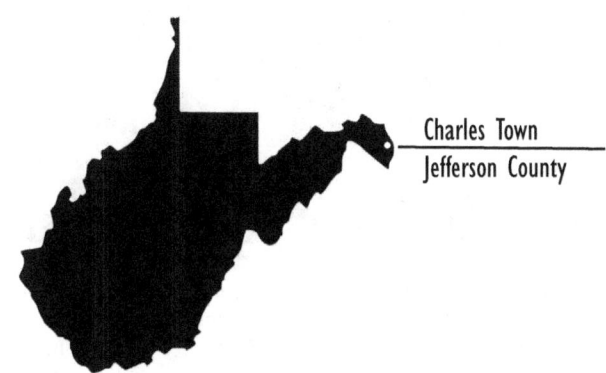

Charles Town
Jefferson County

"The writer has seen many beautiful places at home and abroad, but of all the places that have gladdened his eyes, Harewood is the most picturesque and the most beautiful."
Washington Manor Association
for the Purchase and Preservation of Historic Harewood, 1901

The writer of the opening quote saw Harewood on "one lovely spring day." My visit was on a dreary winter day, but the gray sky and brown mud could not diminish the beauty of the limestone mansion on Smithfield Pike, some three miles west of Charles Town. Indeed, the steel-gray backdrop amplified the magnificence of this mansion built in 1770 for Colonel Samuel Washington, a brother of our first president.

On the day of my visit in 2015, Harewood was the private of home of Walter Washington, a direct descendant of the original owner. It is one of eight surviving Jefferson County homes with connections to the Washington family.

The Washington link to Jefferson County commenced with George

Walter Washington stands in the yard of his Harewood estate, the oldest of the Washington family houses in Jefferson County. The limestone house was built by Samuel Washington, brother to George Washington. Walter is a direct descendant from Samuel.

Washington's first survey in the area in March 1748. While mapping the region, the future president suffered health issues. He found the water at Berkeley Springs to be so beneficial he acquired property there. Two years later, he purchased land in what would become Jefferson County. At one time, Washington owned nearly 2,300 acres in the region. A half-brother, Lawrence, likewise had a passion for what became West Virginia's Eastern Panhandle. After Lawrence died in 1752, his brothers divided the land. Although George didn't build a mansion for himself in the area, he made numerous trips to the Shenandoah Valley over the years to visit his brothers, Samuel and Charles.

Samuel (1734-1781) was the first Washington sibling to venture northwest from the Tidewater and build a house in present Jefferson County. Harewood, made of native limestone and designed by noted architect and Washington family friend John Ariss, took form in 1770. When Samuel died in 1781, he bequeathed Harewood—most likely a reference to the greenish-gray wood of the abundant sycamore tree—and 850 acres to his widow and fifth wife. Harewood eventually ended up in the hands of

George Steptoe Washington, one of Samuel's sons from a prior marriage. George Steptoe married Lucy Payne in 1793, setting the stage for the most spectacular event in Harewood's history.

Lucy's sister was Dolley Payne Todd, a widow engaged to Virginia Congressman James Madison. Dolley married the future fourth president of the United States at Harewood. The wedding was held in the first-floor drawing room, whose walls have not been painted since the 1794 ceremony. The drawing room is also notable for its dark-green marble mantelpiece, said to be a gift to the Washington family from the General Marquis de Lafayette.

The Todd-Madison wedding was perhaps the happiest occasion in the long history of Harewood. Misfortunes beset the property and many members of the Washington family thereafter. There was a succession of Washington heirs who inherited the property only to die young. By the time of the Civil War, Louisa Clemson Washington was living on the plantation.

With the Confederacy just across the county line, the conflict hit Jefferson County residents particularly hard—possibly worse than any other place in West Virginia. Back taxes, demanded by the Union following its victory, bankrupted the Washington family. Harewood became a refuge for the Washington diaspora after the war. At the end of the 19th century, the Washingtons vacated Harewood and moved to Charles Town.

A tenant farmer occupied Harewood until Walter Washington's father, Dr. John A. Washington, in 1951 restored the house and moved in. In 1961, Dr. Washington added a north wing as a more practical living space. He planned the addition with great reverence for the existing structure, blending it seamlessly with the architecture. Walter lived in this section of the house during winter months because the older parts were quite costly to heat. When warmer weather arrived, he returned to the familiar comfort of Harewood's central porch, the historic drawing room and east-wing kitchen.

Dr. Washington also added modern decorative touches, such as wallpaper, to Harewood. He retained the services of Thomas T. Waterman to guide the work and ensure the structure's historical integrity.

Walter returned to the family homestead in 2002 after a law career in Texas. Thanks to his parents, the property needed little in the way of structural attention. However, there was a more pressing threat. Charles

Town was being consumed by the urban sprawl stretching westward from Baltimore and Washington, D. C. Walter wanted to protect the property around Harewood and the structure itself from this invasion of modern development.

He carved out 219 of his 260 acres as an agricultural easement. Some of this land includes a Civil War battlefield also protected by a historic lands easement. His goal was to forever preserve all of the Harewood land from residential and commercial development.

Happy Retreat

An attorney who specializes in real estate, Walter also serves as president of the Friends of Happy Retreat—another Washington family home. It stands on a hill overlooking Charles Town, a community founded by and named for Charles Washington (1738-1799), George's youngest brother. Charles built the west wing of this Federal/Greek revival-style home.

While Walter has a good grip on dates and events for Harewood, Happy Retreat's details are murky. "We don't know" is an oft-heard response a vistor's questions when touring Happy Retreat. A reliable date for the Washington family's presence on the knoll is 1780.

Matt Webster, director of Architectural Resources at Colonial Williamsburg, analyzed the property and determined that the home was developed in three phases: (1) portion of the west wing and old stone kitchen; (2) one-story east wing and brick portion of the kitchen; and (3) second stories above the two wings, tied together by a 2½-story addition. The latter improvements were made in 1837 by owner Judge Isaac Douglass, who presumably fulfilled Charles Washington's original intention to connect the two wings with a central section. Douglass's purchase ended the Washington family's ownership of Happy Retreat. In 1954, the house was bought by Mr. and Mrs. Robert McCabe. Four years later, Mr. and Mrs. William Gavins became the owners and extensively remodeled it.

Happy Retreat was eventually vacated and placed on the market. A 2006 appraisal commissioned by the City of Charles Town suggested that the land be subdivided for residential use. Meantime, the nonprofit Friends of Happy Retreat was formed to acquire, preserve and utilize the property for public benefit.

"It had been on the market for three years," Walter told me. "Someone

Happy Retreat's fan window, a crowning jewel of the Greek Revival facade, is even more striking when viewed from inside. Walter Washington looks out on the grounds of the property, now owned by Friends of Happy Retreat, a nonprofit.

Walter Washington gives a tour of the exterior of Happy Retreat to visitors who recalled the mansion from their childhood. The exterior facade is brick, probably of local clay. The use of standard exterior paints on the relatively soft walls, beginning in the mid-20th century, trapped moisture inside the brick, causing them to crumble.

Happy Retreat was begun by Charles Washington with construction of two wings connected by a breezeway. He anticipated construction of the central block, but died in 1799; Isaac A. Douglass added the central section circa 1837, after his purchase. Only the front section of the wing on the right-hand side, the west wing, is considered to be original in appearance to Washington's era.

would have eventually bought it, and it could have been subdivided and had other houses put on the property."

In 2010, Preservation Alliance of West Virginia recognized Happy Retreat's precarious status by naming it one of the 10 most endangered historic properties in the state. This spurred Walter and the Friends of Happy Retreat into action. As a result of their lobbying, the city of Charles Town purchased 10 acres of Happy Retreat land for a park, leaving the friends group responsible for raising $375,000 to purchase the house and 2.3 acres. The group received two very generous gifts/challenge pledges, and the sale was closed in spring 2015.

During the first nine months of ownership, the Friends of Happy Retreat invested about $80,000 in the property.

"Our initial goal is to get the house into a condition that will allow us to use it for events and weddings," Walter said.

In the past, both the Gavins and McCabes had hired architects to prepare drawings of their renovations to Happy Retreat. These documents provided the friends a pathway to reverse-engineer some changes. Early on, a consultant steered the group away from creating a "house museum" in favor of authentically restoring a only portion to its 18th century appearance. The remainder would be used for educational, cultural and social events.

"There will be only two rooms in the house that will look the way they did when Charles Washington lived here," Walter said.

In October 2015, the Jefferson County Arts Council used Happy Retreat for its first ArtOber event. The mansion's space did great justice to the artists' work, while the acoustics drew praise from both musicians and guests.

The Friends of Happy Retreat's board of directors—stocked with professionals from education, law and government—hired several professional groups to evaluate the property and plan restorations. In 2015, Preservation Alliance of West Virginia, which just five years earlier had identified Happy Retreat as one of the state's most endangered properties, presented its Most Significant Save of an Endangered Site Award to the group.

Claymont Court

On the southwest outskirts of Charles Town, new single-family homes and condos rise on farmlands where cattle once grazed and apple trees grew. Here, Claymont Court stands majestically on a hill, overlooking neglected gardens.

This, too, is historic land. Claymont's 300 acres were originally owned by John Augustine Washington (1736-1787), another brother of George. In 1811, Bushrod Corbin Washington (1790-1851), George's grand-nephew, inherited the Claymont land. Nine years later, he built the mansion that would grow to 59 rooms with 25 fireplaces. At a cost of $30,000, Claymont had a reputation among his neighbors as being "Bushrod's Folly."

Fire consumed his folly in 1838, but Bushrod, a wealthy assemblyman in the Virginia House of Delegates, rebuilt the central portion in 1840 and restored the remainder. This is the building that still stands.

Bushrod died in 1851; his son, Thomas Blackburn Washington, inherited the property but lived only another three years. Bushrod's eldest son, Bushrod Corbin II, was next in line. During the vicissitudes of the Civil War, many Washington family members found refuge at Claymont. Two young Washington men—both Confederate officers—were staying there

Claymont Court rises majestic and stately on the hill of clay from which it derives its name. The mansion was built for Bushrod Corbin Washington in 1820 and again in 1840 following a fire in 1838. He was the grand-nephew of our nation's first president.

during a Christmas furlough, when they were captured by Union troops under George Custer, a former roommate of one of the Washington boys at West Point.

Both men died in a Union prison. To punish the Washingtons for "harboring guerrillas," Union General Philip Sheridan ordered his soldiers to drive all the cattle off the land and burn every fence surrounding the estate. During the war, the Washingtons paid their taxes to the Confederacy; afterwards, the Union came knocking for its share. Unable to meet these financial burdens, the family was forced to sell Claymont for just $10,000, a third of its construction cost.

In an interesting twist of fate, one of the later owners was perhaps more famous than any of the Washingtons who lived there. In 1899, Claymont Court was bought by author Frank Stockton, best known for his short

Chimneys, dormers and windows, nearly 100 of them, create beautiful lines and patterns in the central section of Claymont Court.

story, "The Lady, or the Tiger?" He lived at Claymont for most of the last three years of his life and wrote three books in the house.

Claymont has a tired, yet organic and original feel to it. Although the Georgian-style brick mansion is the grandest in this collection, it feels unpretentious. Perhaps it is due to the way the long narrow driveway winds past a 1930s barn and silo, the scruffy woodsy appearance of the grounds, or the cats that peer out from a second-story window, Claymont Court feels much less ostentatious than its smaller cousins.

Amy Silver, executive director of Claymont, welcomed me to the mansion on a sunny January afternoon—a time of year when the center is usually closed. Amy has lived here since 1982 and works for the Claymont Society for Continuous Education, which has owned the property since 1975. When Amy first arrived on the scene, the society owned 410 acres, and apple orchards still lined Huyett Road. As the trees succumbed to the asphalt and lawns of the housing boom, the society was tempted to sell off some of the property.

"Because of all the development that was going on, running a nonprofit can be financially stressful," Amy said.

The society's finances finally reached a point where nearly 100 acres had to be sold to raise operating capital. "It was pretty much a given that was

Bright, graceful and spacious, Claymont is ideally suited to the work of The Claymont Society for Continuous Education, which has owned the mansion since 1975. The society was led by John G. Bennett, English philosopher and scientist. His nonprofit purchased the property and focuses on lifelong learning and principles of sustainability.

what we had to do. But I think that also informed us that we didn't want to have to do that again," Amy said.

Calling the sale a "big motivator" to become more sustainable, the society placed 265 acres in a conservation easement. Another 25 acres that includes the mansion itself is outside the easement but remains protected by the historic nature of the land.

At 16,000 square feet, Claymont Court is touted as the largest house in West Virginia. It's been used for several film productions, including the movie *Gods and Generals* and an episode of the History Channel's *The Men Who Built America*. The rest of the time, Claymont is essentially a nonprofit retreat center used by spiritual and meditation groups, health care workers, environmental groups and artists. Amy said there's a strong emphasis on organic farming, local foods and sustainability. Rental fees

The Georgian style mansion known as Claymont Court cost $30,000 in 1840. "... he is an innocent good man, and I deplore his weakness and folly in erecting such an expensive building, because a house half or one quarter of the cost would have created as much if not greater real comfort," observed Henry Bedinger, who ran against the successful Bushrod Corbin Washington in the legislative race.

from these various groups provides a modicum of financial support, but the group's nonprofit status as an educational entity excludes using Claymont as a more lucrative venue, like weddings or as a bed and breakfast. And some projects, such as restoring the gardens that once helped defined the mansion's grandeur, simply go undone due to lack of funds.

As an interesting footnote to West Virginia and U.S. history, more Washingtons are buried in Jefferson County than in any other place in the nation. Aside from the Tidewater area of Virginia, no other location is so closely associated with the Washingtons. Harewood, Happy Retreat, and Claymont Court are only three of the eight Washington homes in Jefferson County. They are lavish reminders of a different time and place, but they also underscore an important fact about historic preservation. When even the homes built by our first president's family are threatened by townhouses and subdivisions, are any historic structures safe from modern development?

Few places in West Virginia have had so much controversy about the correct spelling of its name as (according to official sources), Rosbys Rock in Marshall County. Both the name of a town and a boulder, the obscure community was once a thriving hamlet along the Baltimore and Ohio Railroad.

Chapter 17

Rosby, Roseby or Rosbby?

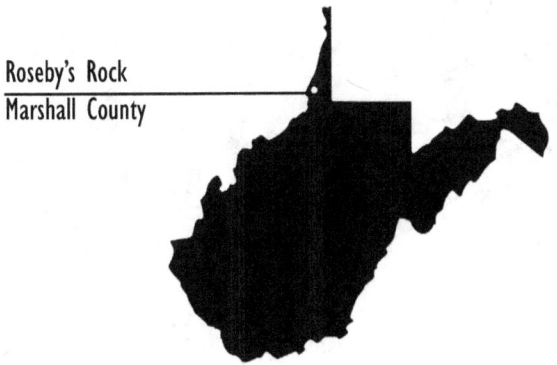

Roseby's Rock
Marshall County

The late Dorothy Lynn Dakan Sedoski was a model of kindness and hospitality. In 2004, she welcomed me and my wife into her Marshall County home at Rosbys Rock, and we spent the afternoon listening to her stories of the remote hamlet and its historical significance. She was a smart, articulate, passionate, determined and thorough researcher of local history, and we enjoyed our afternoon talking with her about her hometown.

Unfortunately, I alienated Dorothy when the editor of *Goldenseal,* John Lilly, went against the grain of her research and declared her hometown "Rosbys Rock, No More, No Less."

"I don't agree with them. I don't agree with them at all," countered Dorothy, who stood by the Roseby's spelling even in death—the author of her obituary used the unconventional spelling. "I use the spelling. I use it all the time," she told me.

Ironically, if one goes by the inscription on the 900-cubic-yard namesake rock, it ought to be "Rosbby's Rock," despite the U.S. Geographic Board's official decision in 1933 to set the name in paper as "Rosbys Rock."

That inscription, said Dorothy, is wrong. It was wrong the day the "well

Dorothy Dakan Sedoski in her Rosbys Rock home, 2004. She grew up in the Marshall County community and insisted upon the Rosbby's Rock spelling.

oiled" stonecutters turned the "e" into a "b," and it's been wrong ever since, insisted Dorothy.

"It was definitely a mistake," she told me as we sat in the living room of her family home near the huge rock. "I don't know why you have to preserve a mistake for posterity."

Dorothy went to great lengths to set the record straight. To celebrate the 150th anniversary of the town in 2002, Dorothy purchased the paint and supplies for four inmates from the Northern Regional Jail and Correctional Facility at Moundsville to paint the inscription and rock so it would read: ROSEBY'S ROCK.

But someone came along and painted in the upper loop on the first "B," once again making it "ROSBBY'S ROCK."

"It's just a shame," Dorothy said. "They really don't know the history of it."

A hollow community along Big Grave Creek, contemporary Rosby's Rock bears little resemblance to the prosperous railroad and farming hamlet in which Dorothy was reared. These B&O beneficiaries had graduated to graveyards by the time I and my wife visited. The new crop of residents were retirees and factory workers or coal miners who drove to Moundsville or beyond for their livelihoods. Most of them lived unaware of their community's history; Robert "Bob" M. Sullivan was the exception.

Bob, who moved to Rosbys Rock in 1973, lived in a farmhouse on the bottoms to the east of the landmark rock and about a dozen yards south of the railroad grade. He had to drive down that old grade to get to his house. Bob recalled a time when freight trains traveled the course that traced his access road. He told me that an average of two freight trains a day crawled past his house in the first few months he lived there.

After the railroad removed the rails and ties, Bob had easier access to his house. But he mourned for what the hollow had lost. "I was heartbroken: No more trains, no more trestles, no more tracks. I liked those tracks and those trains going by," said Bob, a 50-some coal miner in 2004.

Although Dorothy and Bob came from different generations and occasionally clashed over the issue of who had access to the rock—Bob installed a gate across the former rail bed to keep recreational motorized vehicles off the trail—they shared a common respect for and interest in their community's history. Each resident expressed that respect differently.

Dorothy spent much of her free time documenting the story. On the afternoon she met with me at her family home, she brought one bag full of property deeds and a second one of photographs and newspaper clippings, all pertaining to this valley hamlet. These were in addition to two books she wrote, one about Marshall County, a second about descendants of Simon and Elizabeth Martin Dakan.

The story of the rock itself is familiar to Baltimore and Ohio (B&O) Railroad history buffs. The B&O, chartered as the nation's first common carrier, began construction of the line from Baltimore to the Ohio River on July 4, 1828. For the next 25 years, thousands of laborers struggled against wilderness and the Alleghenies' rocks, valleys and heights. On Christmas Eve, 1852, two crews—one working its way east from Wheeling and one working west from Grafton—met at Big Grave Creek and "closed," or completed, the track at 5:20 p.m. (one source states 6:05 p.m.).

A December 28, 1852, article from Wheeling's *The Intelligencer* newspaper states that Roseberry Carr supervised the crew that was working west from Cumberland, Md., while his son, R. Carr Jr., supervised the

Bob Sullivan and his daughter are dwarfed by the huge boulder near their home.

crew working from Grafton. A boisterous celebration was held at the rock upon the track's closing, and speeches were made hailing the great accomplishment.

Stonecutters Hobbs and Ferris were hired to carve an inscription on the face of the sandstone boulder that marked the point of closure. The boulder had most likely fallen off the hillside in an era long before railroad barons made it famous.

The inscription reads: "Rosbby's Rock, Track Closed Christmas Eve 1852." Local legend attributes the misspelling to the stonecutters being drunk, a cumbersome explanation, at best, considering the tedious process of carving a large letter with hammer and chisel. Perhaps, as suggested in a *Goldenseal* article, the stonecutters were simply attempting to abbreviate or phonetically spell Roseberry's lengthy name. Whatever the explanation, the town's name remained a source of debate for decades, even after that official government ruling in 1933.

Although the community's proximity to Moundsville, about eight miles of rail distance, somewhat mitigated its potential for growth, Rosbys Rock nevertheless benefited from the railroad's presence. A school, church, post office, dry goods store/mill, freight/passenger depot and typical services required by a rural community's residents sprang up in response to the prosperity and population fostered by the B&O's presence. The railroad was both employer and economic engine. Farmers profited by raising beef and sheep shipped on the B&O. Every summer, several car loads of wool departed the town on these tracks. The railroad even maintained a stockyard along the Rosbys Rock section.

"It can well be said of Rosbys Rock that it is the biggest little town to be found in a long distance," noted the late Craig Shaw, owner/editor of the *Moundsville Echo*, in 1916. "The town has a business record of which it can well be proud. The good businesses housed there have proved a distinct advantage to all the farmers for miles around, affording them a convenient market for their products as well as giving them shipping facilities at home."

R. G. Dakan, Dorothy's grandfather, was among the businessmen of Rosbys Rock. R. G. was just 19 when he purchased the S. B. Elliott Store in 1882. Later, he also bought out the stock and goods of William Lutes & Son. R. G. had served as a clerk in the William Lutes store and his father's hotel in Clarksburg prior to purchasing the Elliott store.

Dakan's store stocked a complete line of dry goods, notions, groceries, household wares, yard goods, men's work clothing and shoes, farm implements, wagons, and mining and building supplies. He also dealt in cattle and bought and sold wool produced in the Big Grave Creek valley. The store stood on the south side of the tracks. On the north side was the home in which George and Eliza Kull Dakan raised Dorothy and her three siblings.

"We walked out of our front gate and across the railroad tracks to the store," Dorothy recalled.

Their house had been a one-room dwelling that was built a few years before the track was closed. The structure was modified and expanded as each subsequent owner's needs dictated. Henry Faust built the home's second section around 1879. Sometime around 1917, R. G. Dakan purchased the house and shared it with his son George and his family. R. G. eventually moved into an apartment in his store, giving the George Dakan family full use of the two-story frame house. Under the direction of Dorothy's mother, larger windows, a kitchen to the rear of the structure and a row of cabinets along a kitchen wall were added.

Dorothy had nothing but positive memories of growing up in the house and Rosbys Rock. She said that the community's wonderful people defined

Dorothy Dakan Sedoski purchased her childhood home in Rosbys Rock after her mother died. She loved welcoming guests to the home and her community.

Rosbys Rock even more so than the namesake boulder. She fondly spoke of Earl Wellman, his wife and their 11 children, who were like a second family to Dorothy. Wellman was postmaster of the post office in the Dakan store and performed double duty as a store clerk. Joshua "Jot" Hood was assistant postmaster and a first cousin to R. G. Dakan. "They were wonderful gentlemen," said Dorothy, who enjoyed visiting and occasionally playing in her grandfather's establishment.

"We liked to play in the mill, play hide-and-seek in the wool sacks," Dorothy recalled.

The house that belonged to Jot Hood and his second wife, Kathryn (Shutler), stood at the east end of town, near the main bridge that crosses Big Grave Creek from the county road. Dorothy said the owners kept the house in immaculate condition; residents and guests alike were expected to remove their shoes upon entering.

"She even had dollies in the outhouse," Dorothy said. "He had a miniature golf course there, and he was interested in astronomy and would look at the stars and planets from his yard."

Although Rosbys Rock was eight miles from Moundsville and its entertainments, nature provided its own set of diversions for the community's youngsters. They swam in Big Grave Creek in the summer and skated on it in winter. They rode sleds down Bowman Ridge Hill and played football on the commodious, level yards of their neighbors, particularly the former Methodist parsonage that stood to the east of the Dakan family home.

Approximately 1 ½ miles east of the rock is Shepherd's Tunnel, a B&O railroad structure that provided risky recreation for daring youngsters. Dorothy said youngsters who ran through the tunnel did so quickly, although it was not fear of an oncoming train that motivated them.

"The rumor was that someone had once thrown a baby out of the window of the train as they passed through the tunnel," Dorothy said. "That's why we were scared."

The rock was a safer destination. Dorothy said it was a popular place for lads to carve their initials aside those of their sweethearts. Many of these inscriptions remain legible on the boulder's surfaces.

Youngsters who walked the railroad right-of-way to the rock passed the simple home of Jim Lowry, who lived at "Tool Shed Hollow," just below the rock. Lowry's home was a stopover where youngsters could thaw out and be entertained by the antics of this little man who told funny jokes and danced a jig while holding a jug. Dorothy said Lowry also served as the town crier.

"He'd go up the track shouting, 'Rise and shine!'" she recalled.

There were three sets of tracks between the upper (west) crossing and lower (east) crossing, which was near Dorothy's house. One set was the B&O mainline through town. A second set was used for switching, the third a siding that serviced the mill and store.

At the height of the B&O's West Virginia operations, eight passenger and 12 freight trains rolled through the town daily. By the 1930s and 1940s, when Dorothy lived in Rosbys Rock, passenger service had fallen to just two trains daily. Although the massive steam engines passed within a few yards of her bedroom, Dorothy did not recall being awakened by their rumblings, hissing and shrill whistling.

Railroading hobos frequently disembarked at the store and homes in search of a handout. "We got all the hobos at our house," Dorothy said.

"Mother would feed them, but she kept her door hooked. She always had something to make them a nice meal with."

The town faded during World War II. R. G. Dakan died in 1942 and Dorothy's father, who worked in the commissary of the Moundsville Penitentiary, closed the business. Dorothy said an A&P store had opened in Moundsville by that time, and there was no sense in trying to compete. Further, the quality of wool produced in the valley was no match for foreign fibers. Automobile ownership and the trucking industry presented insurmountable challenges for the railroad. The last passenger train stopped in Rosbys Rock on October 26, 1957. Within 15 years, freight traffic on the line had ended, as well.

"By early 1974, there was only one train a week going by my home, hauling supplies out of Moundsville to Cameron. It was just an engine, a couple cars and a caboose," Bob said.

In those final days of B&O operation along Big Grave Creek, many rail buffs made a pilgrimage to Rosbys Rock to visit the tunnel and twin trestles that stood east of it. The railroad contracted to have every trestle removed, the entrances to the tunnels filled with dirt and all the tracks and ties torn out and hauled away.

When I walked back to Shepherd's Tunnel from Rosbys Rock in 2004, I could discern only the top of the stone portal; descending into the abyss would have required the skills, courage and equipment of a spelunker. Further, a large, swampy area—one of Bob's friends calls it a bayou—had formed near the tunnel because of flooding and changes in drainage patterns around the railroad grade. A haven for waterfowl, the bayou was a creepy place inconsistent with the bucolic atmosphere of the Rosbys Rock that Dorothy and Bob once knew. I couldn't walk fast enough to get out of the wetlands with all its copperheads, ticks and mud. I kept thinking, "This would be a great place to dump a body," not that I ever had a need to do that in my life, mind you.

A bit creepy to me, it was home to Dorothy, Bob and a few other souls who found something very special in Rosbys Rock.

"I can remember riding out here on my bicycle when I was 14 years old," said Bob, who grew up in Moundsville. "It was like I found this little place, and it was wow! What is this out here? It was like a whole other world."

"As time went on, I got so I really felt like it was a place to go and collect

Bob Sullivan controlled access to the town's namesake rock on Boulder Road. He had no issues with pedestrians circumventing the gate but was adamant about motorized vehicles otherwise breaking the solitude of life along Big Grave Creek.

my thoughts, and if not that, at least to get away from everything," he said. "I got to thinking, 'I'd like a piece of ground out there.'"

Dorothy left Rosbys Rock after high school and moved to Moundsville but kept close ties to the settlement through her mother, who stayed in the house after George Dakan died. Dorothy helped Eliza maintain the house, which at the time seemed like a burden.

Dorothy's mother, sensing her daughter's passion for the homestead and community, stipulated in her will that Dorothy had first option to purchase the homestead. Dorothy followed through on the opportunity and maintained the home's appearance to that of her childhood, although her primary residence was in Moundsville, where she died May 13, 2015. She was 91.

I wonder if she ever forgave me?

Tom Shipley's painter falling off the barn stops traffic on Route 219. Weather and sun have destroyed several of these dangling effigies over the years he's owned Sharp's Store.

Chapter 18

A Sharp Landmark

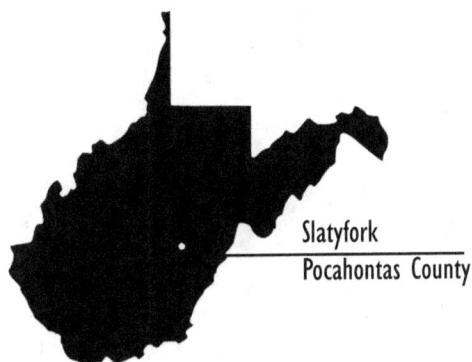

Slatyfork
Pocahontas County

The red covered bridge just off Route 219 at Slatyfork is more memorial than bridge, more "romantic shelter" than transportation link.

Fully functional yet leading only to a pasture and family cemetery, the bridge appeared on the bucolic Pocahontas County landscape in 2005 as a tribute to Dave Sharp, a Cincinnati, Ohio, resident who grew up on the Sharp farm. In 2004 Dave transferred his family's 300-plus acres of farmland and woodlands, tired farmhouse surrounded by a front porch, 19th-century log home, barns, orchards and iconic gas station/museum/antiques store to his great nephew, Tom Shipley, great grandson of L.D. Sharp (1872-1963), Dave's father.

Tom, who grew up in Parkersburg, said his childhood recollection of this historic wide spot on Route 219 centered on its role as a venue for the family reunion. After high school, Tom left the state, became an actor, theatrical producer, wine merchant and antiques dealer far from the mountains of West Virginia.

Through a long and complex chain of events that would endear him to his great uncle, Tom became owner and steward of this tradition.

Tom Shipley had an epiphany as he walked his ancestral property in Slatyfork on New Year's Day 2005. His newfound appreciation for the land shifted his priorities and set him up for a protracted, expensive legal battle.

"I came here at 7 p.m. on December 14, 2004," Tom told me as he stood amid antique showcases and shelves filled with collectibles, museum pieces and homemade items in Sharp's Old Country Store, a Route 219 landmark since the 1920s.

Tom, who had just turned 50 when he was entrusted with the property, felt like his ship had finally arrived. He planned to transport his inventory of antiques to the property and continue his business in the peaceful Little Elk River valley while revitalizing the tourist landmark. He planned to literally "live the high life" by building a modern home on the ridge overlooking the store and tired farmhouse.

"You see things differently when you grow up in the city," Tom told me, recalling his perspective at that time. "I was racking up the dollar signs in my mind."

The morning of New Year's Day, 2005, while strolling around the property following an ice storm, Tom had an epiphany as he took in the stunning landscape.

"It all started welling up inside of me," Tom said. "The tears started

Tom Shipley rings the old dinner bell at his ancestors' home in Slatyfork, property that was slated to become a wastewater treatment plant.

to run down my cheeks. I realized what was so important to my family about this place."

About that time, the Pocahontas County Public Service District notified Tom that his family farm was deemed the best site for the proposed Slatyfork Wastewater Treatment Plant. If necessary, the farm would be taken by eminent domain.

"I was here for an entire two weeks when I got the letter in the mail that called for eminent domain," Tom said. "The county decided it was a good idea to take our farm for a sewer plant."

Tom spent 12 hours a day learning all he could about the eminent domain process, engaged the residents of the county and worked every angle of the debate for three years to block the action. Along the way, Tom learned everything he could about the property and its unique place in Pocahontas County's natural and human history.

"It was the most horrific yet wonderful experience of my life because the people of this county, this state and even this nation came together and fought for us. We ended with this thing called an election, and the people voted out of office every single one of the (project's proponents)."

Tom Shipley's great-grandfather, L.D. Sharp, was the founder of the general store that Tom inherited and has turned into a museum and antique shop along Route 219 between Elkins and Lewisburg.

This happy ending included Tom being installed as head of the sewer district board. But preservation and victory came at a steep personal cost. More than $400,000 and thousands of hours were invested in litigation to defend the property and a way of life. "We were very grateful, but tired and broke," Tom told me in 2008.

It was a test of devotion that not only challenged Tom's commitment to the heritage entrusted to him, but also radically changed his outlook on life. The dollar signs the city boy once racked up in his mind as he walked his property that icy January morning in 2005 morphed into something much more precious. Walk in his store and strike up a conversation with Tom, and he'll tell you about what really matters in his life: heritage, nostalgia, family and Pocahontas County.

The store itself has changed little through the years. Under Tom's ownership it has devolved to its general store roles as a community center and tourist stop. It is, as the signs along the highway tease, "a free museum" featuring "100 years of nostalgia" that Tom loves to share.

"My great granddad, L. D. Sharp, started the store when he was 12 years old, in 1884," Tom said. "There was a one-lane road called the Huttonsvile

Tom's store has a mix of regional merchandise and old stuff.

Turnpike, and if the road went through your property, the state would let you, twice a year, fix the road and then you didn't have to pay taxes."

L.D. went into the retail business selling essentials to the woodsmen who invaded Pocahontas County as the lumber boom engulfed the region. L. D. also dealt in furs as a teenage entrepreneur, according to audio recordings Dave Sharp made of his father.

"He was quite the entrepreneur," Tom said. "He ended up with such a following that they had to build a new store. He didn't want to lose business, so he built the new store on top of and around the little one, and when he was done, he dismantled it and took it out the front door."

The state abandoned the Huttonsville Turnpike in the mid-1920s, necessitating relocation of the store. L. D., who vacationed in Florida during the winter months, decided to add an exotic look to his venture on Route 219. He embedded seashells and coconut shells in the exterior stucco, artifacts that are still there under the layers of paint.

"He did that so local people and travelers could see what Florida was like," Tom said.

The new store catered to the burgeoning automobile-owning public. Four Gilbert and Barker T-26 gravity-fed gas pumps stood in front of the building, which was a Standard Oil, then Esso dealership for many years. Tom restored a couple of those pumps and the store's original red-and-white color scheme.

Ever the entrepreneur, L.D. capitalized on the opportunity that came with a new highway.

"When the road came through in about 1926, he noticed that were a lot of people who would come by and ask for a place to stay . . . and he built about eight or 12 little tourist cabins out of chestnut wood and put that metal-brick facade on them. He loved that stuff and nailed that onto everything he had," Tom said. "He charged a dollar a night, and you got breakfast with that. There were people living in those tourist cabins clear up until the 1960s."

L.D.'s son, Ivan, likewise was an entrepreneur and ran an auto parts store out of one side of his father's general store. Ivan was the oldest of L.D.'s sons, and father of Tom's mother, Ramona, who was born in the farmhouse.

Sharp's was a classic country store in the 1930s and 1940s, a community center dominated by the radio and pot-bellied stove. Today, a modern stereo system that plays digital recordings of old-time string music replaces the radio. As for the stove, Tom said it was sold years ago and is in use in a restaurant, but the owner is unwilling to part with it. He hopes to one day restore it to its place of honor in the store.

"The only thing my family ever sold out of store was that pot-bellied stove," Tom said.

Tom has been more fortunate in retaining many of the artifacts that his grandfather accumulated over the years. Old photographs and curiosities like the skin of a huge Florida rattlesnake fill the front windows. Inside, the paintings of Si Sharp, one of L.D.'s seven children, are randomly displayed.

Silas "Si" used deeply saturated colors to create his folk art paintings that often feature wildlife themes. Tom is constantly looking for Si's paintings, which occasionally show up at sales. He documented at least 40 works attributed to Si. To perpetuate his great uncle's art, Tom sells note cards featuring select works.

Si was the only one of L.D.'s four boys to stay in Pocahontas County. Ivan, Tom's grandfather, eventually left the auto-parts business and moved

Tom Shipley enjoys talking to the motorists who stop at his store to browse the shelves and learn the landmark's history.

to Nitro. Paul went to Texas and Dave to Cincinnati. L.D. transferred the store to Dave when he turned 18, and Dave inherited part of the farm when L.D. died. He acquired the last tract when Si passed. Si, also a watchmaker, either ran the store or hired someone else to do it for him

With the family far flung, Tom grew up not knowing his relatives or the Sharp family heritage in Pocahontas County.

"Three of the four boys had to move out of the area because it was hard to raise a family (here) after the war," Tom said. "So, we didn't know Dave well. "

Dave established himself as a highly skilled and certified watchmaker in Cincinnati, Ohio, but he never lost his love for Pocahontas County. He remained committed to family ownership of the farm and perpetuating the country store, despite its outdated business model. For several years, Dave's daughter, Linda, and her husband, Benny Eduardo, ran it as a grocery store/flea market. Tom said she eventually tired of the restrictive lifestyle.

As Dave neared his 90s, he sought a family member who would carry

Motorists familiar with Route 219 will recall the simple billboards that advertised "Sharps Olde Country Store and Free Museum" to travelers looking for a place to stretch their legs and perhaps buy a souvenir.

on the tradition. Tom, his older brother and sister-in-law made a trip to Cincinnati in 2002 to re-connect with their great uncle.

"Dave was very appreciative of that, and he took us out to dinner. And I remember he left a big old tip for the lady, as he was a very generous man. That was my first introduction to his generosity," Tom said.

Dave's house in Cincinnati was "loaded to the hilt" with antiques purchased at auctions and sales. That common interest provided an immediate connection with Tom, who offered to sell 10 items from Dave's collection on eBay. Dave, 89 at the time, had been planning to dispose of his collection at a yard sale. On eBay, however, the items fetched prices unimaginable to Dave. "Needless to say, I endeared myself to him, he liked me after that. I proved to him I could put fast money in his pocket," Tom said.

The relationship between Dave and Tom quickly moved beyond antiques as Tom continued to help his uncle liquidate the collection.

"Dave needed someone to run the place, and he started calling me at midnight every night for six months," Tom said. "He kept giving me things, trying to get me hooked on the Sharp farm at Slatyfork. And one of the things he gave me was Si's pocketknife. One day he called me, and of course it was midnight . . . I said, 'I happen to be up sitting here at my desk, and I have to tell you, this knife you gave me of Si's is really cool. I use it to cut seeds with, pears and fruit, cut up strings for a package. I just really like that. Thank you for giving it to me.' And he said, 'Oh, that was Si's castration knife.'

"Finally, one day he made me an offer I couldn't refuse. He gave me the farm and the store, and I agreed to give up my home and my business, and I came here. It's been a ride, but I've enjoyed it," Tom said.

Tom commissioned construction of the covered bridge in 2005, during his first year on the farm. The lumber is native poplar for the deck and structural uprights; pine for the siding. Ralph Beckwith sawed the beams; the Hamilton Mill at Huntersville sawed the other lumber. Mill co-owner Pat Hamilton is a Sharp, a direct descendant of the original pioneer settler.

Steel beams that came from a bridge underpin the structure. During a contentious labor dispute, workers blew up the bridge that once led to a coal mine. Dave Sharp bought the steel for scrap and stashed it away with all his other acquisitions on the farm. "He just said, 'I might be able to use that someday,'" Tom said.

When Tom told Dave that he planned to build a covered bridge on the farm to honor him, Dave confirmed his decision. "He said, 'I always wanted a covered bridge . . . and it has to be red.' He said, 'If you'll pay for it, I'll have it built,'" Tom recalled.

Tom selected the site just north of the store because a rope bridge once crossed the creek at that spot. The covered bridge uses a simple king-post truss design and is 50 feet long. Tom estimates the cost at around $40,000.

"Ken Gibson built that in about two and a half weeks," Tom said. "That was a really neat time for me, because we could put our own mark on the farm and see a little progress"

A huge celebration was held for the bridge opening during the family reunion weekend in late May 2005, when all the Sharps return to the farm to decorate graves, honor their heritage and reconnect.

"(Dave) had tears in his eyes," Tom said. "The whole community came out, and we had a fiddler and special music."

Tom's great-uncle, Dave Sharp, made the sign for the covered bridge Tom erected in his honor.

Tom said his great uncle had built, painted and erected along Route 219 several billboards that promoted the store to tourists. During the reunion and bridge dedication, Dave Sharp added another sign to the Route 219 landscape.

"When (the bridge) was finished, Dave came down from Cincinnati. saw him walking around out back. This is a man 90 years old, and he had a saw and an old piece of plywood," Tom said. "I said Dave, 'What are you doing?' And he said, 'I'm making a sign.' And I asked him, 'What's it say?' And he said, 'I'm not going to tell you.' He made an oval sign out of that piece of plywood, and it said, 'Sharp's Kissing Bridge.'"

"I said, 'Dave, a kissing bridge?' He put the date on it and said, 'I need a ladder.' And we went and got it and he supervised me—he did a lot of supervising when he was here—and we put it up there," Tom said.

Dave had to explain the "kissing bridge" concept to his grand nephew.

"When I was a young man, everyone was always out, your mom and pop and all your brothers and sisters, and watching you," Dave told Tom.

Surrounded by history, heritage and the natural beauty of Pocahontas County, Tom Shipley has to admit, "I have a good life."

"And the only place you could get a peck with your girlfriend is when you went to a covered bridge. And that's why it's called a 'kissing bridge.'"

Tom said the red bridge and the store's iconic "falling painter" on the north side of his barn slow traffic and compel many motorists to pull off, snap pictures and tour the store. The painter—an effigy that requires periodic replacing because the sun accelerates destruction of the man's coveralls—was Dave's idea, first placed there more than 50 years ago. Visitors have exported the idea to many other states and venues.

Dave's creative touch also greets visitors as they pass a little car that's parked next to the gas pumps. The car, which has a large "wind-up" key stuck onto its rear end, once stood outside Dave's store in Cincinnati. Tom said Dave stuck a naked female mannequin in the car with her legs protruding through the roof. The mannequin is gone, but in Slatyfork, as in Cincinnati, the car attracts visitors and ignites conversations.

"Come on inside," Tom says to visitors. "Have you ever been here before? No? Well then, I have to be nice to you."

Tom strives to retain the 1926 gas station/museum look of his building

Tom Shipley inherited the log home built by Hugh Sharp, who was Tom's great grandfather's uncle. Robert E. Lee allegedly ate dinner in the structure in 1862.

while generating revenue from the sale of antiques and regional products. He has his own line of jam and jellies made from fruit grown on the farm. The Sharp family had a history of shepherding and beekeeping, and Tom sells local honey and beeswax candles and figures.

Tom plans to restore the log home that was built by Hugh Sharp, L.D. Sharp's uncle, and where General Robert E. Lee ate dinner in 1862. The house stands behind the store and next to the large farmhouse where Tom lives.

For Tom, the eighth generation of Sharps to live in this county, everything has come full circle.

"This is my life," Tom said, as he swept his arm across the property in a wide arc. "It's not the Gettysburg battlefield or anything like that, but I think it's cool. I think I have a good life."

Nearly 15 years after meeting Tom for the first time, I checked in with him again as I worked on this book. He confirmed that their victory in the eminent domain case has held and the land remains under his care. "We have relative peace and quiet now, and it is wonderful!" he said.

Sharp's Store continues to serve the thousands of tourists who travel Route 219 through beautiful Pocahontas County, but Tom has pared back the months of operation to Memorial Day through late October. For hours and days of operation, check the website, https://sharpscountrystore.com.

The Pringle Tree that grows in Upshur County is not the original from the 1700s. It is a grandchild of that tree, which is celebrated at a small park along the Buckhannon River.

Chapter 19

The Pringles' Sycamore

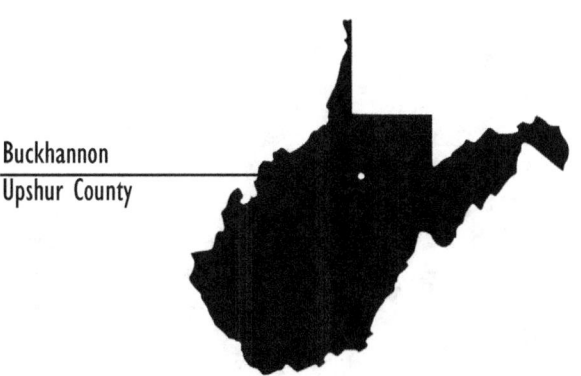

Buckhannon
Upshur County

The pull-off on Route 119 in Upshur County had just enough room for my subcompact, a state historical marker and two picnic shelters before the level ground surrendered to hillside. In its heyday, the spot must have been a pretty one for a picnic or cup of coffee while enjoying a sweeping view of the Buckhannon River.

On this morning in 2014, however, the shingled roofs of the simple shelters gave more sustenance to moss than protection to travelers. It was no place for a picnic unless I would be dining in my vehicle. Just as well; it was the sign, not the potential for "rest" that attracted my attention.

The historical marker declared "Pringle Tree." I immediately envisioned a sharp-eyed youngster shouting for the driver to stop so the passengers could get a better look at the "potato chip tree." Such is the challenge of an economy that monetizes surnames, even those of obscure historical significance.

Born in Philadelphia, brothers John (b 1728) and Samuel (b 1731) Pringle lived on the South Branch of the Potomac River in what was then Virginia. In 1761, while serving in the British garrison at Fort Pitt,

The third generation of the Pringle Tree could not accommodate one person in its trunk.

the brothers and two comrades, William Childers and Joe Linsey, walked away from the fort without permission.

The deserters went AWOL because they despised the king they were fighting for, not because they were cowards. Their journeys took them to Looney Creek in present-day Hardy County, where Childers and Linsey were captured. The Pringle brothers escaped capture and took up with John Simpson, a trapper and trader. Their partnership with Simpson ended at Horse Shoe Bend on the Cheat River; Simpson headed to what would become Clarksburg; the Pringle brothers followed the Tygart Valley to Turkey Run.

Housing was a problem in this wilderness, which made the Pringle Brothers' discovery of a huge sycamore tree with a hollow cavity a godsend. The cavity was so large, a fence rail 8 feet of length could be turned around in it without touching a wall. The question that this often-quoted

The tree's significance to West Virginia's story was recognized more than 100 years ago. The tree that stands there now has been around for at least that long.

fact begs is why would you bring an 8-foot-long fence rail into your hollow tree in the first place?

The Pringle brothers, perhaps securing the opening to that cavity with fence rails, took up residence therein. And they lived in there from 1764 to 1767.

A check with my faithful traveling companion, a dog-eared DeLorme map, indicated that County Road 20-6 would get me within a few hundred yards of the Buckhannon River tributary of Turkey Run, where the tree grew. I headed south on Route 119, toward Buckhannon, and found

County Road 20-6, aka "Pringle Tree Park Road," nestled between the shell of "Christine's Lounge" and a large sign for "BJ's Mobile Home Movers: We move 'em, big or small, one call does it all."

The park road narrowed, and I was soon driving past the beautiful homes I had admired from the overlook. The accommodations looked comfortable and serene, a far cry from the kind of rugged living the Pringle brothers had in this valley. A mile or so down the road, I passed a farm where men were cutting firewood, which raised another question in my mind about this legendary tree: How did the Pringle brothers stay warm in their humble lair? In my experience, trees make good firewood but poor hearths.

A mile or so down the road, I encountered Pringle Tree Park and the culvert over Turkey Run. On this October morning, it was an inconsequential rivulet shaded by weeds and brush for much of its course through a pasture and along the park boundary. The river into which it discharged, however, was substantial and flowing swiftly.

At the far end of the park, near the mouth of Turkey Run, stood the largest sycamore I'd seen in my 60 years. A nearby sign claimed that the tree within the fence enclosure was a grandchild of the original Pringle Tree that sheltered the Pringle brothers.

This ancestor had two massive arms, one of which sent a low-hanging digit some 50 feet distant from the trunk. Its massive brown leaves littered the ground; puffballs of seeds dangled from its twigs, awaiting proper conditions to bring forth another generation of the historic being. And, like its grandfather, there was a cavity in the tree, although not so commodious to accommodate an 8-foot rail.

Back home, with access to technology, I learned from a 2003 message board posting by Jerry Pringle that the original tree fell in the early 19th century; its stump was visible until 1848. The roots brought forth a second tree that a flood washed away in 1880. The current tree emerged at this spot some time afterwards, allegedly an offspring of the Pringle Brothers' famous habitat.

The hardy men eventually ventured back to civilization. By 1768 they had exhausted their supply of ammunition, and John traveled to the South Branch, where he learned at a trading post that the war had ended. Assuming they were no longer wanted by the British, they abandoned their cavity in the sycamore.

Most visitors to the Pringle Tree will say, "Yes sir, that's a big tree," snap a photo and continue on their way. To appreciate it, you need to know the story behind the Pringle Brothers. And, I suppose, to really appreciate its value, you would have to spend a winter living in the wilderness with only a hollow tree for shelter.

Noel W. Tenney, writing in the *West Virginia Encyclopedia,* notes that the Pringle brothers led a small group of settlers into the Buckhannon Valley in 1769. They got off to a bad start when buffalo ate their crops that year. John's path disappears in the wilderness of Kentucky after that.

Samuel finally got the opportunity to militarily show his disdain for the king of England when he served in the Continental Army. He achieved the rank of captain. For all the hardship and difficulties he faced in his life, Samuel Pringle lived to be 99 years old. He is buried in Upshur County.

I wonder if his coffin was made of sycamore?

Orus Ashby "Totter" Berkley walks across the lawn at Sweet Springs Resort, with one of the former cottages behind him. A passionate developer of historic properties with numerous success stories in The Mountain State, he tackled his most ambitious project, Sweet Springs, in the sunset years of his life. Photo from 2021.

Chapter 20

A Vision for Sweet Springs

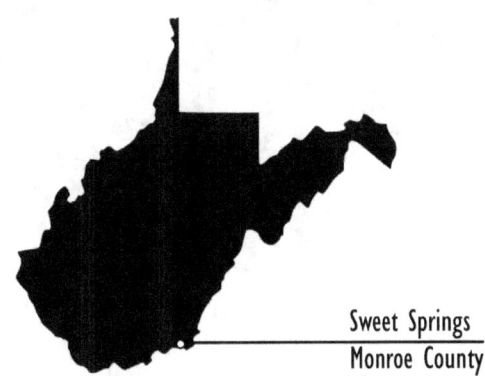

Sweet Springs
Monroe County

Long blades of meadow grass crunched underfoot and deposited frost crystals on my boots as I headed up Peters Mountain toward a lone stone structure set against the hillside. Black Angus cattle bellowed in the distance; crows cawed; the sun yawned, its rays brushing, melting the bucolic landscape. It was Sunday morning, but no church bells rang, no hooves clopped or carriage wheels ground against the curvy macadam of this hamlet a stone's throw from Virginia.

The hotel below this meadow has more than 100 guest rooms, but only ghosts slept there last night. The stone building was once a district courthouse and jail, but this morning could not incarcerate a breath. Like the nearby massive hotel and spring-fed pool, it awaited restoration, repurpose and rebirth on this November morning at Sweet Springs Resort.

Orus Ashby "Totter" Berkley, an octogenarian who lived in nearby Pence Springs, Summers County, was midwife to this labor. The project manager for a 501(c)(3) corporation that owns the hotel property, Ashby has presided over numerous other historic-property rebirths in southeastern West Virginia. They included four historic homes, the Pence Springs

The oldest building on the Sweet Springs property was a jail and county court from the late 1700s.

spring house and the Pence Springs Hotel, formerly used by the Greenbrier Academy for Girls. Owned by Sweet Springs Resort Park Foundation, Inc., this property promised to be a long, difficult birth for Ashby.

"I love to do restoration," Ashby told me as he led a tour of the resort the prior afternoon. "It's not so much about the work, but I like to save the history. To me, that's more important. Otherwise, we're constantly reinventing ourselves. And it is amazing how much more advanced (the builders of these 19th-century buildings) were than we are now. We are not nearly as smart as we think we are."

Old Sweet, as Sweet Springs Resort is also known, was Ashby's most ambitious effort in the realm of historic preservation. It is a massive project, and he correctly prophesied that it would take more years to complete than those he had left. Accordingly, he organized the effort under an umbrella of foundation ownership, with a board of directors capable of carrying on Ashby's vision long after he also became history.

"If the Lord takes me home tomorrow, that's all right," Ashby told me. "But I don't want that to happen, because I want to see this place up and running. I want, for one time, for (Monroe County) and this area to

The main hotel part of Sweet Springs exhibits the influence of Thomas Jefferson in its design. The stunning building has had many uses in its long lifetime, and Ashby Berkley had a vision for developing the property to meet 21st-century needs and interests.

realize that this place can be a gold mine, just like Pence Springs was. You just got to put forth the effort."

Ashby made the purchase in November 2016 after years of pursuing acquisition. In the relatively brief span of foundation ownership, more progress was made toward saving the antebellum resort than was accomplished under the string of owners since 1993, when The State of West Virginia shuttered the Andrew S. Rowan Memorial Home, occupant of Sweet Springs since 1945.

Over a meal of pasta and salad prepared by my host, a retired executive chef, Ashby told me that thousands of volunteer hours and roughly $1 million had already been invested in the foundation's efforts to save the Sweet Springs structures. He felt that the key to its preservation was finding 21st century uses for a 19th-century behemoth. The building in which we met, once a brick cottage where family groups stayed while drinking the spring water and bathing in the blue-green pools, was an example of that vision. The only one of the extant cottages to be restored, it gave visitors a taste of what could be accomplished given enough money, volunteers, vision and cooperation from the state.

We exited the cottage through a side door and walked toward the massive brick hotel with its four neoclassical porticoes and 17-foot-deep piazza extending the building's entire length and intermittently covered by the porticoes. Ashby shared his vision for each section of this structure.

The lawn and trees of Sweet Springs are reasons enough to visit the astounding Monroe County property on an autumn morning.

The east end would be a country inn with a colonial theme. The next section would be for extended-stay lodging, three days to three months. The third section, the one nearest to W.Va. Route 311, would accommodate an eclectic collection of commercial, office, professional and retail space in the former guest rooms. It would become a hotel, conference center, business center and health spa.

He also envisioned a youth center that would serve local disadvantaged and inter-city youth with a soccer field, tennis courts, putting greens, amphitheater and nature-related activities. In shops and other training facilities on the grounds, youth would learn historic trades and skills like wood turning and stonemasonry, then put them to use saving Old Sweet. A veteran-operated organic farm and history museum were part of the plans, as well as a functional bathhouse and pool fed by the spring water that stays at 72 degrees year-round.

"It will be perfect for a sports training facility for children," Ashby

Cottages offered an alternative the springs' hotel rooms for guests who needed more space.

said. "Our objective is to restore this place and use it to the best purpose to support itself. It's just too beautiful to let go."

Ashby recognized that all these activities would not provide the critical mass necessary for sustainability. To fully develop Old Sweet's potential, the foundation needed access to the Peters Mountain land that rises above the complex. However, the foundation owned only 33 acres, the land occupied by the resort, and leased another 600 from the West Virginia Department of Agriculture. When I spoke with Ashby in November 2021, ongoing access to that land was in jeopardy as the state had expressed plans to break the lease. Champions of Sweet Springs and Berkley's work took to social media to pressure the state to reverse its stance.

"I am a native West Virginian," wrote Michael M. Barrick of the *Appalachian Chronicle blog*. "I know there is no place else in the state like Sweet Springs. It must be preserved. The architecture; its unique history in antebellum America, in particular the South; and, most importantly, its many natural springs of some of the purest water in the world, make this a true state treasure."

Ashby Berkley looks into the bathhouse area, which is fed by springs that flow from Peter's Mountain. The alleged health benefits of the water drew guests from all over the East Coast.

Sweet history

This treasure rises above the otherwise prosaic farming community as an architectural oddity, an anachronism and remnant of antebellum-America's fascination with the summer resort and mineral springs. Peters Mountain is the source of at least seven such springs, one of which supplies the water that made Sweet Springs famous and flows as a thread of continuity through a saga of many owners, visions and failures.

William Lynn Lewis and offspring recognized the potential of the springs and made something of it. Lewis got the property through a land grant from King George III—most likely William's share of the 8,000 acres that his father received. John Lewis was founder of Augusta County, Virginia—mother to most of West Virginia, as well as Kentucky, Ohio, Indiana, Illinois, Michigan, Wisconsin and southwest Pennsylvania. Circa 1780, William built a frame house, believed to have been the first west of the Alleghenies, on the property that would become Sweet Springs Resort.

Within a decade of building their homestead, the Lewis family opened

Ashby Berkley walks across the lawn of Sweet Springs with the main hotel building in the background. Construction of the 90,000-square-foot building began in 1833 and took five years to "complete."

the spring's amenities to guests. Individuals stayed in log houses, while families had their choice of furnished cabins with up to four rooms. At least one guest in 1804 considered the accommodations superior to those at White Sulphur Springs. The food was plentiful and, despite the water's medicinal qualities, "the banner of society" flew "above the banner of the invalids," according to one writer.

William's grandson, Dr. John B. Lewis, further elevated that banner with construction of the 90,000-square-foot building that became Sweet Springs Hotel. Approximately 240 by 48 feet, the two-story building was built with bricks made from clay on the property. Construction began circa 1833 and continued for five years.

William Burke, who owned a rival resort at Red Sulphur Springs, admitted that "Dr. Lewis has just now finished a house which for architectural beauty and accommodations is superior to any house for the same use in the United States that I have seen." The main floor dining room was 160 feet long and had additional 40-foot-wide spaces on each end. A ballroom and ladies' room also were on this floor. Thirty-six spacious bedrooms were on the second story, and the ground floor "basement" provided room for the kitchen, mechanical systems and administration.

The generous use of arches and original five-part architecture—three porticoes connected by two "hyphens"—suggested either the drawing pen or influence of Thomas Jefferson. Ashby supports the former, although Jefferson died eight years before construction began. His Jefferson-design stance is based upon court testimony, the opinion of expert architects and Jefferson's practice of not signing his architectural plans. "Jefferson (drew) a design that he did not build," Ashby said. "That's where the confusion comes in."

S. Allen Chambers, in his *Buildings of West Virginia,* presents a case for William B. Phillips as builder. A master builder at the University of Virginia, Phillips would have been familiar with Jefferson's penchant for neoclassical architecture, thus the Jeffersonian influence cannot be dismissed. "In sum, had it not been for Jefferson, Phillips could hardly have designed such a building," concluded Chambers.

The new building elevated the hotel far above competitors in the springs resort market and made it a destination for the antebellum elite. Guests included eight of the nation's first 10 presidents. Other famous users included Patrick Henry, Robert E. Lee, the Marquis de Lafayette and Napoleon's brother, Jerome. That unlikely latter claim was based upon a stage production, "Glorious Betsy," set at Old Sweet and featuring a love story between Jerome and a Baltimore belle.

Building an attraction that appealed to this class of clientele severely stressed Old Sweet's cash flow. By the early 1850s, Dr. Lewis was forced to sell the asset to cover his $34,000 debt. Oliver Bierne and Allen T. Caperton of Union purchased the resort in 1852 and expanded its footprint. The bathhouse, which faces the hotel at the far end of the lawn, was constructed under this new partnership. Attributed to Henry Exall, the bathhouse featured two brick towers interpreted as either ecclesiastical or military bookends to the facade. The towers flanked the open brick arcade fronting the two gender-specific pools.

A row of brick cottages filled the space between hotel and bathhouse. Three survive. Bierne even had plans to build a second hotel, mirroring the grandeur and scope of the first, opposite the original.

Guests—nearly 2,800 of them signed the register in 1859—poured into the valley to enjoy the waters, food and accommodations in the summers before war came and Northern troops took control of the valley. While invaders respected the structures, social, transportation and economic changes in the decades following the conflict were unkind to springs resorts. Sweet Springs struggled through the era of decline, and in 1902, Cam Lewis, son of C.C. Lewis Sr., returned the dinosaur's ownership to the clan. The resort did well for several years, but not well enough to keep Cam out of hawk; Bierne and his brother repossessed it. Cam's father stepped in and redeemed it a few years later. An uncle, John, ran it until 1920, when it was sold out of the family once again. Eight years later, following a string of owners, it was closed.

D.N. Taylor, a Roanoke, Va., investor purchased it for $30,000 in 1938 and "flipped it" to the State of West Virginia three years later for $150,000. There was a short, unsuccessful attempt to operate it as tuberculosis sanatorium. The state was more successful in reinventing it as the Andrew S. Rowan Memorial Home for the Aged, which opened in 1946. The state renovated the original structure and expanded its capacity with a backside addition in 1950. Two three-story wings constructed in 1974 further increased the home's census. The architect, Henry Elden & Associates, replicated the hotel's architecture during that project. Unfortunately, the expansion sacrificed some original structures, and the state showed little regard for preservation of the cottages, former courthouse/jail and bathhouse, all of which fell into disrepair.

Ashby said that the Rowan complex lived up to its "home" moniker. "The old people loved it here. They had these little beds of lettuce, and little flower gardens, and took long walks up to the old cemetery on the hill. It was something else," Ashby said. "And when they closed it, it just broke my heart because they had a home here. It wasn't an institution, you know, and they were all country people, out here in the country, and the (locals) would talk to them about their crops and their food. And the food here was wonderful."

He spoke from experience. His father, Orus Berkley, was a World War II veteran who made his home at Rowan in his sunset years. Grace Smith Berkley, Ashby's mother, worked at the West Virginia State Prison for Women, which was housed in what had been the Pence Springs Hotel.

The hotel opened in 1918 and closed in 1929; the state purchased it and remodeled the hotel as a prison in the 1940s.

Ashby went to school in Charleston, but his weekends and vacations were spent in Summers County, on the south side of the Greenbrier River at Pence Springs. He spent many hours at the prison, where Grace was kitchen manager, correctional officer and assistant warden to its 90 inmates. Ashby said his mother went beyond the call of duty by housing prisoners' children who came long distances for one- or two-hour visits on Sundays.

"And then they'd have to go back home, and God knows when that mother would get to see then again," Ashby said. "Well, my mother would bring (the children) home to spend the week with us so they could spend another Sunday with their mother. We never knew how many or who was going to be at the breakfast table ... we didn't question where mom was because she was either delivering a baby or getting a (deceased) old person ready to go the funeral home."

In *Goldenseal* stories by Maureen Crockett ("Doing Time in Style: The State Prison for Women at Pence Springs" and "Pence Springs Resort Lives Again," Summer 1990), Ashby recalled how he and his childhood friend Ashby Maddy played on the prison grounds and became acquainted with the prisoners. "The boys ran through the prison at will. They played canasta with the inmates," Crockett wrote.

Ashby Maddy also recalled his friend's childhood interest in the restaurant business. In Crockett's "Resort Lives Again" article, Ashby Maddy recalled how Berkley cleaned out a stall in the family barn and converted it to a restaurant setting where he served friends "wine and roast pheasant under glass." In reality, the meal was peanut butter sandwiches under a glass bowl with a glass of cherry Kool-Aid.

Following graduation from Charleston High School, Ashby pursued a culinary career, working as a secretary to pay his way through the Culinary Institute of America. He interned at The Greenbrier and got a scholarship to study wines and food in France and Germany. Back in the states, he turned entrepreneur, purchasing and renovating the former summer home of Governor Henry Hatfield, reborn as Riverside Inn. With Ashby as chef, the Jamestown-period inn received international recognition as one of the world's best 300 restaurants. That led to Ashby's involvement in the West Virginia Hospitality and Travel Association, on which he served

Ashby Berkley saved the former Pence Springs women's prison from demolition and transformed it into a hotel and restaurant. It was home to the Greenbrier Academy for Girls 2007-2023.

as a board member. His impact on the industry extended to consulting and teaching contracts with previous communistic nations that sought to attract American tourists.

"I think it was about 10 years, and during that time, the state loaned me to the federal government. I worked in post-communistic countries teaching tourism and marketing. That was a wonderful job. I did that in six or eight countries," he recalled.

In the early 1970s, Ashby began acquiring properties of both personal and historical significance, including the lowland Pence Springs property, which he purchased with his brother and developed into an outdoor flea market. By that time, the women's prison had deteriorated to the point the state planned to bulldoze it and build a new one on the site. Ashby worked with Fred Long, Steve Trail and the state's Historic Preservation Office to get the property listed on the National Register of Historic Places in 1985. However, convincing the state to stop the bulldozers and sell the property to him required creativity and a bit of deception.

"I said, 'You're going to spend a whole lot more money (building a new prison) and you're going to destroy this historic structure.' I said, 'I'll buy the hotel, and I'll restore it. And they fought me and fought me,'" Ashby recalled.

He attempted to get a meeting with Corrections Commissioner W. Joseph McCoy, but his requests were ignored.

"I'd call every third day or something like that," Ashby recalled. "They were just too important to see me. So, I called him up and told his secretary, 'Please tell the commissioner that I had that property surveyed and that you all built that fence between me and you, and you are 6 feet over on my property.' This was on a Monday. And I said, 'I want to meet with him this week. If I don't hear back from him, if I don't get that meeting, I'm going to take my tractor and I'm going to pull that damn fence down over the hill because it's on my property.' And the phone rang within 30 minutes."

The meeting was scheduled for two days later, and after getting settled into the commissioner's office, Ashby admitted the survey story was a "damn lie" but the only way he could get the audience and attention he needed. "Well, he mellowed out a bit, and we got it. They put it up for auction, and I paid $310,999 for it and restored it," Ashby said.

The project involved eleven banks, most of which had loaned $25,000 each and required its approval for any changes to the work or business. "I had to go through 11 different bank boards, and sometimes it would take six months or more, or I wouldn't get an answer at all. A couple of times I had to pay 18 percent interest when for everybody else it was around 6. But we managed it and got through."

The revived Pence Springs Hotel had 22 rooms and a restaurant with a stellar reputation, thanks to Ashby's culinary skills. Ashby and his wife, Katrina, tired of that hectic lifestyle and decided to move to Mexico. They closed the Riverside Inn in 1996 after a Greenbrier River flood caused extensive damage (the building later burned). And in 2007, they sold the Pence Springs Hotel that was so significant to Ashby on both personal and professional levels. But life in Mexico was complicated, and Ashby missed the heritage of his home state. They returned to the Summer/Monroe counties region, where Katrina died.

"And I got tired of sitting around, so I decided I was going back to work, and this came on the market and I came over here and bought it," he said of Sweet Springs.

The state had donated the property to Monroe County following closure of the home for the aged in 1993. Monroe County borrowed $1.3 million from the Bank of White Sulphur Springs to renovate the property and open a drug addiction treatment center there. That plan fell flat, and the county defaulted on the loan. The property went to auction in 1995 and was purchased by Dr. Vasu Arora of Grundy, Va. His plans to bottle water and re-open the facility evaporated from lack of funding. The next owner, Warren D. Smith, purchased it in 2002 and bottled the water under the Sweet Sommer label. In January 2008, Smith entered the spring water in the International Water Tasting Festival, where it ranked in the top 10 entries.

Smith, a realty company owner and member of the National Trust for Historic Preservation, had ambitious plans for Sweet Springs, but, once again, financial issues thwarted germination. He died in 2010, by which time the West Virginia Division of Culture and History had designated Sweet Springs one of the state's most valuable and endangered historic resources. The property languished for five years as Smith's estate moved through the judicial system.

"We were told that a gentleman wanted to raze the buildings and put in a mobile home court here," Ashby said. "And I thought, 'Oh, my God, we surely can't let this building and all this history go and have trailers in here.' I was so depressed about it, I could sit down and cry."

Rather, Ashby went to the bank and arranged financing. The property went to auction November 12, 2015, and Ashby purchased the site, appraised for $10 million some 14 years earlier, for $560,000.

Ashby applied his experience with the Pence Springs Hotel to Sweet Springs, placing the project under a foundation rather than personally carrying the financial and administrative burdens. The foundation operates on grants, donations and fundraisers. Further, all the staff and board members are unpaid, and the foundation has no debt.

"I'm supervisor, if you want to call me a supervisor. I'm a damned poor one because I'm a butterfly, I flit around too much," Ashby said.

The progress by 2022 included stabilizing the roof on the main building, renovation/opening of one cottage and transforming the former Lewis home into an income-generating hospitality property. There were plans to develop the full potential of the springs, upon whose reputation the entire complex had floated for two centuries.

"They quicken the circulation, impart tonicity and vigor to the system,

Sweet Springs Hotel is just a few feet off W.Va. Route 311 at the Virginia border. It rises against the bucolic countryside like a beautiful anachronism in a prosaic dream.

excite the animal passions, cheer the spirits, and inspire the mind with pleasurable sensations," observed Dr. William Burke of these waters in 1857. Even aged persons, free of organic disease, would "find youth and vigor and elasticity at the bottom of this noble fountain," according to Burke.

"So, it's a case where the springs built the property," Ashby said. "And the springs are going to help save the property."

Potential paths include bottling and marketing the water to Europeans. Based upon his observations of European tastes, he predicted residents would "pay a fortune" to access the water Americans take for granted. He also envisioned a "water club" concept, which would periodically ship a case or two of Sweet Springs water to the subscriber.

Having control of and access to the leased parcel on the slope of Peters Mountain, where the water originates, was essential to success. Ashby said he never would have purchased the place if the lease for an additional 625 acres had not been in place.

"(The) 33 acres (the foundation owns) would not do what we need to do," Ashby said. Having access to the mountain would make the difference between success and one more failed effort to revive and restore the landmark.

"This property will employ between 250 and 400 people," Ashby said. "This is a big operation. There's tremendous potential. It's a great location; we are within five to six hours of 60 percent of the U.S. population."

Walking the property with Ashby that early November afternoon, I felt overwhelmed by the enormity of the task, yet encouraged by Ashby's determination and track record. Understandably, locals did not share his enthusiasm and had been slow to embrace his grandiose vision. They have seen too many projects at the old property run out of steam long before generating any meaningful contributions to the local economy.

"Monroe is an agricultural county," Ashby told me. "(Residents) are still holding their breaths, they don't know what we are doing."

Ashby promised that, under his watch, Sweet Springs would never revert to institutional use; it has the land, heritage and amenities to make it a first-class destination. The nonprofit's volunteer board had already invested $1.3 million. Unpaid volunteer hours leveraged the grants, donations and fundraiser revenues that Sweet Springs received. Several events were held at the resort and drew crowds much larger than anticipated. Encouraged by this response, the board stayed true to Ashley's vision, which is backed by a solid track record.

After Ashby purchased the women's prison at Pence Springs, he heard Senator Jay Rockefeller tell an aide as they toured the building, "This time Ashby has bitten off more than he can chew." But, as Ashley told me before I left Sweet Springs that afternoon, "you got to put forth the effort."

"We will slowly be getting it done," he said.

Orus Ashby "Totter" Berkeley died October 12, 2024. The status and future of his Sweet Springs Project is in the hands of the Sweet Springs Resort Park Foundation, Inc., online at sweetspringsresortpark.org/.

The author, at 5 feet 6 inches, had to bend down to enter Shepherdstown Little House on the campus of Shepherd University.

Chapter 21

The Little House

Shepherdstown
Jefferson County

The imposing McMurran Hall at the northeast corner of German and King streets is arguably Shepherdstown's most iconic building with its Greek Revival architecture and stunning clock tower. But for many tourists and locals, the real icon of this Jefferson County town is about one-tenth the height of McMurran Hall and was built for youngsters rather than county government and higher education.

The Little House is made of sandstone in the Dutch colonial revival style. The 1 ½ story home has three gabled dormers that pierce the gambrel roof and provide a view of West Princess Street. It's the kind of house that any college professor would be proud to come home to at the end of a long day—if only he could stretch out in it and clear the ceiling. The house is but 10 feet at its widest and tallest; first-floor ceilings are 5 feet, 6 inches.

On the ground floor is a 6-by-9-foot living room, the largest room in the house. Amenities include a fireplace, sofa, chair and bookcases. The dining room is 5-by-5½ feet; the kitchen, 3 by 6 feet. Up a narrow staircase, three bedrooms and a bathroom await, with 4½ foot ceilings.

Also known as the Florence Shaw Demonstration Cottage, this beloved

The Dutch colonial revival style Little House is dwarfed by Shepherd University's human resources building on the left and White Hall on the right.

structure is tucked between the human resources building and White Hall on the campus of Shepherd University. The university owns and maintains the structure. It is open, by schedule and appointment, to all who stoop to enter.

"It's the most popular place in Shepherdstown," Jan C. Hafer, director of the Shepherdstown visitor's center, told me back in 2014. "When it's open, we'll get 200 people going through there. It's magical. It's really special."

"It's a cute little house," observed the late Jay Hurley, who grew up in Shepherdstown during the 1940s and loved to tell the backstories related to its construction. "Everybody loves it."

The Little House was a project of Florence Shaw, professor of elementary education, and Edith Thompson, college supervisor of observation and teaching. Charged with developing a summer-session, teacher-training program, Florence and Edith envisioned a miniature farm where student teachers could practice classroom theory on real students.

"It was projected as something which would attract children of 12 and 13 years in the Summertime, so that the teacher-students attending Summer School at Shepherd College might have some 'raw material' with

Charlie "Moustache" Jones was the stone mason who built the Little House. *Scarborough Library at Shepherdstown University collection.*

which to accomplish their training," reported *The (Shepherdstown) Register* newspaper as the building neared completion.

On Princess Street there was, behind the tennis courts, an unused parcel, "a brush patch and dumping grounds." Florence Shaw set her sights on this lot for the laboratory; her project would both raise the teaching skills of the summer-session students and remove an eyesore from the community.

She approached Dr. W. H. S. White, who was president of the Shepherd College State Normal School. He embraced the plan and pledged money from the college's repair and improvement fund to cover expenses. Indeed, he liked the plan so much that he insisted they expand their project to encompass the entire lot and make the structures permanent.

White felt the ambitious but noteworthy project would "solve the problem of adequate enrollment of pupils for Summer Demonstration School." Objectives of that school were:

❖ "Create situations that will provide opportunity for the growth and development of every individual who will in any way be connected with the demonstration school." Specifically, students would feel the joy of work, "whether it be the work of the mind or the hand," and increase their appreciation of the world's workers; and encourage the exercise of

A bedroom in the Little House had scaled-down furniture built for the project.

initiative and self-expression on the part of every individual while maintaining a cooperative atmosphere;

❖ Help both teachers and students realize that "success in life depends on our adjustment to our environment";

❖ Grasp the concepts of the problem method of teaching by providing teachers a laboratory for testing their skills at executing theory.

Public school teachers at that point in U.S. history were being immersed in new teaching techniques such as unit plan, contract, project-problem method and direct experience. Professional literature oozed with these buzzwords, but education professors were uncertain of their suitability to schools in West Virginia. The college's literature for the experiment promised an opportunity for immersion in "creative activity," "group processes" and "democratic procedures."

"It was not easy to bridge the gap between the old traditional type of classroom procedure and the 'problem-project' method, but the group of student teachers who enrolled for Grades 4-6 was made up of mature, experienced teachers who were courageous," Florence Shaw wrote in a description of the project. "They had a fine attitude, too, and lost no time in getting started. The more mature teachers worked well with the younger

The living room of the Little House was comfortable for a child or two.

ones and soon they were all getting enough joy out of achievement that they were ready to try things out with the Summer School pupils who were not to come until the second week."

At the heart of this process was using a real-life problem as a learning experience, to wit: "What adjustments did the pioneers of the Shenandoah Valley have to make to their natural environment in order to establish homes and make a living for their families?"

To Florence Shaw, the neglected lot offered challenges similar to those that existed in the Shenandoah Valley wilderness, albeit on a child-sized level. The lot's overgrowth represented wilderness; piles of construction debris stood in for the valley's limestone mountains. Town Run, a spring-fed brook that rambles through Shepherdstown in a stone-lined course, represented the Shenandoah River. Bridges had to be built so crops could be moved to storage structures and livestock to shelter and market.

The challenges posed by this real-world scenario required a multi-disciplinary approach, from language to math, from home economics to agriculture. Students wrote letters to farm families in the valley and asked questions about their heritage. The customs, hardships, and literature of the settlers were studied. Designing the house and plotting gardens involved mathematics. Committees formed to deal with every aspect of the project led to an understanding of government and democracy.

The summer of 1928 was the first session to use The Little House project. According to a document in the Shepherd University Archives, A.D. Kenamond was director of the summer school that year and I.O Ash was head of the education department. John H. Newcome, head of the agriculture department, assisted with the farm aspects of the project. And Florence Shaw and Edith Thompson supervised the instruction and directed observation.

The demonstration class students (teachers) were Florence Grubbs, Edna Bauserman, Pauline Staubs, Mildred Rowe, Chester White, Delbert Arbogast, Ancile Gray, Laura Thompson, Mollie Trout, Pearl Hutton, Olive S. Cooper, Allison Rider, Alice Harlin, Mary Howell, Hazel Shrader, Lakey Swartz, Martha Warner, George Nolan and Lane Moler.

The summer school got under way in early June. After the first week of preparatory classroom instruction, youngsters arrived on campus to work with the student teachers. The youngsters, in grades in 5 and 6, were Mary Catherine Rouze, Elizabeth Knode, Lawrence Burgan, Charles Owens, Billy Thatcher Jr., Jean Skinner, Louis Whittington, McKee Price, Thadeus Knode, Pershing Knode, Walter Whittington and Eilen Jones.

Committees went to work on the property in the following weeks, drawing plans for the house, garden, bridge and barn. Students did as much as they could to prepare the land for construction of the cottage. A Mr. Martin, who lived near the Little Farm, noticed that the youngsters were having a difficult time staking off the foundation. He went home, grabbed his surveying equipment and helped them complete their task.

Elsewhere on the project, Laskie Stanley and A.J. Stanley worked as carpenters and a Mr. Jenkins and Mr. Sanbower hauled construction materials. Atlas Cement donated the cement and Johns Mansfield Co. of New York donated standard roof shingles, which were cut down to maintain proper proportions on the Little House. Parents of demonstration school children provided refreshments and assistance; Jim Washington, the college janitor, "helped us over the hard places when our work became too heavy for us," Florence Shaw wrote.

Charlie "Mustache" Jones, "one of the finest (stone masons) in the Shenandoah Valley," built the house from native stone.

Jones, who lived on Jones Alley, now Rocky Street, in Shepherdstown, had a reputation for more than fine stonework. Florence wrote that she had been "warned by doubting Thomases that he was undependable and alcoholic." The professors put their faith in Jones and hired him for the task, despite the warning.

The project ran into trouble when Charlie Jones saw their plans for a 10-foot-wide cottage that called for an 8-inch wall. He told the committee that "there never was an 8-inch wall" and stone could not be cut to that dimension. Undaunted, Florence Shaw promised that the students would find a way to cut the stone if he would build the walls. Jones mumbled that he'd see what he could do about it, and the project moved forward—for a while.

Jay Hurley said that the story around Shepherdstown is that Jones reached a point where he grew tired of sobriety and working on the house. Florence Shaw, a diminutive lady, struck a deal with the stonemason; she would get him "a couple of bottles of the good stuff" from a bootlegger in Frog Hollow.

"So, she got in her horse and buggy, went across the bridge and went about eight miles into Frog Hollow," Jay said. "She knocked on the door and the man inside asked for a password. And she said, 'You know,' and he let her in and sold her the hooch. And she took it back to Jones and in front of the committee gave it to him. He was shamed into getting back on the job."

Florence Shaw makes no note of this incident, but she gave a resounding endorsement to Jones and his workmanship.

"The Little House stands today as a monument to his skill and dedication to a cause," Florence Shaw wrote in her story of the project. "He was so proud of his achievement that as long as he was able, he'd walk by and stand and admire it."

Jones received offers outside Shepherdstown to build fireplaces and other stone structures. No matter how attractive the offer, Mustache Jones refused to leave his community.

While Jones worked on the house, the professors, student teachers and youngsters tackled the job of clearing the lot. During the process, a lone grape vine was discovered and an arbor was built for it. Groups of students cleared, fenced and planted garden plots. A professor from the college's science department made a display of common garden pests and shared it with the fledgling gardeners.

Florence Shaw described the soil as soft, black and easy to work. "The soil was just right for everything we planted," she wrote. Rose and mock orange bushes were planted on the site, which was under a large weeping willow tree.

The Little Farm's barn evolved in its purpose and size. Initially, the concept was a simple structure to provide shelter and security for garden tools. But teachers and their students needed a space to construct objects for home and garden; the barn morphed into a workshop. In its final incarnation, the barn became a "club house" for students who worked on the miniature farm project.

Carpenters Laskie and Arch Stanley led the barn construction project, which was aided by student teachers and professors. "There was hardly a space (in the barn) to wield a hammer" Florence Shaw wrote.

Originally much closer to the house, the barn was relocated in 1974. Also, there were originally two bridges across Town Run, since replaced by a single concrete span.

Many of the original furnishings in The Little House have gone by the wayside over the years, and the interior is (sadly) equipped with plastic kitchen appliances and dishes. A newspaper story from the construction period states that Potomac Edison had the house wired for 120-volt service and even installed a small electric stove in it.

President White had a copper box made that was placed in the cornerstone during a ceremony. Its contents were a 1928 Lincoln penny, a listing of all who worked on the project and this declaration: "We who have labored over the building of this little farm leave the results of our labor in the hands of those who follow us. The best wish that we can leave for all who will work on this little farm through all the years that are to come is that the same spirit that guided and strengthened them will reign over them."

What began as a project to build a "temporary" structure ended up taking two summers. It cost the college $1,000; in the history of the institution, it was probably the best grand ever spent on public relations.

The *Washington Sunday Star* ran a lengthy article that was reprinted in the Jefferson County papers. The *Baltimore Sun* and *Washington Post* also reported on it. Children of the American Revolution heard about the project and devoted a page to it in their publication. *National Geographic* and *Better Homes and Gardens* also gave it press.

Broadcaster Lowell Thomas delivered the commencement address at the college and saw The Little House during his visit. That led to a film crew from Universal News Reel visiting the town the following year and filming a segment for the newsreel series "Personoddities."

The film was made during World War II and many troops saw it through the USO service screenings. The sight of their community and The Little House on the big screen buoyed those Shepherd students who had put their studies on hold to serve in the military.

A scrapbook in the Scarborough Library's Shepherd College Collection documents how Shepherdstown's children and families adopted the house and grounds as their special place. It became a meeting place for the children's garden, reading and dramatic clubs. The farm hosted picnics and birthday parties. A circus used the grounds for its Shepherdstown engagement; children dressed up as animals and paraded down the street to the adults' amusement.

Youngsters who came under the house's spell developed affectionate names for the building, calling it "Peter Pan and Wendy's House." Many years after The Little House project ended, Florence Shaw wrote an account of its history. She wrote then what is true to this day, "it still has that 'Strange Drawing Power' for all who love little homes and little children!"

The Little House is located at 120 N. Princess Street, Shepherdstown.

Westbrook's Esso in Kingwood is a restored 1920 service station that serves as a repository for a portion of Tom Westbrook's automotive memorabilia collection. He also owns a former Dodge dealership building in Kingwood, where he secures his collection of classic vehicles.

Chapter 22

A Baby Boomer's Babies

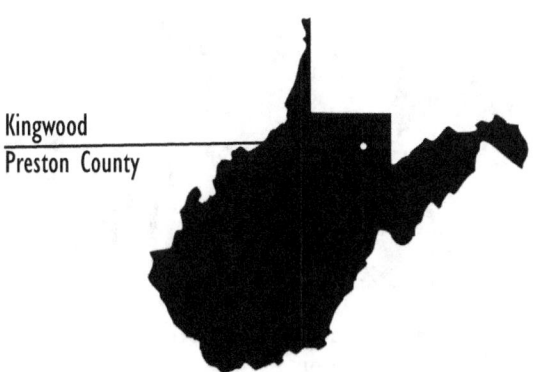

Kingwood
Preston County

Tom Westbrook is a Baby Boomer. So am I. We share a passion for the cool stuff that our made our childhoods a memorable, if not legendary, American cultural experience.

I collect and preserve old photos and films (8mm, 16mm); Tom collects the Great American Road Trip.

His vast collection includes Westbrook's Esso, a landmark 1920s service station in Kingwood, the county seat of Preston County.

You can't buy gas or get your car lubed there, but you can get a nostalgia high. The square building with a simple canopy over the pumps is a repository for Tom's collection of automobile memorabilia. All the big names associated with the glory days of road tripping are represented: Gulf, Pennzoil, Esso, Goodyear, Sunoco, Quaker State, Pure, Coca-Cola—you get the idea.

Tom also owns the "Dodge dealership," a two-story brick building on Tunnelton Street. Built in 1946, it stands in a section of town that once hosted several other dealerships, creating a post-war version of the modern "Miracle Mile" of auto dealers.

Tom Westbrook's collection of memorabilia from the Great American Road Trip was displayed in his Esso service station.

The building's first level is stuffed with 22 classic cars, dealership and service station memorabilia, bicycles and whatever else wouldn't fit in Tom's service station building—a huge quantity. Folks who pull into the parking lot and gawk at the tantalizing selection of sports cars in the showrooms' windows see only a small percentage of the overall collection that lurks in every dingy shadow of this building.

If Tom gave tours and kept regular hours, the service station and dealership could be tagged "museums," but they are more accurately warehouses for fading memories.

"The good thing is there is lots of glass on this building, and people find a way of walking around the building and look in, and they get to see some stuff even if I'm not here," he said. "So that's pretty much it. When I'm here, I'm here. To make this an enjoyable hobby for me, I don't want to feel a compulsion to have to do anything, you know?"

While The Great American Road Trip would be an appropriate tag for Tom's collection, his criteria for acquisition is more philosophical than categorical.

Tom Westbrook stands in front of his Esso service station at the corner of High and Price streets, Kingwood. There's a legend that a team of horses was used to dig the hole for the gasoline storage tanks. One of the horses backed up, fell in the hole, and was stuck there upside down. Straps were put around the animal to extricate it, but it was too late. Tom said the horse was buried "right there in the hole with the tank!"

"I'm preserving something that goes back," Tom said as we talk in his dealership office on a gray February morning in 2025. "I'm preserving things that represent the efforts of people in America when they placed a higher value on the quality of things. It wasn't just about turning the next dollar."

He said Americans' freedom to travel, which was accelerated by construction of the Interstate Highway System, became a metaphor for the other freedoms they enjoy.

"What better expression of freedom could there possibly be than having the ability to jump in a car and go anywhere you wanted to go? Nobody was stopping you, and that made the United States the envy of the entire world," Tom said. "Cars were the conduit of that expression of freedom. And I think that's one of the things that appeal to me about them."

Tom's father, Darrell, worked for a heavy equipment company and covered thousands of miles of curvy, hilly road annually. Occasionally, when

In this photograph from 2009, Tom Westbrook stands in the doorway of his Esso service station, which would soon be joined by a former Dodge dealership as repository for his collections.

his mother got tired of Tom hanging around the house, she sent him to work with his father on one of those trips. "We'd always stop at some little roadside place and get a can of Vienna sausages, a piece of Colby cheese and loaf of bread," Tom recalls. "We'd make our own sandwiches and drink a pop. You remember those things as just good times in your life. So, that was probably in my DNA for liking cars and travel and everything about it."

His collection of the bold signage that sold cars and drew motorists from the byways to gas pumps and blue-plate specials is a tangible link to the memories he and his father created as they traveled through the mountains.

"All this stuff used to be common in the service stations, and it has all been changed to convenience stores now," he said. "Nobody goes out, pumps your gas, cleans your windshield, checks your oil and does all the rest of that stuff. But if you remember it happening, when you used to go with your parents . . . then you remember traveling and seeing roadside America. That was your fun time. We were going some place, either on vacation or to see a relative. It didn't matter, we were just going.

"That was amazing. You were getting out of your little world there. As far back as you can remember, it was your first introduction to travel

Tom Westbrook has nearly two dozen classic vehicles stored in his former Dodge dealership. The garage provides more than storage. He can tinker with the vehicles as time allows and sometimes just sit and admire the craftsmanship.

and something besides your house, your hometown," he continued. "You were going someplace, and you knew what that was. The whole point of it was enjoyment."

Alas, collections built upon collective memories rest on a precarious, shifting foundation. Gray are the heads and dim are the eyes of those who find an emotional connection to the orange Gulf logo brimming with the joy and freedom of motoring, or the "ding" of the air hose summoning the attendant to "fill 'er up!"

"We have such a short window of time, when you think of it," Tom said. "Our lives are a short window of time, and there are only a certain number of people who can enjoy this stuff because there's only a certain number left who can remember when you used to drive down the road and see it."

It's not that these items exist solely in a nostalgic envelope. The bold, metal brand signs are very collectible as man-cave centerpieces. The worth of six signs in Tom's collection was noted by at least one thief who drove off with them in June 2023. Only two signs were recovered. While the suspect has been identified, tracking down the persons who received the

Tools of the mechanic's trade are part of Tom's collection in the former Dodge dealership in Kingwood.

stolen goods is unlikely. Tom has little hope for recovering them or the money the new owner paid the thief.

"These signs have gotten to the point that there are very few of them that are worth less than two or three thousand dollars. Depending on the grade and condition of them, they may go for five to six thousand dollars," Tom said.

Tom could empty the service station and board up the dealership's showroom windows to add an additional layer of security to his collection. But that would deprive honest nostalgia seekers of the opportunity to spend a sliver of their years reminiscing. And, since Tom is one of them, he shares rather than hoards.

"To have it someplace where you can't display it and people can't enjoy it is ridiculous," he said. "I watch *American Pickers,* and I see these people go into buildings where they got this stuff jammed away. What's the point? It's like everybody that appreciates art does not necessarily have the oils and palette. They can't do anything with it, but they still appreciate art. So, I'm kind of the person that has the oils and the palette and all the rest of it, and I put something together that people can enjoy and have a means of displaying it and then attaching it to history."

Full circle in Kingwood

Tom grew up in the downtown Kingwood neighborhood that is home to his business, hobbies and 1875 house. As a lad, he walked and biked past the dealership when it was owned by the Snyder family and the Esso/Texaco/Pure service station when it was the community's equivalent of "Facebook."

"You have to realize that service stations were, at one time, the greatest means of communication in a community," Tom told me back in 2009. "People came through here all day from different towns and conversed with the attendants."

Tom graduated from Kingwood High School, a now decommissioned brick building on High Street across from the service station. He commuted to West Virginia University in a 1963 Plymouth Valiant station wagon that cost him $50. Decades later, Tom located an example of his first car for his collection, which also includes his two brothers' first cars: a 1964 Pontiac Bonneville and 1971 AMC Gremlin.

"Those cars meant something to me. That was the starting point, when you were beginning to drive," he said.

Tom preferred a Corvette to his more practical station wagon, and he painted houses during the summer to make enough money to buy his first used one for $1,000. By driving it to school and parking it at highly visible spots in downtown Morgantown, Tom attracted offers from buyers.

"You're in a college market where there are lots of people wanting sports cars," he said. "And one thing led to another, and I basically put myself through college buying and selling Corvettes."

Tom's capital came from an insurance settlement on his first Corvette, which was totaled in a collision with an uninsured motorist. Tom had paid $5 for the additional uninsured-motorist coverage on his policy and walked away with $3,000. He said a defining moment in his life was when he showed the settlement check to his father, who had doubted his son's wisdom of buying a two-seat sports car.

"It was maybe the first time you were ever able to prove that your dad was wrong about something; that moment was like monumental—like, 'Hey Dad, you know I've listened to you all these years. You haven't steered me wrong or anything, but here's something you don't know anything about,'" Tom said.

Years later, when Darrell Westbrook was so ill that he could no longer drive, he offered his huge Oldsmobile 98 to his son. Still enamored with sports cars, Tom rejected the offer.

"That was my mistake," he admits. "Later on, I replaced it with a car that I have today and reminds me of him. It isn't his car, but it is the thing that reminds me of that episode in life and what he always drove."

The Olds is further personalized by Kathy Mattea's

The 455 Rocket and autographed air filter cover. *Photo courtesy of Tom Westbrook.*

autograph on the air cleaner. His father made a big deal of his car, a surplus state police vehicle powered by a 455 Rocket, also the title of a Gillian Welch/David Rawlings song that Mattea recorded. Tom keeps a cassette of "Love Travels," the album containing "455 Rocket," in the car's cassette deck.

Tom cut his teeth professionally with Corvettes as the vice president of Corvette America in State College, Pa. He came back to Kingwood in 1980 as a family man and worked for a Reedsville filtration company, rising to the position of vice president through years of work and extensive travel.

He retained "the bug" for Corvettes and other classic vehicles and needed a place to work on them. A two-car garage next to the old Esso station was for sale, but it was part of a package that included a warehouse and the service station. He bought the whole deal.

The service station seemed like a sure bet for investors Englehart and Loar when it was built on the corner of High and Price streets in the 1920s. Similar in design to many of the stations of that era, the building has a unique red-tile roof, which was the idea an investor's wife. A century

Tom Westbrook stands with several examples motoring memorabilia housed in the former Dodge dealership building that Tom purchased to house his collection of classic automobiles..

later, the roof remains as a testimony to her wisdom. However, the idea that a service station could support two families was less practical. As reality set in, the owners went into the station's backroom and flipped a coin to determine which investor would retain ownership. Loar won and operated it from 1926 to the late-1940s.

Tom said the station changed brands and affiliated with Texaco in 1961, the period from which he remembered it. "I grew up walking by here every day. It was Kelly's Esso then. He sponsored the Little League team," Tom said. In the 1970s, it became a Union 76 station.

A friend, Bob Hart, had a photograph of the station as it looked in the late 1920s. He suggested Tom restore the building to its original appearance and two-pump island. Bob collected Model A cars, something that did not interest Tom at all because he had no emotional connection to them. Nevertheless, Tom went along with Bob's suggestion and created a Kingwood icon in the process.

The restored building needed memorabilia to complete its story. Appropriately, Tom hit the road in search of relevant artifacts. He approached the task methodically, as a preservationist not a collector, scouring the countryside for rusting signposts that hinted of a former service station site. Tom stopped, talked to the owner and asked if any remnants of the former business might be stashed in a garage or basement.

His portfolio of photographs of the Esso station project helped his efforts to secure signage and more. As he shared his vision with artifact owners, he assured them that their items would have a good home and second life that recognized their contributions to the community, travelers and America's motoring heritage.

"It was not their choice to close their (service station) business," Tom said of the mom-and-pop station owners who contributed materials. "It was (that of) the oil companies. It was something where the little guy didn't have the option to have a business."

The warehouse that Tom bought as part of the service station deal gave him the opportunity to pursue his plan of going into business by the age of 40. His company, Filtersource, supplies American-sourced, high-quality filters to industry, with his largest segments being refinishing (automotive/industrial paint) and hospitals.

"I just transitioned from manufacturing the filter media into selling the finished product," Tom said. Based entirely in Kingwood, the business has five employees and operates on a model of quality rather than scale driven by low prices.

"My goal was to have a business that was profitable, that I made a living from and my employees made a living from," he said. "We were able to have a business that resembles a family more than a corporation, where everybody just kind of becomes a member.

"(When working for other corporations), you see certain components or requirements and standards that a corporation wants, that basically oppose your ethical makeup. And you say, 'OK, so what is this really about? Do I want to be happy, or do I just want to be rich for the sake of getting rich from somebody else and taking advantage of the situation?' And, so, I just decided that's not really me. I just wanted to have something where I have a good business that will withstand the test of time."

Another building

Being a CEO, maintaining numerous buildings and a 150-year-old house would be enough responsibility for one man, but Tom Westbrook's passion for preserving that sliver of time for others to enjoy is boundless. He purchased the former high school building with no concrete plan for repurpose except to save it from the fate of many other structures that held memories for Kingwood natives who returned to visit. In 2025, he was still looking for a nonprofit group with the proper credentials and organization to take over the three-story building. "Hopefully, that philanthropy will result in a venture that benefits Kingwood," he said.

He also participates in Main Street Kingwood as a means of giving back to his community and preserving its small-town atmosphere and infrastructure. Tom's purchase of the former Dodge Dealership building in 2010 was in keeping with that civic commitment and passion for enriching the Baby Boomer's allocation of time.

The stout structure with its two showrooms and large service area accommodated a dealership that relocated from Bruceton Mills to take advantage of the county seat's robust business climate. "So, he opened up Seese Motors here and built this building. And next door, where the Hometown Diner is now, that building was, if not the first, one of the first few, Chevrolet dealerships," Tom said. "That was Central Chevrolet. And, when it changed hands, it became the Ford dealership. And, during that period of time, this was the Dodge dealership. Next door, in the parking lot, there was a little building in the back, and that is where the Brindle Chevy dealership moved to."

Tom said auto dealerships did not require huge lots back then because they carried very little new inventory. The buyer either bought whatever vehicle was in the showroom or waited for months for his order to be fulfilled and delivered. It was only after manufacturers required dealers to stock more inventory that the lots grew to accommodate dozens of options.

"So, this building was kind of a big deal because it actually had a big garage and enough space for inventory around the building. You might be able to have 10 or 11 cars, but that isn't the way it was done back then," Tom said.

Shortly after graduating high school, Tom was presented with an offer to buy the dealership for $400,000. The thought of taking on that kind of debt and responsibility made him physically ill, and he declined. Decades later, he was once again offered the property, this time without the dealership, which had moved outside the city limits.

"We arrived at a price, and I bought it. It serves my purpose well," he said. "There was too much stuff to put in the service station, so all this stuff you see in here is like the leftovers that wouldn't fit in the station."

That "stuff" includes the advertising banners that once hung in dealership showrooms and garages, all manner of signage, servicing equipment, tools and just about any kind of vehicle with at least two wheels, including a wooden wheelchair. In the showroom that was added to the dealership around 1960, Tom displays his collection of bicycles alongside several vehicles. Like much of the signage and memorabilia, the bicycles were offered to Tom by individuals who knew of his passion for preservation.

"The common denominator is just memories," he said, explaining the tangents that his collecting has taken.

He is the curator, owner and impromptu docent of this massive collection, but running Filtersource is still his primary assignment, although he is years beyond the age at which most Baby Boomers retire. If he left his cell phone at work, the service station and dealership could offer an oasis from running a business.

"But that's my world," Tom said. "There is something going on all the time, so when you get to the end of that after a week, you walk in here. Lots of times, I lock the door behind me. I go back here somewhere in the cavern with cars and maybe change an air filter (he has a ready source of them), put air in the tires, dust off a car," Tom said.

"Because this is not your day-to-day transportation, there is no pressure to do any of it on a timeline. You just do it when you want to do it and when you can get around to it. That's the medicinal part of this. You just go back there, turn the radio on and you're not answering to anybody or talking to anybody else. I'm not anti-social, but you get to the point where you say, 'OK, I've given to everybody all week long. It is time for me to give back to myself.' You have to find that balance in life."

The dealership gives him a quiet place to just sit and ponder.

"I can come in and just sit down there with the cars and not do anything, just look at some styling detail or something on a car that I hadn't noticed before—how a molding was put on, or why they put a certain accent on something. Why did they put that hood emblem there? Why does that Cadillac have a winged victory as the emblem and another one a flying duck and another a jet? All of those things were decisions that were made

The purchase of the former Dodge dealership's building in Kingwood gave Tom Westbrook room for showing and displaying his classic cars, as well as storing the service station and auto industry memorabilia he collects.

by somebody that would have been applicable to the time period in which they were building the vehicle."

In the summer months, Tom divides his free time between the dealership and the service station. Tom likes to pull up a chair under the canopy and reminisce with visitors.

"That's where I get my best stories," Tom said. "People would come in and say, 'That was my first job, I worked in a service station ... for 25 cents an hour.' They'll tell you about their lives, and that allows you to make a connection."

Making a connection at the dealership is more challenging, although signs on the windows encourage vehicle owners to call him if they have

Tom Westbrook said he got his best stories by just sitting in front of his Esso station and waiting for someone to come by and start reminiscing.

a classic vehicle for sale. Tom has vehicles in his collection that he knew about for decades but the owners were unwilling to sell until a change in their situation necessitated disposal. He's seldom had to venture beyond the tri-state region to acquire vehicles, and most of the cars came from The Mountain State.

Tom occasionally takes his vehicles to car shows, but it requires considerable planning and preparation. The cars are tightly packed in the showrooms and garage, necessitating moving several vehicles out of the way to clear a path for the featured automobile to depart for the show. While the shows provide Tom with connections to other collectors and sellers, most people have their introduction to him through the service station or former dealership.

There is a sense of urgency about his hobby and making these connections wherever he goes.

"It's a fleeting moment," Tom said. "This stuff isn't going to mean anything to future generations. Will it be interesting? And are old cars and stuff like that always interesting? Yeah, to some degree they are. But even as we transition to electric vehicles from standard modes of transportation and things . . . there really isn't a car culture anymore. It's been relegated to just kind of basic transportation."

Tom said there are still "cool" cars out there, but they are beyond the reach of the average young consumer, which was not the case when a new Roadrunner in 1969 could be had for $3K. And the sports cars that put Tom through college no longer appeal to buyers of that age today.

"Now, the average age of a new Corvette owner is 60," Tom said.

Tom realizes he is part of a fading generation. He knows that within the next decade he will have to liquidate the collections that have given him and many others much joy, fostered many conversations and sparked many memories. Some people look at all he's amassed and chalk it up to one more example of Americans' penchant for consumerism. Tom takes a wider view.

"This may be self-serving to me because I enjoy it and the other Baby Boomers out there may remember it," he said. "That could be all that any of this comes down to when it is all said and done."

Tom Westbrook's "Dodge dealership" building is located at 208 Tunnelton Street, Kingwood. His Esso service station is at 101 West High Street. If Tom's truck is at either location, he is there. If not, peek in the windows!

The next book in the *Wandering Back-Roads West Virginia* series focuses on Tucker County, where readers will meet the late John DePollo, whose Thomas store was transformed into The Purple Fiddle.

Epilogue

As I wrap up my fourth volume in the *Wandering Back-Roads* series, Tom Westbrook's sagacious observations about our "short window of time" hang over my keyboard and gray head. Revisiting the many back-roads journeys I have made, the fine folks I've interviewed and photographed, and the stories I have told during the past 40 years, I realize the window is very small, indeed.

We come into this world hoping for a picture window, but most of us get stuck with an attic sash. When we encounter a place like Westbrook's Esso, we pause to rub the accumulated grime from our pane and bask in the lingering glow of that magical era. We long to linger in this region of memories, but distraction marches across our view and draws us back to the 21st century with its breakneck speed of "progress," vicissitudes, background noise, incessant stream of "news" and ever-present uncertainties.

Collectors seek relief in the analgesic of holding and using something of the past, an era we recall as stable, soothing and even-paced. At the time of our original encounter, the stuff we remember most fondly was boring —things you had to do, places you had to go, people you had to see because Mom and Dad said so. And now, as we take inventory of our years, it turns out that the prosaic was life. Pity the person whose windows have grown so dingy that they no longer admit these gloriously mundane rays of the past.

Traveling back-roads West Virginia as a documentary writer, photographer and filmmaker provided me with many memories as I explored the state through the eyes and stories of its people. This volume in the series focused more on the places that these subjects built or preserved rather than the people themselves. Thankfully, many of these places are intact for us to enjoy. They are places dear to my heart and memory.

Writing these books has allowed me to revisit the places of childhood, youth and adulthood in my waning years. Even as I write these words, I am reminded of my near-death experience in 2020, when I went into cardiogenic shock following a heart attack and open-heart surgery. It was only through the prayers of many faithful friends and strangers that I lived through those very difficult three months of hospitalization.

In the months of recovery, medical interventions and setbacks that followed, I often questioned why I was allowed to live; what purpose and value can I possibly have that so much was invested in keeping me alive?

My family, my wife, son, grandson and, yes, our beautiful animals answer that question daily. Again, the daily, prosaic elements of life are what matter.

The final two books in this series, assuming my window allows me to continue my wanderings, will focus on places and people of my two favorite West Virginia regions: Tucker County and the George Washington Highway (Route 50). I look forward to sharing the stories of these stages where so many of my best memories had their debut.

Thank you for your purchase of this book and support of this work. If you enjoyed it, please take the time to write a review on amazon.com and explore the other books in this series and at our online bookstore, books.by/feather-cottage-media.

I look forward to connecting with you once again when I publish *Wandering Tucker County*.

Bibliography

Much of the material in this book is based upon the author's interviews with individuals. Additional background and historical information was provided through books, periodicals, online resources and newspapers. Readers interested in exploring these resources in greater depth may find this list of value.

Arthurdale
Chambers, S. Allen, Jr. *Buildings of West Virginia.* New York: Oxford University Press, 2004.
Maloney, C.J., *Back to the Land.* Hoboken: Wiley & Sons, 2011.
Stover, Alex, "Wooden Avengers, Target Kites . . . " March 2, 2025, https://theaviationist.com/2024/09/14/arthurdale/.

Berkeley Castle/Wheeling Castle
"Lydia Brimelow," SPLC, Jan. 24, 2025, https://www.splcenter.org/resources/extremist-files/lydia-brimelow/.
Berkeley Springs Castle (website). Accessed Jan. 26, 2025. https://www.berkeleyspringscastle.com/.
Herald Mail Media, "Foundation focused on immigration buys Berkeley Springs castle for $1.4m," Jan. 25, 2025, https://www.heraldmailmedia.com/story/news/local/2020/02/25/foundation-focused-on-immigration-buys-berkeley-springs-castle-for-14m/43684487/.
Brimelow, Peter, "Why We've Suspended VDare and I've resigned after 25 years," VDARE.com, March 9, 2025. https://vdare.com/.
Heitz, Miranda, "The House that Harness Built," Archiving Wheeling, Feb. 11, 2025, https://www.archivingwheeling.org/blog/mt-wood-castle-overlook-wheeling, .

Bruceton Mills Dam
Harrison Hagans (1796-1867) Papers (A&M 0012), Series 2, Account Books. West Virginia & Regional History Center Collection. Morgantown.

"Bruceton," *Preston County Journal (PCJ)*, Sept. 22, 1881, page 2.

Ibid. July 17, 1884, page 2

Ibid. July 31, 1884, page 2.

Ibid. Jan. 8, 1885, page 4.

Ibid. Nov. 19, 1885, page 2.

"The Late Flood," *PCJ,* Aug. 30, 1888, Page 2.

Morton, Oren Frederic & Cole, J.R. *A History of Preston County, West Virginia, Vols. 1 & 2.* Kingwood, W.Va.: The Journal Publishing Company, 1914.

Whitescarver, Ida Lee Armstrong, "Bruceton Mills," **P**reston *County West Virginia History*. Kingwood: Preston County Historical Society, 1979.

Wiley, S.T. *History of Preston County*. Kingwood: The Journal Printing House, 1882.

Buckwheat
Wiley, S.T. *History of Preston County*. Kingwood: The Journal Printing House, 1882.

"Portland District." *Preston County Journal.* June 26, 1884, page 2.

Harpers Ferry
Daugherty, Shirley. *A Ghostly Tour of Harpers Ferry.* EGMID Publishing, 1982-1990.

Locust Heights & Western Railroad
Clarkson, Roy B. **Tumult on the Mountains.** Parsons, W.Va.: McClain Printing Co. 1964.

Wilson, Matt. "LH&W Railroad: A Photographic History," booklet.

Pleasant District Holiness Association
Jones, Loyal. *Faith & Meaning in the Southern Uplands.* Urbana: University of Illinois Press, 1999.

Synan, Vinson. *The Holiness-Pentecostal Tradition.* Grand Rapids: Wm. B. Eerdmans, 1997.

Sweet Springs

Maureen Crockett. "Doing Time in Style: The State Prison for Women at Pence Springs" and "Resort Lives Again." *Goldenseal,* Summer 1990. Charleston: West Virginia Department of Culture & History.

Meador, Michael M. "Sweet Springs." *The West Virginia Encyclopedia,* Ken Sullivan, ed. Charleston: The West Virginia Humanites Council. 2006.

Virginia Furnace

Cuppett, Reardon S., "Harrison Hagans and His Times." "Tableland Trails," Vol. 1, No. 4, Summer 1954. Oakland, Md.

Wiley, S.T., History of Preston County. Kingwood, W.Va.: The Journal Printing House, 1882.

Straka, Thomas J., "Historic Charcoal Production in the US and Forest Depletion," Scientific Research Open Access, May 18, 2025, https://www.scirp.org/html/3-2810039_44438.htm, accessed May 18, 2025.

Index

Town places are in West Virginia unless noted otherwise

A

agritourism 74, 238-249
Air Force, U.S. 125
Albright 212, 213
Algonquin Mill Festival 243
Allegheny Conferance of the Wesleyan
    Methodist Church 237
Allegheny Wesleyan Methodist 227
Allendale Nurseries 76–81
amputation 236
Anderson, Albert 147–148
Anderson, Virgil 138
Andrew S. Rowan Memorial Home
    301–302
  closing 295
  residents' life there 301
Angel of Arthurdale 97
Annie's Project 241
apple-growing region 83
Apple King 83
apple migrations 67
Apple Pie Ridge 84
*Apples: A Catalog of International
    Varieties* 79
Apple Savior 64
apples, commercial production 83–89
apple selection criteria 80–81, 82

apples, heirloom varieties
  Ashmead's Kernel 82
  Baldwin 79, 82
  Ben Davis 79, 82
  Ben Davis (Black) 69
  Cortland 82
  Cox's Orange Pippin 82
  Eglon Post Office 72
  Fallawater 69, 71, 82
  Fall Rambo 69, 71, 82
  Feather, Carl 72
  Fried Apple 82
  Golden Delicious 79
  Gravenstein 82
  Grimes Golden 63, 69
  Jobe Road 72
  July Sweet 76
  June Sweet 82
  Kelly Farm 72
  Kines, Dr. 72
  Pride of Preston 72
  Railroad Red 73
  Rainbow 66
  Roxberry Russet 79, 81
  Sheep's Nose 76
  Sissaboo Red 63
  Stemple, Scott 72
  Yellow Transparent 62, 65
  York Imperial 66
apple variities charateristics 82
Arbogast, Delbert 314
Archiving Wheeling 49, 133
Ariss, John 252
Armstrong, Norma Francis 158
Armstrong, "Uncle" Rufe 137

Arora, Vasu Dr. 305
Arthurdale 90–109
  blacksmith shop 92, 101
  community center 93
  crops 99
  decline after government withdrawal 104
  educational resources 98
  factories 100, 107
  farms 98
    issues with 99
  homesteader rent 102
  homesteaders 104
  house types 92–93
  industry 100
  kites 107
  outsiders' view of 103
  rent cost 92–93
  sale of properties 102
  schools 101–102
  site issues 101
  social atmosphere 103
  teachers 102
Arthurdale Heritage 93, 104–105
Arthurdale Heritage Day 91, 106
Arthurdale High 101
Arthurdale High School 108
Arthurdale Historic District 105
Arthur, Richard 96
Ash, I.O. 314
Associated Investors Group 38
Augusta County, Va. 298
Aurora Pike 72

B

Baby Boomer generation 333
Back to the Land 97
Bailey, Jason 67
Baker, Shannon 184
Baltimore & Ohio RR 53, 265-266
  closing track at Big Grave Creek 266
  trackage in Rosbys Rock 269–270
Bank of Morgan County 36
Bank of White Sulphur Springs 305
Barbour County 236
Barrick, Michael M. 297
Bath 30
Bauserman, Edna 314
"Beacon Light" song 166
Beckwith, Ralph 281
Bedinger, Henry 261
Beegley, Emanuel 220-221
Bellamy Brothers 144
Bennett, John G. 260
Bennix, Howard "Big-Eared" Zip 157
Berkeley Castle 28–41
  compared to English 41
  construction of 33–34
  cost to construct 34
  deaths in 35
  dimensions 33
  gargoyles 38
  ghosts 37, 40–41
  modernization of 35, 37
  operating costs 39
  post-Gosline years 42
  renovations under Gosline 38–39
  tunnel legends 41
Berkeley County

apples 83
Berkeley Springs 28–41, 252
Berkeley Springs Castle Foundation 42
Berkeley Springs Yule Tea 30
Berkley, Grace Smith 301–302
Berkley, Katrina 304
Berkley, Orus Ashby 293–308
  chef career 302
  childhood 302
  disputes with state 297, 304–305
  love of historic restoration 294–295
  property developer 302–304
  training as chef 302
  vision for Sweet Springs Resort 295–296
Berkley, Orus (Sr.) 301
Berry, Joseph 60
Bible walk, Morgantown 44–47
Bierkortte, Herb 133
Bierne, Oliver 300, 301
Big Black 16
Big Grave Creek 264, 265, 269
Bird, Water 37
Bishop, Gordan 150
BJ's Mobile Home Movers 290
Black Hills Free Methodist 231
Blackie (cat) 130
Blamble, Dan 70
Blamble, Don 69
  destruction of orchard 71
Blosser, Granny 149
Blue Bonnet Girls 155
Blue Bonnet Mineral Crystals 155
bluegrass music 146
blue pike (Lake Erie) 122
Bolyard, Darlene 98, 104-108

Bonaparte, Jerome 300
Boone, James H. 195
Bowden, Gary 206
Bowman, Glinda 118, 124, 126–127
Bowman, John 118, 124–133
  antique shop 128
  boats modeled 132
  books authored by 124
  knowledge of history 126
  military service 125
  model builder 128–133
  sales career 125
Bowman Ridge Hill 269
Boyd, H. H. 33
Brady, Bill 15
Brady, Kristi (Mason) 15, 21
Brady, Kyla 21
Brady, Will 21
Brandon, Jonathan 213–214
Brandonville-Morgantown Road 213
Brandonville Pike 213
Brave, Pa. 152, 154
Bretz (Preston County) 96
brevity of life 323, 332–333
Bridgeport 21
Bright, Brian (Rev.) 230, 233
Brimelow, Lydia 42
Brimelow, Peter 42
Brindle Chevy dealership 329
Brown, John 55, 59, 60, 61
Brown, John raid on Harpers Ferry 60
Bruce, Robert 220
Bruceton Mills 63, 220-221, 236, 329
  flooding 221
Bruceton Mills Dam 220-221
Buckhannon River 287

buckwheat 99, 174–187
  Arthurdale crop 99
  botanical classification 176
  Evans Mill 174–187
  Heritage Milling 187
  milling process 181–185, 187
  nutritional value 176
  Preston County history 176
  processing in old times 175
  sourced from 180–181, 187
  ways to use 185
buckwheat cakes 109, 176, 187
Budge and Fudge 158, 160
Bunner, Jack "Hardrock" 141
Bunners Ridge 134–149
Burford, Thomas 65, 79
Burgan, Lawrence 314
Burke, Dr. William 306
Burlington Apple Festival 63
Bushrod's Folly 257
Buskirk Family 137, 158
Butcher, Oscar 138
Byers, J. F. 16
Byrd, Harry F. 86

C

Calvary Chapel Morgantown 43, 47
Canaan Valley 63
Caperton, Allen T. 300
caribou 196
Carlile, Walter "Wat" 215
Carpenter, Darrell 136
Carr, R. Jr. 265
Carr, Roseberry 265
castles 28–41

Centennial Exposition 32
Centre Market (Wheeling) 118–133
Chambers, D. Allen 300
Charleston High School 302
Charles Town
  urban sprawl 254
  Washington family properties 250–261
Cherokee Sue and Little John program 159
Cherokee Sue (Harriet Dieckerhoff Graham) 151–152, 158-161
Chesapeake and Potomac Telephone 111
Childers, William 288
cider 75, 76–77, 81
Cincinnati 279
City of Sistersville II ferry 198–211
City of Wheeling 129
Civil War 31, 53, 85, 254, 258
  Organ Cave and 193–194
Clapp, Elsie Ripley 101
Clarksburg 13–27, 111, 288
Class A Climax 16
Claymont Court 257–261
  financial challenges 260
  largest house in W.Va. 260
Claymont Society for Continuous Education 259
cleft graft 65
Cleveland Clinic 169, 170
Clifton Mills 178, 221
climber's school 114
Clise, Jim 136
Clonch, Gladys 159
Clonch, Joan 159

coal miner 265
  at Arthurdale 97
coal mines 116, 202
coal mining 149, 150
Coco-Wheats 160
Coleman fish sandwich 122
Coleman, Jodi (Carder) 123
Coleman, John 120
Coleman, Nellie 120
Coleman, Renie 122
Coleman, Robert 121–123
Coleman's Fish Market 120–123
Comet river steamboat 127
Confederate Army
  saltpeter supply 193
Connor, Carolyn 162, 167
Connor, Don 167
consumerism 333
Continental Army 291
Cooper, Olive S. 314
Corder, Gerald 15, 21
Corvette America 326
Costello, Father ghost story 58–59
Cottrill, Rick 159
country music 134–161
  wages 160
Country Music Association of West
    Virginia 140
covered bridges folklore 282
COVID-19 142, 107, 170
Cowboy Loye 137, 143
Cow, Flip 150
Crane, Paul 140, 147
Cranesville Swamp 16
Crichton, Malcolm 35
crime 236

Crockett, Maureen 302
CSX Railroad 53
Cunningham, Bob 137
Cunningham, George 37
Cuppett, Reardon S. 217
Currence, Elizabeth 164
Currence, Jimmie 166
Currence, Loren "Lodi" 166
Curry, Dave 112
Curry, Florence 155
Curry, Lillie 155
Curry, Sylvia 155
Custer, George 258

D

dairy farm sustainability 68
Dakan, Dorothy (Sedoski) 263–271
  childhood memories 266–270
  childhood recreation 269
  memories of childhood home 267
Dakan, Eliza (Kull) 267
Dakan, George 267, 271
Dakan, R. G. 267
Daughters of the American Revolution
    218
  Elizabeth Zane Chapter 289
Davisson Brothers Family Band 144
Deen, Amy 201
DeGarmo, Alan 241
DeGarmo, Mary Kathryn 241
Delco generator 195
Dellslow 149
Depression of 1893 35
Depression, The Great 96
desertion from British forces 288

Dewey, John 101
Diamond Hill Cathedral 47
Dickens, Little Jimmy 137, 138, 148
Dieckerhoff, Harriet (Sue). *See* Cherokee Sue
Doberman pinscher 30
Dougherty, Ann 56
Dougherty, Pat 52
Dougherty, Shirley 51–62
Douglass, Isaac 254
Durst, Lynn 132

E

Eastern Panhandle
  apples 83–89
Eddy, George 112
Edison, Joe 158
Eduardo, Benny 279
education
  Little House role 310–311
Eglon 73
Eisenhower Executive Office Building 33
Eisentrout, Bill 138, 140
Elkins 115
Elliott, Gary 113, 114, 115
eminent domain 275–276
Eskew, Garnett Laidlaw 127
Evans, Dayton 178
Evans, Doug 174–186
Evans, Harry Wayne 180
Evans, John G. 175–187
Evans Mill 175-186
  bagging operation 183–184
  building history 179
  equipment 179–180
  formulating mix 183
  process of milling Buckwheat 181–185
  steam operation 180
  stones 182–183
  toll basis milling 180
  waterpower 179–180
Exall, Henry 300

F

Facebook 143, 170
Fairmont 110, 152
Fairmont Armory 137
Fairmont Telephone Museum 110–117
Falbo, Jack & Cindy 148
Farmington 115
farm mechanization 85–86
Farris, Britney (Hervey) 239–249
Farris, Charlie 239–249
Farris, Grady 238, 249
Farris, Mylah 238, 249
Fayette County, Pa. 220
FBI 237
federal penetentiary, Georgia 49
ferry service in W.Va. 198–211
fiber arts 106
Filtersource 328, 330
Fisher, Grant 149
Floral Hills Memory Gardens 160
Florence Shaw Demonstration Cottage 309. *See also* Little House
Fly, Ohio 198–211
Foil, Henry 37
Fort Pitt 287
Franciscans 44

Franklin 16, 18
Fred McCabe/Liberty Marine Photos 133
Free Methodist 227
Friends of Happy Retreat 254
Frog Hollow 315
Frontier, utility company 111
Frost sledding hill 79
Frost (town) 76–81
Fruit Hill Farm 33

G

Gandee, Sam 231
Garden Fresh Markets 160
Garland, Amelia 50–62
Garland, Rick 51–62
gas pumps 278
Gavins, William 254
General Assembly of the Commonwealth of Virginia 200
Gerrardstown 84
Gettysburg 57
ghosts 41, 50-61
    explanations for 56, 58
Gibson, James 215
Gibson, Ken 281
Gilbert and Barker 278
Glen Dale 119
Glorious Betsy play 300
Gods and Generals 260
Godshall, Robert 196
GOLDENSEAL magazine 71, 363, 364
Golden, Willard "Sam" 232
Good Counsel Friary 44–47
    Bible walk 44–47

Gorby, John 21
Gosline, Andrew 29–40
Gosline, Mark 30
gospel music 150-152, 162–173
grafting 65
    process of 79
    timing of 73–74
Graham, Eva 152
Graham, John (son) 159
Graham, "Litte" John
    children 159
Graham, "Little" John 137, 151–159
    music training 152–153
    naming of 154
Grand Ole Opry 137, 138, 153
Grandpa Jones 137
Grant, Ulysses S. 31
Gray, Ancile 314
Gray, Robert 223–235
Great American Road Trip
    memorabilia 319–333
    memories of 321–322
Green Bank 81
Green Bank Elementary-Middle School 76
Greenbrier Academy for Girls 294
Greenbrier County 188–197
Greenbrier River 304
Greenbrier, The 302
Green Valley Park 151, 158
Greenville Furnace 215-216
    fGreenville Furnace and Mining Company 215
Grubbs, Florence 314

H

Hadley, Steve 201–202
Hafer, Jan C. 310
Hagans, Harrison 213–214
Hagans, H.C. 213
Hagans Store 213
Haggard, Ben & Strangers 144
Hall, Robert E. Lee 95
Hall, Tonia 178
Hall, Worthy 15
Hamilton Mill 281
Hamilton, Pat 281
Hampshire County
  apples 83
Handley, Robert 197
Hanke, Al 241
Hank the Cowhand 158
Hannibal 201
Hannibal, Ohio 120
Happy Retreat 254–257
  renovations 254
Hard Cider Band 138
Harewood 250–254
  bankruptcy 253
  Madison wedding 253
  renovations 253
Harlin, Alice 314
Harmon, Gilbert "Dib" 204
Harmony Grove 96
Harness, Dr. Andrew Jackson 48–50
Harness, Mable 48
Harness, Mary Louise 48
Harness, Myrtle 48
Harpers Ferry
  Federal Armory 53
  ghosts of 51–62
  ghost tours of 51–63
  violence 60–61
Harpers Ferry ghosts
  Dangerfield Newby 59-60
  Father Costello 58–59
  Jenny 52–54
  photographic evidence of 61
Harpers Ferry Merchants Association 56
Harpers Ferry railroad tunnel 52
Harpold, Randy 21
Harrison Community Church 163–173
Harrison County 13–27
Hart, Bob 327
Hastings, Frank 155
Hatfield, Henry 302
Haun, Dave 141
Hause, Captain Herman "Bo" 198–211
  how he got job 204
  licensing 204–205
  mechanic 205
  navigational challenges 206–207
  nickname 204
  retirement 208–209
  tribute to 206
Hause, Sue 204
Hawkins, Hawkshaw 148
Hayes, Rutherford B. 31
Hayhurst, Blaine 138
Hayhurst, Donald 136, 138
Hayhurst, Glenn 138
Hayhurst, Paul 138, 139
Hazelton Mill. *See* Evans Mill
Hazelton Milling Co. 175–187
Heinz family 93

heirloom apples 62–89
Heiskell, Vernon 138
Heitz, Miranda 49
Henderson, Dorothy *See* Radio Dot
Henline, John 70
Henline, Lawrence 71
Henline, Wilma Mae 70–71
Henry Clay iron furnace 212
Henry Elden & Associates 301
Henry, Patrick 300
Henry, William 129
Heritage Milling 187
Hervey, Britney *see* Farris, Britney
Hervey, Cathy 240, 249
Hervey, Fred 240, 249
Hervey, Mamie 240
Hervey, Mattie 240
Hervey, William Judson 240
Hickok, Lorena 97
Higgs, Charles (C.Y.) 129
Hindenburg 154
Hobbs and Ferris 266
hobos (railroad)
   Rosbys Rock 269–270
Hodgson houses 92–93, 97
Hoffman, John 220
Hog Alley 59–60
holiness 228–233
Hood, Joshua "Jot" 268
Hopkins, Howard 154
horses
   farming orchards with 85–86
Hot Dog Haven 51
Hotel Morgan 114
Howdershelt, Brandon 136, 141
Howell, Mary 314

Howson, Jimmy 162, 172
humor 283
Humphrey, Blanche 192
Hundred 155
Hurdle, Sam 120
Hurley, Jay 310
Hutson, Bill 147
Hutson, Debbie 141
Hutson, Helen 147
Hutton, Pearl 314
Huttonsvile Turnpike 276
Hyde House 213

I

Immigration and Nationality Act of
   1965 42
Inland Library 133
International Maple Conference 241
iron furnaces 212–219

J

Jackson, Stonewall 58
Janik, Rachel 42
Janoske, Bill 136-148
Janoske, Lisa 136-148
Jefferson County 250–261
   apples 83
Jefferson County Arts Council 257
Jefferson, Thomas 191–192
   Sweet Springs Resort 300
Jetsville 16
Jewell, Nancy 132
John Brown's Body song 57
John Mansfield Co. 314

John Roger's Stage Coach Stop 193
Johnson, Bob 141, 148
Johnson, Chris 141
Jones Alley 315
Jones, Charlie "Mustache" 314
Jones, Eilen 314
Jones, Grandpa (Marshall Louis) 137, 138, 154
Jones, R.C. 158
Josephine Furnace 218 *see also* Virginia Furnace
Jr., Billy Thatcher 314
Jude Mili, Father 44–47

K

Kapphan, Bill 21
Keefover, John 141
Keesecker, Dr. Ward W. 37
Keller, Mayola 234
Kelly's Esso (Kingwood) 327
Kenamond, A.D. 314
Kennet, Levi 214
Kentucky, early settlers 291
Kidwell, Everett 185
King, Ed 146
King George III 298
King James Version 229
Kingwood Lion's Club 218
kites, target (military) 107
Knode, Elizabeth 314
Knode, Pershing 314
Knode, Thadeus 314

L

Lafayette, Marquis de 253, 300
Lambert, Dustin 162, 164, 171, 172
Lamm, Skip 136
Laskie Stanley 314
Laurel Run 215
Leach, A.C. 218
Leach, George 150
Lee, Mrs. Robert E. 193
Lee, Robert E. 285, 300
Lenox, Preston County 102, 237
Leonard, Donnie 141
Lewis, Ardith 227, 232–233
Lewis, Cam 301
Lewis, C.C. Sr. 301
Lewis, John B. Dr. 299
Lewis, Victoria Evans 178
Lewis, William Lynn 298
LH&W RR. *See* Locust Heights & Western RR
Limbertwig apple varieties 82
limestone caves 189–197
Linsey, Joe 288
Little Farm 314
Little House
   barn 316
   bridges 316
   builders 314–315
   gardens 316
   landscape features 313
   students 314
   students 1928 314
   time capsule 316
   utilities 316
Living Bible Museum 47
Locust Heights 14
Locust Heights & Western RR 12–27

caboose 18, 20
holiday runs 25
jobs on 19
locomotive 16
operating expenses 26–27
preparations for running 23–24
sawmill 18
track & bed maintenance 23
volunteers 22
volunteers' commitment 26
whistle 24–25
Long, Little Roy & Lizzy 148
Loudon Heights 52
Loughry, Brandy 184
Lowry, Jim 269
Lynch, Hiram "Bill" 5

M

Mabie 161, 162–173
MacDonald, Charles (Rev.) 225
MacDonald, John (Rev.) 225–236
Madison, Dolley 250
Madison, James 250
Mail Pouch 132–133
Main Street Kingwood 329
Maio, Dorothy 146
Maloney, C. J. 97
Manning, Carlos 64-68, 75, 89
Manning, Crockett 66
Manning, Mavis 64, 89
Manno, Sam 136
Manno, Samuel 148
Maple Meadow 64
maple syrup 239
    challenges of making in WVa. 239

value added products 241–242
Marietta 128
Marion County 135–156
Marshall County 262–271
Marshy Dell 84
Martinsburg 84, 86
Maryland Heights 51
Mason Climax locomotive (No. 1) 16-17, 18, 22-24
    preparations for running 23–24
Mason, Jean 14, 16, 21
    caring for husband 26
Mason, Keith 12, 13, 14-16, 18, 21
Mason, Kristi 15
Mason Machine Shop 15, 17, 21
Mason, Michele D. 15
Mason, Tammy 15, 18, 21
Masontown 104, 108
Mattea, Kathy 148, 326
Maust, George 217
Mayle, the Rev. Winfield 227, 236–237
Mayse, Budge 160
Mayse, Paul 158
Mayses Brothers 158
Mayses, Paul 158
McConkey Church 225
McCoy Ferry 200
McCoy, John 200
McCoy, W. Joseph 304
McKinney, Michael 201
McLaughlin, Glenda 99
McLaughlin, Joseph Harvey 90, 94–96
McLaughlin, Linda 99
McLaughlin, Nellie Jane (Hall) 90, 94–96

McLaughlin, Robert (Bob) 90, 94–96, 108–109
McLaughlin, Robert Francis Sr. 94–95
McLaughlin, Wendy (Feather) 94–96, 108–109
McMillen, Leo 136, 141
McMurran Hall 309
Meek, Tom 209–210
   training on ferry 199
Megalonyx Jeffersonnii 191
Memphis 129
Merrill, Sue 111–117
migration
   W.Va. residents to Ohio 94–95, 164, 167
Milford (Bruceton Mills) 220
Miller, David 85
Miller family apple orchards 83–89
Miller, Frank 88
Miller, Frannie 87
Miller, Isabella Wilson McKown 84
Miller, John Douglas 84
Miller, John II 88–89
Miller, John M.
   extent of orchards 86
   frugality reputation 86–87
Miller, John McKown 84–86
Miller, John M. II 89
Miller, John M. III 84, 86
Miller, Madge 83
Miller, Madge Sherrard 84
Miller, Sarah 89
miller's trade 181
Miller, William Smith 84–89
millstones 182–183
   maintaining 183

Mitchell, Curley 137
Mitchell, Tex 137
Moatsville 236
Modern Johnny Appleseed 64
Moler, Lane 314
Molina, Duane 14, 21
Monongalia County 152
Monroe County 292–307
   ownership of Sweet Springs 304–305
Monroe County (Ohio) River Museum 133
Monte-Vita 37
moonshine 236, 315
Morgan County 28–41
Morgan, Janie 188–197
Morgan, Sam 189–197
Morgantown 43–46, 91, 96, 97, 111
Morrison, Austin 21
Moundsville 266, 270
Moundsville Penitentiary 270
Mountain State Melody Boys 137, 150
Mount Wood Castle (Wheeling) 47–49
Mozena Boat Works 132
Mozena, Marshall 129
Muddy Creek 214, 217
Muddy Creek Furnace *See* Virginia Furnace
Muddy Falls 217
Mullet, A.D. 33
Murphy, Alicia 184
Murphy, Dana 136
Murray, Arthur & Elizabeth 149
Murray, Bill 137, 149–150
Murray, Ortha Lorn. *See* Murray, Bill
Murray, Rachel 150
Musgrove, Rick 141

N

National Housing Agency 102
National Register of Historic Places 31, 91, 92, 105, 303
National Road 121
National Sweet Sorghum Producers & Processors Organization 243
National Trust for Historic Preservation 305
Nedrow, Peter 220
Nettle Creek Farm 243
Newby, Dangerfield 59-60
Newcome, John H. 314
New Deal 91, 93, 96-103
New Martinsburg 201
New Matamoras 211
New Stanton 141
Nicholas County 154
Nichols, Ray 113
Nitro 279
Nolan, George 314
Noose, Phil 150
North American Maple Syrup Council 240
Northern Panhandle 47-49, 118-133, 262-271, 238-249
Northern Regional Jail 264

O

O' Be JoyFull ghost tour 50-62
Ohio 128, 158, 210, 211
Ohio County Library 133
Ohio River 213, 198-211
Ohio River ferries 198-211
Ohio River steamboat history 127-128
Ohio River storms 207
Old Factory Antique Mall 42
Old Mule 64
Old Pardner, The (Murrell Poor) 157
Old Sweet. *See* Sweet Springs Resort
operators, telephone
   benefits 114
   dress code 114
   family responsibilities 111
   hours 114
   job expectations 111
   pay 114
   tasks described 115-116
Organ Cave 188-197
   acquisition of by Morgans 189-190
   bats diversity 197
   burials in 197
   commercial section amenities 195-196
   commercial tours history 192
   discoveries 195-196
   discovery of 191
   employment during Civil War 193
   fascination with 190
   organ 195
   ranking 190
   saltlpeter production 192-194
   sloth bones discovery 191-192
organic farming 261
Ormet Aluminum Plant 201
Owens, Charles 314

P

Pack, Loye Donald (Cowboy Loye) 137, 143, 154-155, 158
Paden City 119
Paradox Book Store 124
Parkinson's Disease 13, 25–26, 44, 47
Patterson, Robert 215
Patterson, S.B. 218
Patterson, Terry 113, 114, 116
Payne, Lucy 253
Payne, Ruthie 250
Pelham, Rosa. *See* Suit, Rosa
Pence Springs 295
Pence Springs Flea Market 303
Pence Springs Hotel 294, 301, 304
Pence Springs spring house 293
Pendleton County 15
Peter Pan and Wendy's House 317
Peters Mountain 293
Philippi 157
Phillips, William B. 300
Philosophical Society in Philadelphia 191
Pierce 73
Pierce, Larry 226-227
Pierce, Vernon 224-235
Pietro castle 43–47
Pietro, Thoney 43
pig iron production 215-218
Pioneers, The 140
Pleasant District Holiness Association 222–237
   camp as tradition 226–227, 232
   camp rules 228–229
   compensation of speakers 233–234
   early years 234–235
   facilities 224
   structure 224
   tabernacle 222
Pleasant District, Preston County 222–237
Ploughboys 137
Pocahontas County 76, 272–285
   lumber boom 277
Point Pleasant River Museum 133
Poor, Murrell 137, 157
   car crash 157
   funeral 158
Porter, Herb 154
Potomac Edison 316
Potomac Street 52
Prairie Dingle farm 84
Preservation Alliance of West Virginia 256, 257
Preston County 68-76, 90-109, 174–187, 212-221, 222–237
Preston County Board of Education 101–102, 108
Preston County Buckwheat Festival 176–177
Preston County Historical Society 218
Price, McKee 314
Priest, Buddy 140
Priest, Floyd J. 147
Pringle, Jerry 290
Pringle, John 286–291
Pringle, Samuel 286–291
Pringle Tree 286–291
Pringle Tree Park Road 290
Proud, Tom 15, 18, 19, 21
public inquiry accounts (radio) 156

Q

Queen Rosa 34
Quiet Del 160
Quinn, Luke 59

R

Radabaugh, Cameron 104
Radabaugh, Opal 104
Radcliff, Rev. F.L. 158
Radio Dot & her Jubilee Boys 153–155, 157
Rainbow 64
Raleigh County 140
Randell, Neal 51
Randolph County 163
Ravenswood 35
Rawlings, David 326
recycling 73-75
  farm waste 248
Reed, Larry 142, 148
Reed's Mill 177
Reedsville 91, 102
Reedsville Project. 97
Reese, Casey 138
Regal guitar 149
religion 222–237
religious experiences 226
Rhythm Rangers 137
Rich, Mary 123
Rich Mountain 166, 170
Rider, Allison 314
Riverside Inn 302, 304
Riverview Restaurant (Fly) 202–203
Roach, Mason Kenneth 21, 27

Roach, Sarah Grace 14, 21, 27
Roach, Tre 14, 15, 17, 21, 22, 23, 24, 27
roadside parks 218, 287–288
Rockefeller, Sen. Jay 307
Rocky Street 315
Romney 63
Roncerverte 188–197
Roosevelt, Eleanor 90, 91, 97, 101, 109
  ongoing at Arthurdale 101
Roosevelt, Franklin D. 96–97
Rosbby's Rock. *See* Rosbys Rock
Rosbys Rock 262–271
  21st century life there 270–271
  changes to community after WWII 270
  historical significance 265
  in mid-20th century 266–270
  naming controversy 263–264
  wool production 267
Rosenberger, Pam 184
Rothwell, Roger 246
Round-Up Band 136
Route 50 83
Route 92 92
Route 219 272–285
Route 311 306
Rouze, Mary Catherine 314
Rowe, Mildred 314
Roxberry, Mass. 81
Rush, Gary 241, 246
Rutherford, Bud 197

S

Sagebrush Roundup 137-140, 149-161
  final show 140

performers 137–139, 149-161
Sagebrush Round-Up (contemorary) aka W.Va. Country Music Hall of Fame 134-150
  campground 148
  live streaming 143, 148
  stage history 137
  type of music played 146
Salem 117
saltpeter 192–194
  hoppers 193
  hoppers left in Organ Cave 194–195
  production process 193
Salt Sulphur Springs 192
Sanford, John 126
Sardis, Ohio 210
Saterfield, Elizabeth 98, 100
S. B. Elliott Store 267
Scarborough Library 317
Schwartz, Dave 15
Scott, Dave 21
Scotts Run 96-99
Seese Motors 329
service station, vintage 92, 283
Sharp, Dave 273–285
Sharp, Hugh 285
Sharp, Ivan 278
Sharp, L.D. 273–285
Sharp, Si 278–279
Sharp's Kissin' Bridge 281–283
Sharp's Old Country Store 272–285
  covered bridge history 281–282
  history of 276–278
  unique exterior 277
Shaw, Elizabeth 226
Shaw, Florence 310–317

Shaw, Jonas 215
Shaw, Sam (Rev.) 226
Shenandoah River 313
Shenandoah Valley 313
Shepherd's Tunnel 269-270
Sheridan, Philip 258
Shipley, Ramona 278
Shipley, Tom 272–285
  eminent domain battle 275
  epiphany 274
  love of heritage 274, 276
  relationship with Dave Sharp 279–280
Shiveley, George 195
Shrader, Hazel 314
Shutler, Kathryn (Hood) 268
Silver, Amy 259-260
Simmons, Joey 164, 166
Simmons, Lena 165
Simpson, John 288
Singing in the Hills 161, 162–173
  food concessions 173
  history of 167–169
  reunion nature 172
Sisler, Janice Cale 218
Sistersville 198–211
Sistersville Ferry 198–211
  and lack of bridges 201–202
  cost savings to passengers 201–202
  cruises 210
  deckhands 207
  "Dib" Harmon years 204
  history of 200–201
  operating challenges 206–207
  operating schedule history 202
  power options 200

staffing challenges 207
tourism impact 203
traffic on 207
unusual loads 210–211
Skinner, Jean 314
Slatyfork 273–285
Sleepy Creek 36
sloth bones 191
Smith, Jimmy 157
Smith, Steve 134, 144–145, 148
Smith, Warren D. 305
Snyder, Kevin 15
sorghum
  harvesting techniques 246–247
  history in US 243
  press 244–245
  prices 248
  production process 242–248
South Branch of the Potomac River 287, 290
Southside Lumber 100
Stagecoach Band 136, 149
Stanley, A.J. 314
Stanley, Arch 316
Stanley, Laskie 316
Starcher, Buddy 154, 158, 159
Star Mills 177
Staubs, Pauline 314
Stemple, Clifford 72
Sterling Faucet 102
St. Mary's 201
Stockdale, John 152–153
stock market crash, 1929 87
Stockton, Frank 259–260
stone houses (Arthurdale) 93

St. Peter's Roman Catholic Church 51, 57–58
St. Peter's Shrine 47
Suit, Aurelia 32
Suit Land 34
Suit Land mansion 32
Suitland, Md. 32
Suit, Pelham 36
Suit, Rosa (Pelham) 29–41
  children 37
  death 37
  escapades of 34–36
  financial difficulties of 35–36
  regrets 41
Suit, Samuel Taylor 31–34
Suit, Samuel Taylor Jr. 36
Suit, S.T. Fruit Grower 32
Sullivan, Robert M. 265, 270–271
Summer Demonstration School 311–312
Summers County 293, 302
Summersville Nazarene 231
Swamp Angel locomotive 16
Swartz, Lakey 314
Sweet Springs Resort 292–307
  bathhouse 300
  Civil War years 300–301
  employment potential 307
  financial difficulties 300–302
  hotel architecture 300
  hotel builder 300
  hotel dimensions 299–300
  notable guests 300
  ownership history 298–301, 305
  restoration under foundation 305
  state ownership 301–302

Sweet Springs Resort Park Foundation 293
Sweet Springs water 298, 306

T

Taylor County 225
Taylor, D.N. 301
Teets, Aaron 68
Teets, Amanda 68, 74
Teets apple orchard 68–76
Teets, David & Wilma Mae 70–73
Teets, Elissa 74
Teets, Kevin 68, 72, 74
Teets, Paul and Karen 68–76, 82
telecommunications history 110–117
telephone linemen 114
telephone technology 110–117
Tennessee 129
The Men Who Built America 260
The Pageant of the Packets 127
Thomas, Bob 150
Thomas, Donna 166
Thomas, Ely Lumber Co. 16
Thomas, Hunter 187
Thomas, Lowell 317
Thomas, Thaddeus S. 129
Thomas (town) 20, 72
Thompson, Edith 310–317
Thompson, Laura 314
Thornbur, Jim 139
Throckmorton, Joseph 210
TikTok 143
Todd, Dolley Payne 253
Tolley, Lawrence 136
tongue-and-whip graft 65

Tool Shed Hollow 269
Toothman, Virgil 138
tourist cabins 278
Town Run 313, 316
Tradin' Post Gang 137, 157, 158
Trout, Mollie 314
Tunnelton Street 319
Turkey Run 288, 290
Tygart Valley 288
Tygart Valley Dam 236
Tyler County 198–211

U

Union Fish Market 121
Uniontown, Pa. 226
Universal News Reel 317
University of Virginia 300
Upshur County
   Pringle Tree 286–291
U.S. Geographic Board 263

V

Valley Junior High 108
Valley Point 222–237
Vanata, Maddie 112
Vandergrift Brothers 140
VanGilder, Edwin "Bud" 147
VDARE 42
Virginia Furnace 212–221
   ledgers 218–219
Virginia House of Delegate 257
Virginia Scientific Research 37
Voorhorst, Taylor 37
Vulcan locomotive 25

W

Waggoner, Gene 113
Wagner homes 93, 94
Wagner, Steward 93
Ward, Rex 136, 137, 138
Ware, Mark 15, 16, 21, 22, 24, 25
Warm Spring Ridge 33
Warner, Martha 314
War of 1812 192, 196
Warren, Bill 46
Warren, Gail 46
Warwood 125
Washington, Bushrod Corbin II 258
Washington, Bushrod Corbin 257, 261
Washington, Charles 254
Washington, Dr. John A. 253
Washington family
  trials during Civil War 258
Washington, George
  land holdings in Western Virginia 252
Washington, George Steptoe 253
Washington, Jim 314
Washington, John Augustine 257
Washington, Lawrence 252
Washington, Louisa Clemson 253
Washington properties 250-261
Washington river steamboat 127
Washington, Samuel 251-254
Washington, Thomas Blackburn 257
Washington, Walter 252-254
Waterfall Room 196
Waterman, Thomas T. 253
Waters, Norma 5
Watring, Abraham 69-70
Watring, Benjamin 69
Waynesburg 154
WBOY 160
WDNE 165
Webster, Matt 254
Welch, Gillian 326
Wellman, Earl 268
Wellsburg 124, 238-249
Wells, Freddie 154
Wesbrook's Esso 318-321, 326-328
  theft of signs from 323-324
Wesley, John 230
Westbrook, Darrell 321-322, 325
Westbrook Dodge dealership 319
  history of 328-333
Westbrook, Tom 319-333
  approach to collection 327
  auto collection 320, 323
  childhood 325
  Filtersource business 328, 330
  first vehicles 325
  reason for collecting 321, 324
Western Case sorghum mill 245-246
Western Maryland Railroad 20
West Princess Street 309
West Virginia and Regional History Center 218
West Virginia Country Music Hall of Fame *see also* Sagebrush Round-Up 146-147
West Virginia Department of Agriculture 297
West Virginia Department of Education's Governor's Schools 172
West Virginia Division of Culture and History 305

West Virginia Hillfolks 160
West Virginia History Hero Award 133
West Virginia Hospitality and Travel Association 302-303
West Virginia Music Hall of Fame 147
West Virginia Road Commission 123
West Virginia Senate 200
West Virginia Six Pack Band 140
West Virginia State Prison for Women 301-02
Wheeling 118-135
Wheeling Area Historical Society 133
Wheeling Arts Commission 49
Wheeling Castle 47-49
Wheeling Jamboree 137
Wheeling Jamboree Hall of Fame 148
Wheeling National Heritage Area Corporation 124
Whetzel, Vernon "Mutt" 113
whiskey 32
White, Chester 314
White Cross Insurance 160
White, Dr. W.H.S. 311
White's Clock Shop 124
White Sulphur Springs 192, 299
Whittington, Louis 314
Whittington, Walter 314
Willaimson, Kevin & Debbie 148
William Lutes & Son 267
William (town) 73
Wilson, Patricia 166
Winchester, Va. 85
Winfield Community Building 140
Winfield District Country Music Association 140
Wiseman, Dorsey 161
    cancer 168
    desire to perpetuate sing 170
    faith 166
    heritage 163
    humor 169
    ministry to cancer patients 169
    Ohio years 167–168
    Singing in the Hills 162–173
    songwriter 166
Wisemans, vocal group 165
Wiseman, Tippy 164
Wistar, Casper 191
WMMN 137, 150–153, 154, 157, 158, 160
Wolfe, Esther 148
Wolfe, "Foxy" 154, 158
Woolen Mill Church 237
WPDX 160
WWVA 137, 154

Y

Yocum, Bob 119–120
Yocum's Antiques 119, 119–120
York Imperial 89
Young, Charles "Wiliam" 76–81
Young, Christina 77
Young, Stormy 140
YouTube Live 143

Z

Zinn, Gerald 106
Zinn, Jeff 104–106
Zinn, Luther 104
Zinn, Marie 104
Zinn, Maxine 106

About the Author

Carl E. Feather and back-roads wandering buddy, Edison.

Carl E. Feather is a seventh-generation Preston County resident; his fourth great-grandparents, Jacob and Mary Feather (Vätter), settled at Crab Orchard in 1803. The story of his German-Swiss Palatinate immigrant ancestors and their relationship to the Allegheny Mountains is told in *My Fathers' Land,* also by Carl. His book, *Mountain People in a Flat Land* (Ohio University Press), relates the story of migration from West Virginia to Ohio in the post-World War II years.

Carl is married to Ruth Evans Feather, a retired Certified Ophthalmic Technician originally from eastern Pennsylvania. Carl and Ruth have been residents of Bruceton Mills, West Virginia, since 2020.

A retired journalist and professional photographer, Carl has freelanced for West Virginia's traditional life magazine, *GOLDENSEAL,* since the mid-1980s, and more than 100 of his stories have been published on its pages. He continues to write and shoot for the quarterly. Follow his adventures and video at his website/blog, thefeathercottage.com and his video content at YouTube.com/@FeatherCottageMedia.

Wander More W. Va Back Roads

If you enjoyed this book, please consider other titles in this series, as well as *My Fathers' Land,* and Carl's books about another aspect of Appalachia—Ashtabula County, Ohio. All books in this series are available from our online bookstore, Books.by/feather-cottage-media.

To subscribe to *GOLDENSEAL* magazine, visit the West Virginia Department of Arts, Culture & History website: https://wvculture.org/discover/publications/goldenseal/.

Other books in this series:
More Wandering Back-Roads West Virginia
Even More Wandering Back-Roads West Virginia
Still More Wandering Back-Roads West Virginia
Wandering Tucker County, West Virginia (2026)
Wandering Route 50 West Virginia (2027)
(all with Carl E. Feather)

As an independent author and publisher, reviews are our lifeline to gaining new readers.
Please support our work by reviewing this book at
amazon.com
good reads.com.
Booksellers: We would love to have you stock our independently published books. Please send your inquiry to carl@thefeathercottage.com.

Order Feather Cottage Media books online at
books.by/feather-cottage-media

Subscribe to Carl's Substack posts:
@wanderingbackroadswva

www.ingramcontent.com/pod-product-compliance
Lightning Source LLC
Chambersburg PA
CBHW070335240426
43665CB00045B/2003